Lc

Year of the
TIGER

Year of the
TIGER

By **Lewis Moody**
with Paul Morgan

VSP

To my family. Nan and Grandad for all your

support, Nellie and Basil always in my

thoughts and especially to mum and dad for

constantly inspiring me whatever the weather.

Finally to my gorgeous fiancé Annie,

for always making me smile.

Vision Sports Publishing
2 Coombe Gardens,
London, SW20 0QU

www.visionsp.co.uk

This First Edition Published by
Vision Sports Publishing in 2005

Editor: Karen Buchanan
Editorial Director: Jim Drewett

Designed and typeset by Neal Cobourne, ourkiddesign@btinternet.com

Set in Bembo 9.5/14

Printed and bound in the UK by Cromwell Press

A CIP catalogue record for this book is available from the British Library

ISBN 0-9546428-5-6

Contents

Foreword

By Martin Johnson

Lewis Moody first walked into Welford Road as a skinny 17-year-old, fresh out of Oakham School and hunting a career in the game.

Back in those days rugby had only just turned professional and over the years – as you can imagine – I've seen a number of wide-eye teenagers come and go from our club. But Lewis always stood out. He was very quick, very raw and very talented. With pace and athleticism you always have a chance, but it was his fearless streak (bordering on reckless!) that marked him out in his first game, against Boroughmuir. Almost a decade later those qualities are still standing him in good stead.

Lewis was a teenager not afraid of anything and not overawed by senior rugby. The same can be said today. He's a guy who loves to fill up his life and you'll rarely find him doing nothing, which I think is reflected in his diary of my last season in the game. He had Leicester and England to fill his time, along with the lovely Annie, so only Lewis could think, with all that going on, to take up the guitar.

Everyone at Leicester has a good word to say about him. His approach to the game – and life in general – is one of the reasons why I am delighted to write the foreword for his book.

We all know he is a lunatic – on the field – that's for sure and mad enough, as you will read in later in the book, to square up to me at a Leicester training session earlier in the season. I remember that after he clashed with another player I stepped in and before I knew what had happened he had walked onto my fist and was on the floor.

I had no intention of hitting him and he genuinely walked on to it. I thought, "Oh no, I have hurt him!" But in typical Lewis fashion did he hold a grudge? Did he even get grumpy? Of course he didn't. He loved it and, as he had just come back from a serious injury, he was delighted to be back in the thick of it with the lads.

His love of the team, whether Leicester, England or the Lions, is perhaps his greatest attribute. He is a real team man and that is one of the reasons why he is so well liked in the game. Since retiring at the end of the season it is the team I have missed the most. The craic we have when we win and when we lose, good times of which Lewis has played a big part in over the years.

In the game it is at kick offs where Lewis is best-known and a couple of great stories have arisen through the way he chases re-starts. If you haven't seen him play look out for it next time. Basically he chases them like a stone-cold lunatic.

There have been a couple of times when the crowd has held its breath after Lewis has done a mid-air somersault and hit the ground with a thud. I remember one particular occasion, at Quins, when he took out two of their players at a kick-off and hit the floor so hard we thought he might never get up. I trotted over, looked down and there he was laughing to himself as the two Quins guys stayed down!

Not many people play like Lewis Moody, thank goodness! He's a public schoolboy at heart and at Leicester we certainly believe his parents would have been far better putting that money in the bank. He's a lovely guy and I was so pleased to see him get his chance with England while we were away with the Lions in 2001 and obviously delighted that he was on the pitch with me when we won the World Cup, in Sydney, two years later.

I hope you enjoy his diary of a season — *The Year of the Tiger.*

October

Monday 4th

Leicester A 14 – Northampton A 20

Leicester A: M Smith; Alesana Tuilagi (rep: Anitelea Tuilagi, 80),
T Gregory (rep: Anitelea Tuilagi, 49-57), D Hipkiss, A Dodge, R Warren,
S Bemand (capt); P Cook (rep: M Hampson, 30), J Buckland (rep:
R Cockerill, 60), D Morris (R Green, 74), T Croft, S Herrington, D Montagu,
L Moody (D Maguire, 78) and A Shaw.

It's 7pm and I'm sitting in the home dressing room at Welford Road.
Nothing unusual in that. I've sat here many times before, amid the usual jumble
of Ralgex, sweaty socks and the bustle of players jostling for position. It's
somewhere I feel comfortable, somewhere I could almost call home. But this
time feels different. Odd, even. It's a place I thought I might never enter again
as a Leicester Tigers player and I sit in a blur in the middle of this technicolour
world, lost for a minute, drifting back into the monochrome world I've lived
in for the last ten months.

A year ago I had been one of the luckiest rugby players on the planet. I was
a member of the England team that won the World Cup in Sydney. Since then,
however, I have played just two halves of rugby and certainly haven't worn my
England jersey in anger. As we walked out across the Heathrow tarmac to

catch our plane to Australia last October I felt a twinge in my foot. I put it down to the flip flops I was wearing, but the pain continued over the next few days. I thought it was just an annoying niggle that would go away, but it didn't.

Foolishly, perhaps, I kept the injury away from the medical staff for a few days – I certainly didn't want to be one of the players who went home before the first match. I got through the first game against Georgia all right. I was struggling at the start of the training sessions but once I got warmed up out on the field I didn't even notice it. Perhaps adrenalin took over?

I noticed it in a match for the first time when we played Wales in the quarter-finals. It was starting to stop me from running at full speed so I finally told the physios and doctor and they ordered a number of tests, including an ultrasound scan and an x-ray, neither of which showed anything. It seemed that no-one knew what was wrong with me and I began to think I'd almost imagined it.

When I got back to Leicester after the World Cup I threw myself straight back into training, even starting the match against Bath on the following Saturday. After 20 minutes, however, I knew something was wrong and at half-time I said I would have to come off.

I made it on as a sub against our next opponents, Stade Francais, and then, a few days later in training, someone accidentally stamped on the top of my foot and I collapsed in a heap. Leicester sent me for an MRI scan which confirmed a fracture, a crack in the navicular bone in my right foot. They told me I would be out for four months. I was devastated enough with that... but in fact it ended up being ten frustrating months on the sidelines.

I had some really bleak days. It's hard training on your own, building up your upper body strength in the gym, going swimming and then meeting up for lunch with the rest of the guys back in the tea room, their faces all ruddy from being in the great outdoors, their smiles all knowing from jokes shared in the changing room. I really missed the banter, the sense of belonging, of being part of a team. I was on the sidelines in every way.

The guys were great, don't get me wrong. They were a real support to me when I was feeling down, but it's hard to talk to your team-mates when you're feeling really low. I guess I didn't want to show signs of weakness. We all go through it and I guess you have to just get on with it, deal with it. It's part and parcel of being a professional sportsperson and to crack on about "me, me, me" all the time would have somehow seemed a bit disrespectful to the others who've also had lengthy lay-offs.

The thing that really annoyed me, though, was that having worked towards getting back in four months I kept having little flare-ups. It's been a really teasing injury. I'd finally start running and the injury would hurt like hell, so I'd have to stop and go back to pushing weights in the gym. So near and yet so far. I constantly felt like I was taking two steps forward and hobbling back three. It wasn't like I could escape by taking a holiday or deciding to do something else until I was better. It wasn't as if I had a finite date when I knew I'd be okay. Every time I relapsed I'd plunge further into the gloom, torturing myself with the thought that, "This is it. Game over".

I put my girlfriend, Annie, through hell. After several relapses I wasn't allowed to put any weight on my foot for two months and Annie had to look after me, the world's worst, most impatient, patient (although luckily she only had to pick me up mentally!). I'm not sure I can apologise enough.

What's especially frustrating is that I know I'll never get that time back. I'm 25 now and in my prime years for rugby. There's no way I'll be able to replicate my form of the last couple of years when I'm 35. So it's dead time, gone, never to be explored or revisited at a later date. The question is, and one of the reasons I'm sitting here lost in space, can I still do it, even today? Sure, I'm worried whether my body will hold out but, truth be told, I'm even more worried that even if it does I might not be able to play this game again to the same level, the same standard of performance I'd set myself before.

I don't want to sound arrogant, but I would hate to be average. That's the thing that scares me most of all. This is the only thing I've ever been good at and knew I would succeed in. I always, always give it my all when I step onto the pitch. Bob Dwyer, one of my previous coaches at Leicester, once said to me: "Good players have good games and bad games. Great players have good games and great games." Simple enough. I know I've been given great opportunities and I would hate to feel that I'd let myself down – the fear of not doing as well as I know I can has always plagued me.

But here in the dressing room I push these thoughts to the back of my mind and shake myself back into reality. My career is about to start again as Leicester take on Northampton in a Zurich A team game. It's basically a reserve team match, but I don't care. I'm still feeling a bit uncomfortable from the injury, but I care even less. I'm back. I'm about to play again. That's all that matters. Nervous? Yes. Excited? Oh yes. Bring it on!

When we arrived back from the World Cup, at Heathrow Airport, to find

8,000 rugby fans waiting for us was a shock. Remarkable. But it was nothing compared to what is waiting for me at Welford Road tonight.

Reserve team matches are not usually that well attended (although there are usually more than two men and a dog) but tonight at Welford Road there are 9,209 people in the ground, and this is the same night that just 6,751 are at the Walkers Stadium (just down the road) for Leicester City's Carling Cup tie against Preston North End.

I know they're not all here to watch me as we are playing local rivals Northampton – and the Tigers are going well - but when I run out to an enormous roar it sure feels like it and gives me a massive boost.

The odds against me actually finishing the match are huge. Not so the lads' odds on me getting a yellow card. After ten months of frustration, my team-mates know that I'm really pumped up for this – completely psyched. Thud! I've always played a very physical game and it feels fantastic as I crunch into tackle after tackle. In my head it's a mass brawl and I almost forget there's a rugby game going on!

I've got so much pent-up energy I play the ball hardly at all. I go from ruck to ruck, people keep cheap-shotting me and I keep getting stuck into them. One young lad from Northampton takes me out as I'm about to play the ball and I absolutely leather him before an almighty fight breaks out and I'm sent to the sin bin.

I manage to calm down a little and realise I've been a bit crazed. I've just been going around trying to hurt people. I've not been playing any rugby at all, just hitting people. Outside rugby I'm a fairly placid guy, but once I'm on the pitch I go hell for leather. I become almost psychotic. I actually dream about hurting people on the pitch – and, in my defence, ten months' worth is a lot of dreams! Thing is, rugby is a battle; you fight tooth and nail for your mates, you have to be prepared to lay your body on the line for them. I suppose I am a bit of a loose cannon though – every time I've come back from injuries or whatever, I always get sin-binned for whacking someone. Rugby's such a release, mentally and physically, that I go a bit mental before working it out of my system and remembering how to play the game.

Unusually for me (but I guess not surprisingly, given the circumstances) I am feeling pretty emotional and when I finally get over the try line to score I think I'm going to cry. The final whistle goes and I'm exhausted and elated. I want to go up to each and every one of those 9,209 people at Welford Road and thank them, tell them the huge difference that each and every one of them making the effort to come along tonight made to me and my performance. Our fans are top-notch. Leicester are easily the best-supported club in England, perhaps in the world.

It's great that people haven't forgotten about me after all this time. A girl came up to me in the summer and said: "I can't wait until you get back playing again, I miss watching the way you play."

A simple statement but it meant a lot to me. Just knowing that people enjoy watching you do what you do is a great feeling. Sky Sports are here and quite a few of the first team lads have come to support me too. Despite my trip to the sin-bin, I'm declared the Man of the Match. Okay, I scored two tries, both from push overs, but I think it was more of an emotional award than anything else.

My Leicester contract is up at the end of this season and it is this sort of day that will come back to me during those negotiations, it will come back to me when I am deciding whether to stay or go. Right now? God, it feels great to be back!

Tuesday 5th

Before I even open my eyes, I wiggle my toes. Phew, still there. Actually I don't feel too bad this morning, especially given the, um, cavalier way I was tearing around last night.

I'm delighted with the way the club, the players and the supporters have stuck by me through my days of injury hell. And it is at times like this that I am glad I play a sport like rugby union. I need the boost, the strength that comes from being part of a team and, equally, I love being able to gee up team-mates when I'm on a roll. I don't know how I'd cope with an individual sport, such as tennis.

I remember back at school, my coach Ian Smith used to preach about the importance of the team against the individual. He used to say the important thing was "the pill" (the ball). He used to show us the ball in the dressing room and say: "You have to do everything to keep this. You have to put your body on the line to keep this ball for your team-mates, even if you end up shoeing one of your own team-mates; that's okay. As long as you keep the pill."

That aspect has always appealed to me and it is on days like this, as I reflect on my comeback to rugby, that I cherish those values of a team sport, and especially one where the physical confrontation is so important.

Wednesday 6th

My England team-mate, Richard Hill, was carried off against London Irish at the weekend and today we hear he could be out for as long as six months with a serious knee ligament injury. I feel for him, but knowing Hilda he'll be back stronger than ever before.

After my comeback on Monday I've been hoping I might get a run out – even from the bench – when we take on Bath this weekend but Wellsy (first team coach John Wells) decides I would be better off playing another A team game against Loughborough University. My initial reaction is, "You ******, let me get out there", but I suppose I can see where he is coming from, although it's hard to accept. Bath are one of our fiercest rivals so I would have loved it. I go from very happy to very deflated, very quickly.

Thursday 7th

It's my first day back training with the full squad and I get an especially warm welcome from Martin Johnson – a left-hander! I suppose, given that I've been running around like a lunatic all morning, desperately trying to make up for all those months on the sidelines, that something would bubble over, but trust me to pick a fight with a guy who's 6ft 8ins and a national hero. Where is Harry Ellis when you need him?

It happened when we were doing an attack-against-defence drill. I was one of the defenders, holding a tackle pad, and the session wasn't going well. I didn't think the other guys holding the pads were taking it seriously enough, they were just letting people through and I was getting a bit annoyed. Alex Tuilagi was next to try and crash through and he just flew through us. He bounced the first pad, crashed the second guy to the ground, bounced another pad, and I just thought: "What the hell is happening? I'm not having this. We don't train like that at Leicester."

So I threw my pad on the ground, took off after Alex and when I grabbed him the ball flew into the air. Johno marched over:

"What the **** are you doing?"

"What the **** are you doing?"

Before I knew it we had grabbed each other. He was holding me with his right arm and I was holding him with my right arm, then Johno's left arm caught me and I reeled from the blow. He near enough knocked me out. I have to admit I saw stars for a few brief seconds. I still had hold of his shirt, so with as much dignity as I could manage, I pulled myself up and tried to swing back at him with my left, but I was a bit woozy and didn't connect. It was very embarrassing. Luckily, before it went any further Alex's brother, Henry, stepped in between us.

Back in the changing room, Johno comes over straightaway.

"You alright, mate? Sorry about that!"

I assure him there are no hard feelings, these things happen. He pauses for a second and grins a bit.

"You were being out of order though!"

Even Wellsy – who normally loves a good scrap - has a word.

"You've got to calm down a bit," he says.

I know, but give me a chance – I've only just got back!

Saturday 9th

Loughborough 15 – Leicester A 56

Leicester A: M Smith; T Varndell, T Gregory, A Dodge, Anitelea Tuilagi, R Warren, A Wright; R Green, C Whitehead, D Young, T Ryder, J Hamilton (capt), D Montagu, L Moody and A Shaw.

Another second team outing, another huge reception... not. At Lough-borough University today there are literally two men and a dog watching us at times. The pitch is in the middle of campus, surrounded by other pitches, so we're vying for attention.

It really hits home playing here. The first team are taking on Bath, while a year ago I was in Australia playing to packed stadiums. I know it's probably the right route for someone returning to fitness, but I haven't played a game like this since I was around 16 and playing for Oakham Town, so I'm finding it hard to psyche myself up for it.

Having said that I'm keen to show the rest of the lads that I'm committed to this. I have trained with many of these guys before so I'm probably going over the top to show them how keen I am. I don't want them to think I see their game as a run out or that I'm too big for the A team.

It seems to work. Before the game, captain Tom Ryder, does a lot of talking and says: "We have a World Cup winner in the dressing-room with us and he is more fired up than we are. Come on!"

As it turns out I play pretty badly (although I still manage to niggle a few people and stand on their fly-half) but we run away with the game. Unfortunately we drove ourselves to the game so we can't go out for a few beers afterwards. Doh!

Sunday 10th

The first text arrives at around 6.30am. It's from one of my mates who works in the City.

"What have you been doing?"

Eh? Okay, I'm awake now. Can't remember accidentally shagging a page 3 girl, signing up for *I'm A Celebrity Please Let Me Be On TV* or wearing the wrong jacket and tie to an England dinner..

Over the years I've had a pretty good press – some criticism of my abilities but I've managed to stay on the back pages and off the front. No more. Apparently I'm splashed all over the news pages of the *Mail on Sunday*. The story refers to a comment that I'm supposed to have made, but can't remember, to the then Culture Secretary, Tessa Jowell, in the dressing room after England's World Cup win in Sydney.

According to page seven of the *Mail on Sunday* I said: "Look sweetheart, I don't know who you are, but can you **** off?' Can't you see we're having our picture taken?"

The story appears in Will Greenwood's autobiography but Shaggy (Will) hadn't told me about it. So, in the spirit of revenge being sweet, here's my chance to get even. Well it was 2001 and Will and I were in The......Only joking Will!

But I'm not laughing this morning – my phone is going into hypermode, bleeping hysterically with texts and calls. It was chaos in that dressing room after the game and I can remember the pictures being taken, but not who was there with me. So I spend most of the day either talking to my agent, Mark Spoors, random friends who have seen the story or other journalists trying to follow it up.

Monday 11th

Not a drop to drink last night, but the hangover from hell continues as the

Tessa Jowell story mushrooms. I'm besieged with calls from journalists every ten minutes or so.

After talking with Mark we resolve to write a letter of apology to Tessa Jowell and the Labour Party. The last thing I wanted to do was offend anyone… it was simply a case of something that happened in the heat of the moment, at the end of an historic World Cup. I wasn't in a fit state to know who anyone was, let alone a government minister.

Will Greenwood texts me to apologise for the fuss it has caused. Of course I'm annoyed, but I know he didn't mean to drop me in it and I accept his apology. Until the next time I see him.

Tuesday 12th

Great news! I find out that I'll finally be pulling the first team shirt back on again this Saturday at Harlequins, albeit from the bench. I have mixed emotions: I'm wickedly excited to be involved again, but disappointed not to be straight back on the pitch. I'm not used to being on the bench (mind you, I suppose I've not been used to playing at all lately) and I don't like it, as it gives you more time to brood and get nervous. Plus it's hard to keep focused, even more so for me because of the length of time I have been out.

Still, it could have been worse. I was half expecting Wellsy to say there is another A team or under-21s game this weekend and you can play in that one as well, which would have really annoyed me. At least I can see the light at the end of that proverbial tunnel.

Wednesday 13th

I am very nervous about training with the first team today (not just because my jaw's still a bit sore from Johno's punch). I know I am not in the starting line-up but I presume I will get some time off the bench and today feels 'proper'. Before I picked up my injury, training was a walk in the park. I loved it, everything was so easy. I hit a fantastic vein of form for two or three seasons, from my England debut in 2001 to the 2003 World Cup, and I was enjoying my rugby at Leicester so much. When things are going well you don't worry about anything, but this injury has knocked my confidence. It's taken an edge off my personality (although not, obviously, my ability to run around like I'm in *Reservoir Dogs*) and today I'm really feeling it.

Friday 15th

The worst-kept secret in England is out. Andy Robinson is today officially confirmed as new coach of the England team, taking us through the next World Cup, in 2007. Well, we had won the World Cup less than a year earlier with Andy as Clive's number two so who else would they have gone for? I am always happy when there is as little change as possible: we players worry that a new coach might not like the way we play or want to radically shake things up.

Clive's departure was more of a shock than Andy's arrival, especially when he was linked with a job in football at Southampton, but I can understand him wanting new challenges and I wish him all the best with his new appointment as Lions coach, for the tour to New Zealand next summer. I hope to catch up with him then.

Saturday 16th

Harlequins 9 – Leicester 15

Harlequins: G Duffy; G Harder, W Greenwood, D James, S Keogh; J Staunton, M Henjak; C Jones, T Fuga, M Fitz Gerald (rep: M Lambert, 71), R Winters (rep: K Rudzki, 57), S Miall, N Easter (rep: A Tiatia, 59), T Diprose, A Vos (capt).

Leicester: G Murphy; S Vesty, O Smith (rep: M Cornwell, 21), S Rabeni, J Holtby; A Goode, S Bemand (rep: H Ellis, 57); D Morris (rep: G Rowntree, 60), G Chuter, J White, M Johnson (capt), B Kay, M Corry, W Johnson, N Back.
Sub unused and unhappy: L Moody!

Harlequins: Pens; Staunton (3).
Leicester: Pens; Goode (5).

I do my best to catch Wellsy's eye. I warm up for what seems like hours on the side of the pitch slap bang in front of him, doing a great work-out, jumping up and down, strutting my stuff... everything short of running up to him, doing star-jumps, beating my chest and screaming: "Look at ME!"

But it doesn't work: every time he sees me he just puts his head down and studies the ground, desperate to avoid eye contact. I think an 80-minute warm-up's got to be some kind of record. I've never been so tired after a game I haven't played in!

Wellsy had told me he would try and get me on, but the game was so tight I suppose it was much harder for him to make a change. Mind you, he threw a couple of other guys into the fray, although that was down to backs coach Pat Howard. I was ear-wigging their conversation and Wellsy said: "I've got someone here who is dying to come on."

Hey, maybe all my frantic dancing hadn't been in vain. Except it had – Pat won, so, with 15 minutes to go, I went up to Wellsy and said: "Don't worry about today if you guarantee me a start next week." He agreed so that kept me happy. Frustrated, but happy.

It seems the rest of the team noticed my little performance. Will Johnson came up to me at the end and said he wished he could have done more – like score a few tries – to get me on the pitch. He could see how much it meant to me. I was so hyped up today I was like a ten year-old queuing for the new Harry Potter.

I hope the other players didn't think I was being a right pain in the arse. Even before kick-off, I was going around the dressing room trying to psyche everyone up, slapping players like Wig (Graham Rowntree) on the arse. You just try to do what you can to help, but they must have been thinking, "Who the hell is this bloke?".

Monday 18th

My great mate Leon Lloyd of Leicester – and sometimes England – doesn't get out that much, so I'm delighted to allow him to step into my shoes for a corporate engagement today as I'm away on an England training day.

The job is opening the new branch of residential and commercial property company, Pygott and Crone, in Grimsby. Not the most glamorous event you may think, but one of the company's owners, Tim Downing, is a big Tigers fan and even has a hospitality box at Welford Road. Leon and I met him at a game and, with his assistance, are building a couple of houses in Lincoln as an investment.

So Leon gets the glamour job, while I'm at Loughborough for the first England training day since Andy Robinson became head coach. Robbo is keen to take some of the sessions away from London, just to ease the travelling load on those of us based 'oop north' and to freshen things up a bit. Ironically, Leicester had been playing in London at the weekend, so another session at our usual England base at Pennyhill Park in Bagshot would have been perfect!

We're not expecting any radical changes from Clive Woodward's right-hand man but, in our first meeting, we're delighted when he stresses that he isn't big on formality and wants to cut down the number of meetings we have. Sometimes in the past we'd had meetings about when we were going to have meetings. So what else is different, apart from the fact that Clive was a back and Andy a forward? Robbo is certainly a sterner character, but that's about it. So far.

The big change for me is on the playing side. Since I was last involved with England, almost a year ago, some of the biggest names in English rugby, like Jason Leonard, Lawrence Dallaglio, Martin Johnson and Neil Back have retired. As I look round it feels odd not to see them, players who have been involved with England since I made my debut. There are also 10 or 11 Leicester guys and a lot of new guys, however, so I am not as nervous as normal.

When I first started going along to England sessions I was so intimidated seeing all these huge names – people I'd grown up watching. Now there are so many new, young guys that it feels like the start of a new era. I am now one of the most senior players, with the extra responsibility that brings. It's weird going from the new guy to seasoned pro – elder statesman – in such a short space of time. Even weirder is the idea that some of the new guys might have grown up watching me play. I guess I'm getting old. Well, so my accountant, Oscar Wingham, keeps telling me. He used to play for Leicester, but had to retire with arthritis at the age of 29. He says he remembers thinking, "What am I going to do now I'm old?", and delights in pointing out that he's now a young 33 year-old accountant, whereas I am an old 26 year-old rugby player.

Wednesday 20th

I'm sure there aren't many people in Leicester who think of Calvisano with that much affection, but they'll always have a special place in my heart, along with today's date. Wellsy's as good as his word (well, his latest word; I was a bit sceptical as he'd promised me I'd come off the bench in the game against Quins, but that didn't happen did it?). I'm finally starting for Leicester, after ten long months, as we kick off our Heineken Cup campaign against the Italians. My heart leaps when Wellsy confirms it during training. My last first team game was as a replacement against Stade Francais on 6th December 2003.

Unfortunately, I haven't come back into a contented Leicester side. Wellsy leaves us in no doubt that he is far from happy. He tells us that he feels standards have slipped and that we need to knuckle down and put in some hard yards in the coming weeks. Success in the Heineken Cup is crucial for a club like Leicester and we know that. Even with our tough group, the minimum the club and supporters will accept is a place in the quarter-finals. No pressure, then.

Thursday 21st

No sooner have I started to get used to the idea of having a new England captain than I hear that Jonny Wilkinson will not play international rugby again until February at the earliest after suffering heavy bruising to his right arm. I really feel for Jonny: he must be gutted, especially as the upcoming autumn internationals were due to be the start of a long run as captain. I'll have to remember to give him a call, although he'll know we're all thinking about him.

I was looking forward to playing with Jonny again, particularly after what we shared in Australia last year. He was the perfect replacement for Lol (Lawrence Dallaglio) as he has excellent leadership qualities, in particular he's brilliant at organising people. Off the field you couldn't find a quieter guy, but once he crosses the white line he doesn't shut up. He does most of the talking when we go into a huddle before the game and carries on from there. We're happy to listen though; he is respected, knows his job and he takes control. Jonny arranges the attack superbly, calling all the moves, and everyone knows how reliable he is in defence. He is always clear about what he wants and the moves he wants to run. That is all you can ask from a ten.

Friday 22nd

There are a few lads out to prove a point during our team run this morning. Austin Healey is back in the team and a certain Richard Cockerill will be on the bench for us on Saturday. Cockers, an England and Leicester legend, is back in the playing squad after returning from Montferrand to coach the forwards. We've got something of a hooking crisis at the moment, with a few injuries about, so Cockers is delighted to swap his coach's tracksuit for a playing kit.

Cockers was around in the days when Leicester, famously, had letters on their shirts rather than numbers. He was the 'B' in the legendary 'ABC club'. He is one of those fanatical people who loves the combat and competition of first team action. He's completely over-excitable, always shouting, kicking and banging his head against the wall in the changing room before a game, so we will have a little floor show to look forward to again tomorrow, even though he is only on the bench.

He made a big impression on me when I first arrived at Leicester. He was one of the guys who saw it as his job to take on the youngsters, particularly in training, testing them to see if they had the mental and physical abilities for professional rugby. He saw it as his sole role in training and, to be fair, the club needed to know if you could hack it, to see if you have the nerve and the bottle to play rugby at the highest level. At one of my first training sessions on Astroturf, as an 18-year-old, we were split into groups of three. I was with Cockers and Darren Garforth, his front row colleague, and Cockers gave me a few clips around the ear, to see if I was made of the right stuff for Leicester. He doesn't disappoint today, wasting no time in getting stuck back in. At the moment he is dealing with the Academy guys and what he says is law. He may have to change his style slightly when he starts working with the first team on a regular basis but I'm delighted he's back: he's great at keeping everyone motivated, a character in the Martin Johnson mould.

It's an early night for me; I'm way too excited about the game. I just need to focus now. I'm not worried about my injury – the medical team have told me that I'm stronger than ever and that it will never come back. You can't afford to worry about injuries recurring or you would drive yourself mad.

I've been boosted by a larger than usual postbag this week with maybe 50 good luck cards and some really sweet drawings from kids of me diving over the line. Thanks, everyone, they really have cheered me up and inspired me.

Saturday 23rd

Leicester 37 – Calvisano 6

Leicester: S Vesty; J Holtby, S Rabeni, D Gibson, A Healey (rep: A Tuilagi, 40min); A Goode (rep: M Cornwell, 72), H Ellis; G Rowntree (rep: J White, 19-30, 40), J Buckland (rep: R Cockerill, 52-65), D Morris, M Johnson, B Kay, B Deacon, I Moody, W Johnson (rep: H Tuilagi, 71).

Calvisano: P Vaccari; L Nitoglia, G Raineri, C Zanoletti, A Tuta Vodo; G Fraser, P Canavosio (rep: P Griffen, 40+2); G Bocca (rep: M

Castrogiovanni, 56), A Moretti (rep: G Intoppa, 62), S Perugini
(rep: G de Carli, 64), J Purll, V Bernabo, M Ngauamo, R Mandelli,
M Zaffiri.

Leicester: Tries: Moody (2), Ellis (2), Rabeni. Cons: Goode (3).Pens:
Goode (2).
Calvisano: Pens: Fraser (2)

When I dive across the line in the second half, for my second try of the game, I hurl the ball in the air in triumph. God this feels good. I feel like I am a professional rugby player again. Okay, so it's only a push over try so not much to write home about, but who cares? I'm actually very close to tears. Again. God, I sound like a right poof!

The last time I scored two tries for Leicester was on my debut against Boroughmuir. That day they both came from the half-way line. I remember passing Iwan Tukalo to get in at the corner for one of them and Rory Underwood shouting behind me, "Go on, you run it in!". But on my return to the first team today I'll take them from anywhere.

It's a big relief to get across that line again. For most of the last week I've been bricking it. It's not one of my greatest games, but I do enough and get through it; that's the most important thing.

I have never particularly liked night games but I think I might change my mind after this one. Or maybe not: as we didn't kick off until 7.45pm there's no time to go out and celebrate afterwards, so it's just home for a pizza and a video.

Sunday 24th

I dash out early to buy all the papers. I've got a new spring in my step and I'm buzzing so much I almost feel like kissing the newsagent. Almost.

Monday 25th

I manage to clear another big hurdle today. It's just three weeks since I returned to any sort of competitive action, but when England announce their 40-man squad for the autumn internationals I'm in it. Yes! Get in! A text arrives saying "Congratulations" (we always find out this way) and tells me to check my email for the exact details of where we need to meet and what we need to do over the next few weeks.

All my mates and the press are convinced that, with Lawrence Dallaglio retiring and Backy (Neil Back) going after the Six Nations, I am going to be England's new number seven. Hold on guys, I just don't see it that way. I haven't played many games so to be even thinking about stepping into Backy's shoes on a permanent basis is way too far from reality. I've missed a whole Six Nations campaign and a trip to New Zealand and Australia last summer, so just to make the initial squad of 40 is a relief. I don't even want to think about the starting 15 yet.

I don't think anyone can see themselves as others do. I rarely recognise the bloke they are talking about on TV or in the papers. You can never afford to believe your own press and there is plenty about me at the moment. You perform at your worst when you think you are certain to make the England team. The competition for places is huge and nothing is certain, so I wish everyone would stop talking as though it were.

Wellsy tells us the Leicester team a day earlier than usual (in person, rather than by text, that would be a bit odd at the training ground) as I'm off to Buckingham Palace tomorrow to collect the MBE the World Cup winners were awarded. I'm a bit worried about tomorrow: all the procedure and ceremony, hoping I don't make an idiot of myself, wondering how to tell my great Leicester mates Geordan Murphy and Leon Lloyd that their late bid to be one of the three people I'm allowed to take has failed...

Oh, the team? Thankfully, I'm in it.

Tuesday 26th

Call the Queen "Her Majesty" first, then "Ma'am". Don't talk to her unless she talks to you first. Don't fall over. Don't, for God's sake, burp or lose control of other bodily functions. Don't grin like an idiot. That's right, put one foot in front of the other... easy does it...

I make it out of my chair and up to Her Majesty the Queen without mishap. I, Lewis Moody of Oakham School, Rutland, am walking up to get an MBE. Me! I wouldn't have believed it myself unless I'd been here.

It is particularly special for me because, as well as being accompanied by Annie, my mum and dad have flown in from Jakarta, where they now live due to my dad's work, especially for the day. I feel so proud knowing they're watching.

Annie and I came down to London last night for a celebration dinner with my parents. It was the usual deal: mum got all emotional and teary about her "big son" and dad got all awkward and made a toast to me. A very fine speech as well, actually, dad. I was quite touched.

My dad doesn't really do emotional: after the World Cup final we were doing our lap of honour and I managed to find my parents in the crowd straightaway and invited them onto the pitch to celebrate with me. My mum was sobbing her heart out and came onto the pitch and hugged me immediately, but I couldn't persuade my dad to join us. I suppose he didn't want to take any of the glory away from me – although I think he might have been crying too.

Luckily Mum just about manages to hold it together for the MBE presentation. As there are so many of us we are told to go up in groups, rather than individually, to receive our MBE from the Queen. I'm up with Cozza (Martin Corry), Lol, Hilda, Backy and Shawsy (Simon Shaw). She speaks to each of us in turn and asks me if I have been playing for a long time. I wish!

"I've just come back from injury Your Majesty," I manage to reply, without falling over, gurning or dribbling. Phew. Well done me!

I always assumed that Her Majesty pinned the medal on you, but she actually hooks it onto a loop they attach to your suit – presumably to speed things up. And the $64 million dollar question? No, I didn't steal anything, although I think Annie had a good look for something that wasn't nailed down. She wasn't the only one – everyone seemed to be looking around for something like ER soap.

As we walk out there are queues everywhere to have your picture taken, a bit like when you go on one of the rides at Alton Towers. Luckily we spot that Dave Rogers of Getty Images has somehow managed to sneak in so we head straight over to him and ask him to take our picture in various poses, in front of various backdrops, with mum, dad and Annie. Dave has been taking photographs of the England squad since long before I started playing (I think he saw Martin Johnson's first game, and his last!) and was in the dressing room at the end of the World Cup final taking similar shots.

All in all it's a surreal day. Once the ceremony's over I have to dash back to Leicester as we have a big Heineken Cup game this Saturday, in Biarritz; but not before I pop in to see my nan and grandad who live just outside London, to show them the medal. They're chuffed to pieces. I'm not sure I deserve an MBE just for winning the World Cup, but it's a great honour.

There is only one duty remaining before dashing back up the M1, to give my MBE to my dad. They are going back to Indonesia tomorrow and my dad deserves my medal more than me after all the effort he has put in during my career, driving me all over the country to games when I was a lad; spending a fortune on kit and petrol and giving up huge amounts of his precious free time. He deserves it more than me for the sacrifices he made on my behalf. I can tell it means a lot to him.

Wednesday 27th

It's back to the day job today and back to earth with a bump. Quite a few of us missed training yesterday, so we have to work twice as hard today.

Wellsy's funny. He's a legend but he's quite old school. One of his classic drills is to split us into groups of four, give one of the guys the ball and then shout abuse as the other three try to prise it out of his hands. It's quite hard, because whoever's got the ball is in a very strong position, with it tightly locked in their arms. We'll be wrestling the guy and trying to rip it out of his arms when Wellsy comes up and screams:

"What are you doing? You don't do it like that! Bend his fingers back!"

I sometimes think he'd be happy if at least five of us broke our fingers in training – then he'd know we'd given it our all.

We knew we'd be in a tough Heineken Cup group, but we didn't realise quite how tough. Wasps, Calvisano and Biarritz. Blimey, it's going to be tight. Only the five group winners and three best runners-up make it through to the final stages, and we only qualified as England's seventh side, so we're going to have to pick up some results away from home and that starts this weekend.

Friday 29th

We are pretty confident as we set off this morning because, out of all the English clubs, we have the best record away to French teams, over the years recording victories in Pau, Toulouse, Perpignan and Beziers.

I've managed to go from one palace to another this week as the hotel in Biarritz is awesome, right on the beach. It actually used to be a palace years ago. Far too good for us.

I am sharing a room with the Samoan, Henry Tuilagi, and by the time I get back from having some hot chocolate he is fast asleep, so I go to Sam Vesty's room to watch *Thirteen Days* on DVD with a few of the boys. It's a pretty good film, if a little too long.

Henry is a great guy to have around the squad. He's very quiet and God-fearing off the field, like many of the Islanders I've played with, but on it he's a different man completely. He is quite simply a beast. I'm certainly glad to have him on my side rather than running at me.

Saturday 30th

Biarritz 23 – Leicester 8

Biarritz: N Brusque; P Bidabe, F Martin Aramburu, D Traille (rep: T Lacroix, 60), J Marlu; J Peyrelongue, D Yachvili; P Balan (rep: Avril, 75), B August (rep: J-M Gonzalez, 62), D Avril, J Thion (capt), D Couzinet (rep: O Booyse, 59), S Betsen, I Harinordoquy, S Malonga (rep: C Milheres, 68).

Leicester: G Murphy; J Holtby (rep: A Tuilagi, 44), S Rabeni (rep: M Cornwell, 80), D Gibson, S Vesty; A Goode, H Ellis; G Rowntree, R Cockerill (rep: J Buckland, 49), J White, M Johnson (capt), B Kay, L Moody, W Johnson (rep: H Tuilagi, 44), N Back (rep: B Deacon, 70).

Biarritz: Tries: Arramburu, Marlu. Cons: Yachvili (2). Pens: Yachvili (2). Drop goal: Yachvili.
Leiceter: Try: Rabeni. Pen: Goode

What a nightmare. This has to rank as one of the worst days I've ever had for Leicester. Were we too cocky, too confident? We didn't underestimate Biarritz, but we did seem to take our foot off the pedal after a great start. They scored a try and that was that. What's even more disappointing is that the two tries they scored were from turnovers. We gifted it to them.

I know there was a lot of talk about the fact that Johno was away in Singapore at the start of the week, but the club had allowed him to go. Not having him around for some of the training sessions was a little bit disruptive, but it wasn't even part of the reason we lost. No-one knows how to prepare for a match better than Johno and you know what you'll get from him – a consistent performance every time. He's never going to turn up for a match under cooked and today was no different.

The nightmare on the pitch could have got worse off it were it not for Sam Vesty. I made the massive error of judgement of going to the casino in

Biarritz after the game. If Vesty hadn't been with me, I would have lost a ridiculous amount of money. I normally play poker but they didn't have any at this casino. In the end I gave Vesty all my chips and got him to lend me a few now and again to play with. I was in a strange, restless mood and wanted to bet loads on every turn of the roulette wheel. Luckily Vesty was there to say: "What the hell are you doing?"

The night had started well with a few drinks with Henry and his brother Alex, but while I was in the casino it must have all kicked off. I got back to my room at about 2am to find Henry fast asleep in his bed and Alex out for the count in mine. They had had a big fight – I think they'd knocked each other out. Vesty had a family room so I kipped in a kid's bed for the night.

The perfect end to a perfectly awful day!

Sunday 31st

The club decide to have our recovery session in the sea. For me and some of the other boys it is a recovery from our hangovers, more than from a match I'd rather forget. I don't know what the locals must think – all these big rugby players splashing around, body surfing. The water's pretty rough and Whitey (Julian White) gets dragged down the beach by the current. I'm a bit worried about him as he's getting buffeted by the waves, but he manages to drag himself back to the shore, although he does look something like a stranded porpoise. Battling the sea is working brilliantly as a way of venting our frustration and we all start to cheer up. Except those of us with hangovers; I feel good for about ten minutes and then the pounding of the headache becomes even stronger than the battering from the waves.

Almost as soon as we touch down at East Midlands airport I have to meet up with England for another training session. I manage to get home for about three hours, just time for a shower, change of clothes and a quick chat with the missus, before heading south to Pennyhill Park.

I miss Annie when I'm away, but Pennyhill really is a wonderful place. Nothing's too much trouble for the staff. Michael Wright is the man in charge of looking after VIP guests, which I suppose is what we are. He's brilliant. Whatever we want, he somehow manages to track it down. Mind you, nobody's asked him for an elephant yet (I'm sure we annoy him enough as it is) but, if asked, I'm sure Michael could produce one within a couple of hours. He's that kind of guy. Top man.

November

Monday 1st

I'm still pretty wary about doing too much in the early part of any week and setting back my recovery process, so I'm limited in what I can do with England at the moment. England tend to try and dovetail what you might do with your club, so today we are doing weights at 9am before an outdoor training session in the afternoon.

The weights are fine, but the afternoon session might be tricky so I quickly check in with the England doctor, Simon Kemp, who confirms that my afternoon session needs to be modified as I've only just started my comeback. Slightly to my surprise the coaches give me a heads-up that I will probably be starting the Saturday after next when England kick off their autumn internationals at home to Canada. I'm thrilled, but a bit surprised, considering how little rugby I've had. I know I could get through the next two matches, including my return to the England team, but I want to make sure I am coming back at my best. I'm concerned that the Saturday after next might be too soon and that, if I do play, I am running the risk of letting myself down and psyching myself out for the future. As usual, I'm anxious...

Tuesday 2nd

There's an England defence session today before we head back home to our clubs. I have to say I find it quite disruptive moving from club to country and back again in the same week. Apart from traipsing up and down the bloody

M1, packing, unpacking, re-packing, remembering this bit of kit and that, the calls are all different and you have to suddenly focus on different team-mates and try to click instinctively with them in terms of your style of play. If I had my way the games would be played in blocks with all the internationals together, probably at the end of the season, so things don't get chopped and changed. It would make far more sense and it would make it easier for the players to focus on playing for one team at a time.

The integration between club and country is as good as it can be at Leicester, but there is no doubt that international weeks are very disruptive, especially for us, as we can lose as many as ten players for training sessions. The most frustrating thing is a week like this: Biarritz for three days, up to Leicester to see the missus for five minutes, down to London, back up to Leicester. But enough of my whingeing, I still know where I'd rather be.

Wednesday 3rd

Today is perhaps the most significant day for me since I arrived at Leicester as a teenager. I am, for the first time, selected ahead of Neil Back, on the openside, which gives me a big spur in training. Bizarrely, I was selected ahead of Backy for England in 2002 but it has never happened at Leicester. I remember telling a newspaper reporter once that I thought it was easier to be picked above Backy when I play for England rather than at Leicester. When he saw the report Backy confronted me and said he presumed I had been misquoted, but it's how I feel. It's not a major problem – I've always known that at Leicester, I have to shift over to the blindside.

Wellsy has always seen him as the security, the incumbent. Fair enough. I knew I'd get my chance and my first loyalty is always to my club. I think Wellsy thought I was happy at six, which I am, although I'm delighted to have my chance at seven. At Biarritz last weekend I was playing six and at the start of the second half Backy was taken off and I was moved to seven, so it's a natural progression to keep that line-up going.

When I'm at six I tend to get more ball around the park, more ball in hand because you run later and support lines, whereas at seven, more often than not, you are hitting a ruck and clearing out the backs rather than getting the opportunity to run with the ball; you tend to be chasing the ball around the field more. Also, the way both Leicester and England play means I tend – when playing six – to be left out on the wing more often, which further increases my chances of getting the ball in hand.

A six probably does a lot less defensive work, while at seven you could be putting in 20-odd tackles a match. Also at seven you are hunting the opposition outside half. Your goal is to get to the ten so you can push the rest of the backs out and create a defensive overlap. In my preparation I don't focus too much on the opposition ten. You can do stuff like discover which foot he kicks or sidesteps off, so you can try to push him on to his weaker one, but that obviously doesn't work when you play against a ten like Jonny Wilkinson who is happy off either foot. He is a very tough ten to play against. Even in training he has so many steps he is difficult to read and he passes so well off each hand.

I used to play centre until I was 16. But having failed in the county trials in that position a year earlier, my coach switched me to the back row and I've been there ever since. I'm probably a fraction of a yard short of pace to be a good centre, although sometimes I do wish I'd stayed there because now I'd be playing touch rugby rather than snapping my fingers off.

Wellsy knows that those of us who were with England yesterday ran a pretty heavy defence session so he offers us some time off this afternoon as we're all pretty knackered. I'm tempted to head home for the sanctity of the sofa, but I've been out of the side for so long that I don't want to miss any more sessions unless I really have to. Partly that's for show – never give up, never surrender! – partly it's because I don't want to let my mates down and partly because it just feels so bloody good to be back.

Thursday 4th

After the coaches' hints on Monday that I will be starting against Canada I'm not that surprised to get a text saying, "Congratulations, you are in the 30-man squad". But it's nice all the same.

I'm not sure whether I'm an idiot or just overly keen, but this afternoon I volunteer for the 'Walk of Shame'. No, I haven't agreed to be the weakest link on *The Weakest Link*: every day at Leicester after training those players who have made mistakes are made to line up under the posts, then they have to catch three high balls – kicked by anyone (there are another 20 guys randomly, and wildly, kicking balls in their general direction) before they can leave the pitch. I actually trained pretty well today, but our coach Pat Howard has been giving me some abuse so I think, "I'll show him!". Ross Broadfoot and James Hamilton are in there with me and I'm delighted to say that I manage to catch my three missiles in just a few minutes. Ross and James? Let's just say I've caught colds quicker.

I'm completely knackered afterwards but, being the amazing mate that I am, I manage to summon up enough energy to do a friend of mine, Dodge (Roger Woodall), a favour. I even summon up enough energy to rope Geordon Murphy (Geordy) into it too, as there's no way I'm doing it on my own. Dodge has organised a student night at a club in Leicester and he'd put on his flyers that a World Cup winner would be coming along. He claims to have asked me about it first, although I'm not sure I can recall that conversation too clearly, mate!

These events are always a nightmare because everyone is smashed out of their heads and I'm there sober. Tonight is no exception: slurring blokes tell me and Geordy "I ****king love you" and both the lads and the girls are queuing up to get us to sign various parts of their bodies – nothing too rude this time, thank God.

Saturday 6th

Leicester Tigers 28 – Gloucester 13

Leicester: S Vesty (rep: R Broadfoot, 80); D Hipkiss (rep: A Tuilagi, 53), S Rabeni, D Gibson, T Varndell; A Goode, S Bemand; D Morris (rep: G Rowntree, 61), J Buckland (rep: R Cockerill, 78), J White, M Johnson (rep: B Deacon, 27-39; L Moody 80+4), B Kay, H Tuilagi (rep: B Deacon, 65), L Moody (rep: N Back, 71), M Corry.

Gloucester: J Goodridge; M Garvey, T Fanolua (rep: N Mauger, 71), H Paul, J Bailey; B Davies, A Page; C Bezuidenhout, C Fortey, P Vickery (rep: G Powell, 78), A Eustace, M Cornwell (rep: A Balding, 58), P Buxton, A Hazell (rep: J Forrester, 54), J Boer.

Leicester: Tries: A Tuilagi (2), Rabeni. Cons: Goode (2). Pens: Goode (3)
Gloucester: Try: Paul. Con: Paul. Pens: Paul (2).

I'm out on the pitch about 20 minutes before the other lads today. It's only two weeks since I made my return to first team action and I still need a lot more time to get myself ready for the game. My able assistant, fitness coach Darren Grewcock, is there beside me once again. Darren has been a tower of strength for me in the last few months, doing all my rehab work. He's a top man. He works so well one-on-one with people and is a great motivator – he's got to take a lot of credit for my return. He oversees all my personal training, conditioning and fitness work and is always there for me if I need to do an extra session. He's here for me again now, watching me stretch, warm up and, er, do two tuck jumps.

"What the **** are you doing?" he laughs.

It's my little pre-match superstition: every time I go onto the pitch I have to do two tuck jumps. I have no idea why. But I have to do them when we go out to warm-up, when I go back out to start the game and after half-time. I'm trying really hard to kick my superstitions into touch. I never used to have them, but they do make you focus better and stop you worrying about other things. Like coming back from injury...

Actually, I'm not as bad as some. Cozza has to be the last person out of the changing room and has to make sure he turns the lights off as he leaves (I'm not sure if that's because he's particularly energy-conscious or just tight). Austin Healey always used to have this lucky T-shirt, which was actually emblazoned with the words 'Lucky T-shirt'. I haven't seen it for a while; I think the fact that we all took the mick in a major way might have something to do with it.

No, I'm fairly sensible really. I mean I'm just wearing my match shirt underneath my warm-up top because it's really, really cold, not because I started doing it a while back and I just can't stop. I used to have a really weird superstition: sat on the bench in the changing room before a game, I'd always squirt some juice or water from my bottle onto my gum shield so it wouldn't stick to my teeth (hang on, that's not the weird bit). Obviously some of the liquid would fall on the floor (wait for it), so I'd have to take a swig of drink and spit some out in exactly the same place as the previous spill. The thing is (and this is the weird bit), it would really bug me if I missed and there were unconnected little splashes or spots of liquid, I couldn't stand it. So I had to keep going until they were all joined together in one great big globby puddle. Yes, even I eventually realised that was a bit sad; that's why I don't do it any more. That and the fact that a couple of the lads threatened to deck me if they slipped up on my spit one more time.

But we all have our little routines. I'm a bit worried today because me,

November

Geordan and Leon (Lloyd) didn't get to go to the cinema together yesterday. We started going on the day before a match about five or six years ago, to try and find a jam from whatever film we watched to use as a try celebration. It kind of stuck, as a good luck thing, despite the fact that when we went to do our bowed heads prayer routine from *Crouching Tiger, Hidden Dragon* after Geordan scored once, me and Leon charged 50 metres up the field to celebrate with him and ended up clashing heads and nearly knocking each other out. If we can't get to the cinema together, I'll always watch a DVD at home (popping out for some popcorn just to keep it real) and actually that works too, so maybe the fact that I didn't do either last night might not matter. Oh God. Who knows?

The worst thing a fan or well-meaning friend can do is give a sportsperson something for 'luck'. This creates a huge dilemma in the already pre-occupied mind of the athlete: do I keep it? (in which case I'll just worry about losing it) or do I throw it away? (in which case I'll just worry about bringing seven years bad luck on myself). Or do I just scream at said friend not to be so bloody insensitive. I remember on one Six Nations tour we all got given poppies to wear to a game. Of course, as I had a really good game I had to keep the poppy and wear it to every game after that. I still have a poppy somewhere in my car, although I'm not prepared to admit whether it's the same one.

Darren and I finish my warm-up and I head back in, thankful that neither Leon nor Geordy are playing. That's my final superstition: when we're all playing me, Leon, Geordy, Vesty and Goodey (Andy Goode) have to do 20 keepy-ups before every game. It's just to relax us really, but we're quite strict: we can't go in until we do. Luckily, we're not too bad, so we haven't had to ask for the start of the game to be delayed yet...

Talking of which, I'm chuffed to be playing seven ahead of Backy today. My foot holds out fine (thanks Darren) but I'm not sure I acquit myself too well, as Backy comes on for me in the second half, although I do manage to come on again in injury time. It is my first game with our new Fijian wing, Seru Rabeni, who is making a huge impact around the club. It's not hard to see why: Seru runs onto a long, flat pass from Goodey to score his eighth try in ten matches, from 40 metres out.

Equally impressive is the performance of Goodey himself, who marks his 100th game for Leicester in style, landing five kicks, and surely moving his name into the minds of the England selectors. Nice one, mate.

Sunday 7th

How do I feel today? God, please let me be fit. As I wake up I nervously check myself over. Limbs? All present and in the right places. No breaks, no strains. Just the usual post-match aches and pains. I'm reassured. Today's a big day for me: I'll be able to report fit to the England camp, in preparation for Saturday's Test match against Canada, and give myself every chance of making my international comeback.

It's quite a stressful day, but not because I'm worried about my place in the final 22, which will be decided tomorrow. Annie works in interior design, she's trying to set up her own company and she's been under a lot of stress, so we spend hours writing letters and sorting out problems, under the watchful eye of her little sister, Bailey. I'm sorry that Annie's got all this hassle, but grateful for something to take my mind off rugby – and I'm really proud of her and interested in the work she does.

I did Design A-level and studied business for a year at Uni, before realising that I have no interest in quantitative this and qualitative that. I'm not mathematically tuned in. It's just not my thing: like a lot of people I ended up doing that degree because my parents thought it would be a good thing for me to have under my belt, but I hated it. A year after I started at Uni, rugby went professional and I knew I couldn't do both – I had to commit to Leicester or Uni. You've got such a short career in rugby, so I took the chance and have never regretted it. With the possible exception of now... it would be quite handy right now to be able to take some of the stress away from Annie by surprising her with a load of spreadsheets and flow charts. I do at least do my own finances and accounts – even if it is only about once every five years!

Before I know it it's 5pm, time for me to hit the M1. My heart lurches, not just because I won't see Annie for five days, but at the thought of the journey ahead. My house is, conveniently, at junction 21A of the M1 (well, nearish, it's not actually at the services) but sometimes it takes hours just to get to junction 20. And then there's the M25...

Every Sunday before an international we have to report to Pennyhill by 8pm so that they can assess our fitness. Even if you've just got a nagging ache, it's worth turning up to be given the once-over by Simon Kemp, the head of England's medical team. He and the physios check you out and decide whether or not you're fit to train and what your plan for the week should be.

Joe Worsley – who I think is a dead cert for a place in the back row – picked up a leg injury playing for Wasps yesterday, but he still turned up as Pennyhill is only a 20-minute drive for him. I think he's hoping the physios will work their magic, but sadly he has to pull out. The only consolation, of sorts, is that it's vindication of him coming off in the game yesterday. His coach, Warren Gatland, accused him of having "Test-itis".

Of course, we all worry about picking up an injury in a game just before any England international, but it would be absolutely ridiculous to try and hold back in your club game to try to avoid getting hurt. Leicester is my bread and butter so I'd always give them my all (mind you, it would have been impossible to try and get away with it yesterday against our arch rivals Gloucester without looking like an idiot). But holding back is just a recipe for injury: if you want to get injured, going in at 50 per cent is the best way to do it.

I drag my weary body up to my room and am delighted to open the door and discover that this time I'm sharing with my Leicester team-mate Whitey (Julian White). It's pot luck who you get to share with, and I really don't care who it is, I get on with most people. It's great if you have a room to yourself when the missus is allowed to visit, but Whitey's not a bad substitute. Well, he makes me laugh at least as he has such a dry sense of humour.

We head down for dinner, although I decline as I ate before I left, and then get straight down to the supposedly serious business: money. It's not often we all get together as a team so when we do we've usually got some major issues to discuss, in this case our bonus structure and payments for playing for England. No-one wants a repeat of 2000, when the squad came close to a strike over pay and we put rugby in the headlines for all the wrong reasons. At that time the players were trying to negotiate a new structure. The RFU wanted more of our bonus to be based on us winning but we wanted more of it as a match fee, which led to the confrontation. That time it was settled before the players had to miss a match but we hope this time it won't come to that and we can negotiate sensibly.

So, to make sure we get this sorted and can focus on our game for the rest of the week, we send Ben Kay and Danny Grewcock to represent us. Well, we're not stupid: they're both 6ft 6inches (mind you, I'll be checking that the second-row forwards don't get an extra special bonus).

Actually, don't tell the RFU, but I'm quite relaxed about these things: I see my England money as a bonus to the salary I earn at Leicester. The meeting, with the PRA's chief exec Damien Hopley, goes well despite Wally (Steve

Thompson) stressing that he needs three weeks notice before doing anything – as he likes to be very organised – and everyone suddenly feeling the need to throw their twopence in, and by 10pm there's a broadly agreed deal in the hands of the lawyers and we're ready for bed.

Well, ready for room service at least. I order my usual: a club sandwich. It's tempting to go over the top as England are paying for it, but the lads know the limits. So, ten minutes later, the champagne and caviar arrive on a silver platter... just kidding. I think most people think we have a very strict diet but, while we do have a chef preparing our meals, nothing is off-limits to us and if we want a bowl of chips we're allowed them. We're supposed to be healthy all the time, of course, but we do stray. Steak sandwiches and chips is the preferred vice of most of us. When I first joined the England set-up I remember being a bit shocked by Dorian West who, on the first night we all met up, would always order a huge tray of club sandwiches and a massive hot chocolate, just for himself. Without fail. He's never been exactly the slimmest player, so I was a bit surprised. The thing is, as he said, he got his first cap at 29 and played until he was around 36 or 37, so I think he thought, "I've got this far eating what I want, why should I change now?" Fair play to him.

At 21, when I got my first England cap, I wanted to be seen to be doing the right thing. Five years on, I know what suits me and what I can and can't do. The odd ice-cream or steak and chips isn't going to make much difference. We eat so well at Leicester and I try to maintain that at home. The missus does most of the cooking. If it's my turn to cook, we tend to eat out! The only thing I'm really capable of making is a salad, but my salads are the best – I generally won't eat anyone's else's. They've got to have chicken and avocado, then I add mozzarella, baby plum tomatoes, those sweet little orange peppers, cucumber, pine nuts and sometimes – when I'm feeling extravagant – bacon. All topped off with a German sauce called Maggi – it's similar to soy sauce and I've been obsessed with it ever since I was about four and used to drink it out of the bottle. Mmm... I'm starting to get hungry again.

Monday 8th

Days like this are rugby's equivalent of the *X-Factor*. Minus the high-waisted trousers, of course. Eight people will be going home today, as the squad gets cut down to the final 22. I can't wait, tell me now.

I hate mornings and find it really hard to get going, but today I don't get much choice. Whitey is up at 6.30am, crashing around, as he has a visions skills session. These are designed by our visual awareness coach, Sheryl Calder, who worked with us at the World Cup on improving our peripheral vision. We do exercises on a computer or on the training field, as she believes the eyes are muscles that need to be trained like all the others.

I hadn't planned to be up until 7.20am as the team meeting is not until 8.30am, so cheers Whitey. At least I won't be late: that's a cardinal sin and there's no excuse when you're upstairs in the hotel the night before.

After the meeting, which sets out what we are doing for the week, there is the little matter of a weights session over at Twickenham's superb gym, just 20 minutes drive away. After a good workout, the normal sort of stuff you'd see in you local gym but perhaps done to a higher intensity, Robbo says we need a line-out session which means he has to tell us – earlier than normal – who the forwards will be for the game.

Out on the pitch Robbo announces the starting eight with a cursory point of the fingers.

"You, you and you."

Luckily I am one of the "you's". After ten months out, the finger of fate points to me again.

Back at Pennyhill we huddle around the flipchart and the rest of the team is revealed with a bit more ceremony, as Robbo pulls back the top sheet to reveal the team, including the eight who won't play. We very much believe the whole squad of 30 is important. I was on the bench for the World Cup Final, but I remember, when the starting side ran out onto the field, players who didn't make the 22 – like hooker Ronnie (Mark) Regan and scrum-half Andy Gomarsall – were cheering on the boys for all they were worth.

Unfortunately Ronnie won't be featuring this time either as today he has decided to retire from international rugby after not making the 30. That makes him the eighth World Cup winner to retire in less than 12 months since the final. He is a real character and will be sorely missed in the dressing room, where he's been a fixture as far back as the Brian Moore days.

Tuesday 9th

Today is a media day and I have a date with *The Funday Times*, so I need to swot up – not just on my rugby knowledge but to make sure I know which is my favourite dinosaur. We have one day to get all our media duties out of the way in every Test week. We're quite cool with that. We know there's a huge need to promote the game as rugby is still a young sport in professional terms.

It's fairly casual and easy, really. We all sit round in one big room, doing our bits and pieces, and while the RFU media department doesn't tell us what to say they do prepare answers to some questions that may come up. Still, they're a useful prompt if you have time to swot up.

I generally get through these sessions fairly quickly, but I'm in demand today. Something to do with being back in the team after a year out, maybe? So I mentally grab the ball, put my head down and plough through as if I were out on the pitch. I start off with a group interview with Rob Kitson from *The Guardian*, Dean Wilson from Hayters and Chris Goddard from the *Leicester Mercury*. From there it's *Five Live*, the Sky Sports *Rugby Club* and lastly *The Funday Times* over the phone. (It's T-Rex by the way).

I had been selected on to the openside but Robbo breaks the news that, as we suspected, Joe Worsley isn't fit after all which means I have to switch to the blindside, Andy Hazell coming in on the openside for his first England cap.

Four days ago Andy and I had been knocking ten bells out of each other as Leicester took on Gloucester and now I'm in the same England team as him. Andy seems a good guy. I try never to make my confrontations in any match personal. For me it is about focusing on the shirt in front of me rather than the player in it. If you try to get someone back after they've whacked you, you tend to spend all your time following them around rather than the ball. I have enough to think about without conducting vendettas and trying to give opponents a slap.

Wednesday 10th

What is a restaurant's worst nightmare? Twenty-two very hungry rugby players heading towards them at 100 miles an hour, looking for food and wanting it now. Every Wednesday before a Test, one lucky establishment has the dubious pleasure of hosting the traditional pre-match Wednesday night team meal. It all goes on the RFU credit card and tonight, as usual, we're going to absolutely pillage it.

We get through mountains and mountains of food at these meals. Most guys will have three starters and two or three mains – and no matter how much you eat, I think you can always find room for puddings.

We head into the private room reserved for us to find a mountain of pizzas waiting for us. It's like our pre-dinner aperitif. I make a beeline for anything with anchovies on – I love 'em. My favourite is pepperoni, olives and anchovies. Then we move on to the steaks – with potato wedges, rather than chips – our one concession to healthy eating on these nights. Of course, there's never any salad in sight at these dos; you don't make friends with salad! Then it's time for the calamari or veal escalopes – all washed down with a gallon of lemonade or Coke. We're not allowed to drink Coke in the hotel as it's full of caffeine and if you want to get the best out of the caffeine supplements we take before training or matches we're not supposed to have too much during the week.

A few of the lads enjoy a beer or a glass of red, but most of us just shovel the food into our mouths as quickly as possible. We're in and out within 45 minutes. Some might stay for an hour and a half, just chilling, but most of us want to get back to our partners and enjoy the night before our day off tomorrow. We're like a human whirlwind: in, refuel, out, attempt to squeeze behind wheel of car, spend day off recovering.

Friday 12th

Our video analyst Biscuit (Tony Biscombe) shows us a motivational tape he's prepared: clips of England players putting in big hits, scoring great tries and making good breaks. Normally, these are culled from recent matches, but we've lost five out of our last six games so Biscuit must have been tearing his hair out – he used a load of World Cup footage in the end!

I love those tapes as they remind me of how good this England team is and they really get me in the mood for running out at Twickenham. Not that I need any motivating at the moment. Robbo gives us a rousing team talk, then the coaches leave the room and we are addressed for the first time by our new captain, Jason Robinson. Marks out of ten? Ten. As you might expect Jason – who is the sort of guy who keeps himself to himself – doesn't do that much talking, but stresses how many people in the room have the golden opportunity to start (or re-start in my case) their England careers. Stirring stuff.

Saturday 13th

England 70 – Canada 0

England: J Robinson (Sale, capt; rep: B Cohen (Northampton, 51);
M Cueto (Sale), M Tindall (Bath, vice-captain), H Paul (Gloucester),
J Lewsey (Wasps); C Hodgson (Sale; rep: W Greenwood Harlequins, 57),
A Gomarsall (Gloucester); G Rowntree (Leicester), S Thompson
(Northampton; rep: A Titterrell (Sale, 63), J White (Leicester; rep:
A Sheridan (Sale, 51), D Grewcock (Bath; rep: B Kay (Leicester, 57),
S Borthwick (Bath; rep: H Vyvyan, Saracens, 70), L Moody (Leicester),
A Hazell (Gloucester), M Corry (Leicester).

Canada: D Daypuck (Castaway Wanderers); D Moonlight (Univ of
Victoria); R Smith (Brampton Beavers), M Di Girolamo (Aurora),
S Richmond (DeA Tigers, Hong Kong); E Fairhurst (Univ of Victoria; rep:
J Cannon, Coventry, 39-41; rep: D Spicer, Univ of Victoria, 75) P Fleck
(Meralomas); K Tkachuk (Glasgow, capt, D Pletch, Oakville, 78), A
Abrams (Castaway Wanderers; rep: M Lawson, Velox Valhallians, 49), F
Gainer (Dublin Univ; rep: G Cooke, Benevento, 49), J Jackson (Leonessa),
M Burak (Old Boy Ravens), J Cudmore (Grenoble; rep: S O'Leary,
Meralomas, 24), S McKeen (Pacific Pride; rep: C Strubin, Capilano, 66), C
Yukes (Agen).

England: Tries: Robinson (3), Lewsey (2), Cueto (2), Tindall, Hodgson,
Greenwood, Moody, Vyvyan. Cons: Hodgson (2), Paul (3).

Finally! The months of agony are over. I'm buzzing, bouncing off walls. I can't wait for the game to start and I'm a lunatic all morning. It doesn't really sink in that I'm back in the England side until 2.30pm when I run out onto the turf at Twickenham and hear the national anthem. The hairs on the back of my neck are twitching.

I'm delighted to hear we have won the toss and are kicking off. At Leicester my job from kick-offs is to simply smash into anyone I can and it's the same for England, so I know I can get into this game from the first whistle, which suits me well, as rather than supporting one of my own players from a kick-off, I can wait until one of their guys catches it and then smash into them and I'm straight back into it.

I feel really excited as I take up my position, waiting for the whistle, ready to stand up and be counted, ready to take my place in this new era for England. But the Canadians start well and absolutely batter us in the first 20 minutes. They've got some big ball carriers and soon we're all feeling bruised.

We get a lot of ball, the backs spreading the play wide, so us forwards spend most of the first half chasing the backs around the field, running more than we usually would, and I'm quickly getting knackered. It's a slightly shaky start, but we soon stamp our authority on the game and are well in control at half-time. We're 40-0 up, to be exact.

Clive Woodward set great store behind half-time, certainly more than any England coach before, and this has been carried into the Andy Robinson era. We know we must squeeze every second out of this crucial ten-minute period. The first thing we do is change our kit as it creates the feeling that we are starting all over again, that what has gone before is in the past and it's 0-0 again. Clive used to talk about making 100 things one per cent better and changing our kit is one of those 100 things. On its own it won't win you a rugby match, but when it is part of a bigger picture it certainly helps.

Once I have taken on some fluid, changed my kit and the coaches have made a few points, Danny Grewcock calls all the forwards together. You would think – because of the way Danny plays and trains – that he would be thumping the table during his half-time pep talks. But he's actually quite a softly-spoken, considered speaker and he calmly goes through a number of objectives for the second half. We talk about some of the technical issues: scrum time, the line-out and the importance of not giving any penalties away in the second half, especially at the breakdown –our objective is always to be in single figures. We want to nil the Canadians, as it is rare that an England team manages to do that to anyone. We've only done it once since I've been in the team, against Romania back in 2001.

Bruised I may be, but I'm thoroughly enjoying the game and the icing on the cake arrives late in the second half when I dive over the line for a try on my comeback. I don't have much luck when I score tries for England. I remember getting clattered by a couple of All Blacks when I scored against New Zealand a few years back, but this time it is my own team-mates who do the damage, three or four of them collapsing on top of me as I go over. I would love to jump up and celebrate but, as the ball is under my stomach and almost breaking my ribs, all I can do is scream, "Get off, get off!" Not exactly the celebration I had in mind.

We win 70-0 in the end, but I leave the pitch a worried man because I have picked up a shoulder injury that could threaten my place in the side for the next game, against South Africa next Saturday.

Unlike during the Six Nations, there are no formal dinners after the autumn internationals, but for this series the RFU have come up with a new system. We're having an informal meal in the 'Spirit of Rugby' room – nice and near to the dressing rooms so we don't have to hobble far – and each player is given six tickets, effectively a table each. However, by the time I've done my media interviews and paid a visit to Leicester's hospitality area, like the rest of the players I don't make it up there until around 6pm. The game ended two hours earlier, so unfortunately most of my guests – and those of the other players – have headed home. Only the missus and one of her friends have waited around, so we end up sharing a table with Danny Grewcock.

Oh well, at least the non-event means we can go to a charity dinner that has been organised by the missus. Before the World Cup I could have slipped into a similar event without being noticed, but so much has changed since that day in Sydney. I don't mind people coming up and chatting though.

I can't sleep at all in the hotel afterwards, tossing and turning and waking Annie up every half an hour. I alternate between replaying the match over and over again in my mind and worrying that my shoulder injury will put the brakes on my England career, just as it's beginning again. Here we go again? I hope not.

Sunday 14th

Ouch! The shoulder is still hurting this morning. It's even more painful knowing that it was such an innocuous bloody challenge and that, instead of chilling out on my day off, I'll have to book in later to see the England physio, Barney Kenny, for treatment. Damn.

Monday 15th

Big surprise: despite Andy Hazell getting the defence award on Saturday after making an incredible 21 tackles, he is relegated to the bench. Joe Worsley comes back into the side, giving us the back row that was originally selected for the

Canada game before Joe had to pull out injured. I think that because South Africa are one of the most physical teams in the world, Robbo feels we will need our biggest players on the park, which is fair enough, but it's pretty hard on Andy.

Of course, it also means that I need to move back from the blindside to the openside, although I'm well aware there could be one more change that no-one knows about – me! I've got to have faith that England's superb medical team can somehow get me out on the pitch.

The last time I played against South Africa was just over a year ago, when I came on as a substitute in our World Cup pool game. I won't forget the game in a long time. It's not just the brutal nature of the match that sticks in my mind, but that I was lucky enough to charge down Louis Koen's kick in the second half, which led to Will Greenwood grabbing the ball and going over the line. It was a strange game for me: I know I didn't play that well, but I was in the right place to charge down the kick that led to our try, so got lots of praise. I guess it proves the old adage that it's all about being in the right place at the right time is sometimes more important than anything else, but I felt a little bit of a fraud.

Oh God, please let me be fit to play on Saturday!

Wednesday 17th

After consuming the number of calories a supermodel would eat in an entire year at the England meal, I'm grateful not to have to drive back to Leicester as the missus has my car. I can sit back, relax... oh no I can't. I've stupidly accepted a lift from Wig (Graham Rowntree) who just loves his Gangsta Rap, particularly when it's blaring out at 10,000 decibels. I'm not sure why we call him Wig – I think it's because he had a crazy flat top when he was about 18 – but we only call him Wiggy when we really want to wind him up. Like I do now.

"Turn that rubbish off Wiggy you idiot!"

Thursday 18th

Yet another day of the media fawning over the Springboks, going on about how physical and just all-round world-class their back row have become. The lads and I are sick to death of reading it. It's a real motivator for me, Joe and Cozza – there is no way they will match us in terms of physicality. No way. Anyway, I think it's their weakness as that's all they have to offer. A lot of their attacks are route one and it makes it easier to defend against.

Friday 19th

I'm up early for more physio from Barney. He's right; my shoulder has responded well to his treatment this week and I should be fine for the game. There's another good omen for tomorrow, too: the final team run doesn't go very well. We're at Twickenham by 10.15am and, although the moves are working, the final pass is going astray and we keep dropping the ball just as we are about to score.

It's not the best build-up to the game. We're determined to finish on a high, so we keep going beyond the usual one hour, 20 minute session until we can score five in a row. I'm not telling you how long we spend out there.

After lunch it's time to tip the odds in our favour with a quick trip to superstition land. Me, Ben Cohen, Will Greenwood, Steve Thompson and Joe Worsley head off to the local cinema.

"A pint of Tango and a bag of strawberry milkshake bottles please", (the latter in honour of Annie, who loves them).

Under The Sunset, with Pierce Brosnan turns out to be extremely easy watching – just what the doctor ordered. The other lads often want to go see a horror movie but me and Ben aren't too keen on the scary stuff.

We race back from the cinema as the England management get out the chocolate biscuits on Fridays at around 4pm and they're always quickly polished off. Today we get a result: we make it back in time to grab the last five!

Saturday 20th

England 32 – South Africa 16

England: J Robinson (Sale Sharks, captain); M Cueto (Sale Sharks), M Tindall (Bath), H Paul (Gloucester; rep:W Greenwood, Harlequins, 73), J Lewsey (London Wasps); C Hodgson (Sale Sharks), A Gomarsall (Gloucester; rep: H Ellis, Leicester, 68); G Rowntree (Leicester), S Thompson (Northampton), J White (Leicester), D Grewcock (Bath), S Borthwick (Bath; rep: B Kay, Leicester, 73), J Worsley (London Wasps; rep: A Hazell, Gloucester, 73), L Moody (Leicester; rep: Hazell, 7-15), M Corry (Leicester).

South Africa: P Montgomery (Newport Gwent Dragons); B Paulse

(Western Province; rep: J Fourie, Lions, 73), M Joubert (Western Province), D Barry (Western Province), J de Villiers (Western Province; rep: B Habana, Lions, 73); J van der Westhuyzen (NEC), F du Preez (Blue Bulls); J du Randt (Free State; rep: C J van der Linde, Free State, 17-25), J Smit (Kwa-Zulu Natal, captain), E Andrews (Western Province; rep:Van der Linde, 44), J Botha (Blue Bulls), V Matfield (Blue Bulls), S Burger (Western Province), A J Venter (Kwa-Zulu Natal; rep: D Rossouw, Blue Bulls, 55), J van Niekerk (Western Province).

England: Tries: Hodgson, Cueto. Cons: Hodgson (2), Pens: Hodgson (5), Dropped goal: Hodgson
South Africa: Try: Habana (76). Con: Montgomery. Pens: Montgomery (3).

There's a lot of chat out on the field this afternoon. If you make a mistake the South Africans like to remind you of it, so we give as good as we get and rub their faces straight back in it. A few of them give our players the odd slap on the head: nothing too bad, just an attempt to wind us up. But we keep our cool, despite a brutal opening 20 minutes.

In fact we play out of our skins. Players like Cozza, Wig and the second rows (Danny and Steve) have never played better in an England shirt and that's probably the platform for our victory. The last time we played one of the southern hemisphere giants – Australia, last summer – we conceded 50 points. Since then South Africa have beaten Australia to take the Tri-Nations title, so for us to turn that form around, albeit at Twickenham, is nothing short of remarkable.

I'm so pleased with the way the back row unit performed. It's only the second time me, Joe and Cozza have played together as a three, the first being in Canada, in 2001. Joe's tackling and commitment is superb and Cozza carries the ball extremely well. It's great for us to have taken our chance to emerge from the shadows. Everyone knows England's starting back row at the World Cup was the most prolific of all time. No back row had played together – for any country – as many times as Neil Back, Richard Hill and Lawrence Dallaglio. Maybe one day we can emulate that success, although right now I'm just pleased we had a good game rather than worrying about whether we'll become the next Holy Trinity.

I'm joined at the dinner afterwards by my godparents, my missus and her sister, Bailey. Robbo presents Os Du Randt with his 50th South African cap and my Leicester team-mate, Harry Ellis, with his first England one. Harry's a lucky sod. As we're part-way through a series, he manages to avoid the normal fate of someone winning their first cap, which is to take a drink with every other member of the team. Don't think we'll let him off though – we're merely postponing Harry's big drink until after the match against Australia, when we can enjoy it properly.

After dinner Danny Grewcock, his girlfriend Natasha, myself and Annie head into Richmond for a few drinks at the Slug and Lettuce, right on the riverside. It's always nice when people come up to say "well done" and tonight we are accosted by quite a number of South Africans saying we beat them fair and square, which is even sweeter. Fair play to them.

Sunday 21st

I've got a little extra time off as I don't need to report back to England until tomorrow lunchtime and Annie and I are staying at the Pennyhill Park tonight. England are very relaxed about your partner staying with you – although obviously it isn't something you could do if you were sharing with another player. I'm not sure what Whitey would say if I turned up with Annie at midnight. Having our partners – and in some cases children – staying with us during the tournament really helps us and our concentration. We know when to switch on before a game.

So after a visit to Starbucks for an Egg Nog latte, Annie and I head to nearby Kingston to meet one of Annie's friends, Geordan Murphy's girlfriend, Lucie Silvas (yes, Lucie Silvas the singer!) for a spot of early Christmas shopping and some lunch before heading back to Pennyhill.

The squad are delighted about yesterday's win and I'm in a pretty good mood. It was crucial after such a bad run to show we can still beat one of the top teams, perhaps the top team in the world considering they won the Tri-Nations. Everyone in the team is so proud of the way the front five performed, giving us the platform to go and win the game. The drive and passion is there, I can feel it.

Monday 22nd

It is exactly a year since we lifted the World Cup and it is fantastic to be able to celebrate the one-year anniversary with the majority of the squad.

It seems like about five minutes ago that Jonny Wilkinson was kicking his winning drop goal and we were running around the pitch at Sydney for our lap of honour, with *Wonderwall* blaring out over the loudspeaker.

We've all got cars to take us to Battersea for Kyran Bracken and Paul Grayson's testimonial dinner, but unfortunately I am in one following Will Greenwood's cab. Will decides to make a detour to his home in Wimbledon as he has some papers to pick up. After what seems like hundreds of twists and turns later (and a good few circuits of London) we eventually make it to Battersea, far later than planned. The night's a complete sell-out, with almost 2,000 people turning up. A few toasts from the boys, a whole heap of memories – well we're not going to forget that glorious day just yet.

When I was injured I found the dinner circuit quite difficult to handle and even had to stop going to these sorts of events because people – obviously well-meaning – would quiz me constantly about the injury and when I would be back. But now I'm not trailing around on crutches I don't mind attending the odd dinner or two, especially on the anniversary of our World Cup Final win.

Sometimes I think I can't be arsed to go but once I get there I normally enjoy these events, especially when Annie is able to come with me. At many of them we have to do Q&As or photoshoots, but tonight is just about enjoying ourselves, although not too much – I have to be up at 7am tomorrow for a 7.30am physio appointment. Anyway, you'd never dream of going mad in an England week – even if it is the anniversary of our World Cup win. Did I mention we won the World Cup a year ago? Happy days

Tuesday 23rd

"It's all over". That's my first thought as my ankle buckles under a couple of bodies at today's contact session. Immediately I think it's snapped. Nightmare. I hobble over to sit on the side of the pitch and start to calm down a little. My ankle is at a funny angle, but there seems to be no serious damage, thank God. I think I just pressed the panic button in my mind.

The physios immediately compress and ice the ankle and then give me some intensive physio, they're clearly not giving up on me. I don't think they were hoping to see me again quite so soon as I've already been in this morning for more work on my shoulder. The South Africa game made it a little worse and it's quite bruised, but the treatment worked well.

Wednesday 24th

I have to sit out today's training session because of my ankle and with Joe Worsley also struggling with a stomach bug, Andy Hazell is slotted into the team for today's attack-focused session, while Joe and I sit gloomily on the side of the pitch, watching and encouraging.

I head off to Pennyhill's swimming pool for more rehab from Barney which cheers me up. I'm starting to feel some improvement in my ankle already and I'm feeling more positive about making the game. A bit negative about not making it home to see Annie, though, as I'm tied up on the treatment table all day.

Thursday 25th

Oh no! I want to crawl back under the duvet and stay in bed all day. Not because of my ankle, or my shoulder – they both seem a lot better this morning – but because it's not even quite daylight yet and already the texts and phone messages are flying in.

Today, you see, is my first appearance as a model. I'm 'starring' in a poster campaign for Timberland. As part of the arrangement I'm also going to the Timberland store in Richmond later today to help them launch a new range of clothes.

I haven't seen the posters but I know there is one at Twickenham train station because that's the one that brings me the most stick as the morning progresses.

"Seeing your ugly mug when I got off the train ruined my morning mate!" being a typical example.

Ah, that old green-eyed monster strikes again, lads.

The advert is also in Saturday's matchday programme, so that will bring yet more grief from my team-mates. At least the missus likes the pictures (although she won't admit it), although to be honest if I didn't get stick for doing something like this I'd know something was wrong.

In the afternoon I have two very successful physio sessions and, for the first time since Tuesday, I know I will make the pitch on Saturday.

Friday 26th

A stomach bug has been sweeping through the side this week and the worst affected is Mike Tindall. There is no question of him missing the match as there aren't enough wild horses in the Twickenham area to grab hold of him and keep him from the pitch. He is ill enough to miss the team run, though, so we all know he must be bad.

After the run, which is pretty sharp this week – is that a bad omen after last week? – the usual gang head for the cinema, Tango, popcorn and sweets-fest. Then, back at Pennyhill, a beaming Tony Biscombe has been able to prepare an inspirational video, with all the material drawn from our last two matches! Nice of us to make his job that bit easier...

Saturday 27th

England 19 – Australia 21

England: J Robinson (Sale, capt); M Cueto (Sale; rep: B Cohen (Northampton, 74), M Tindall (Bath), H Paul (Gloucester; rep: W Greenwood, Harlequins, 24), J Lewsey (Wasps); C Hodgson (Sale; rep: H Ellis (Leicester, 70), A Gomarsall (Gloucester); G Rowntree (Leicester), S Thompson (Northampton), J White (Leicester), D Grewcock (Bath), S Borthwick (Bath), J Worsley (Wasps), L Moody (Leicester), M Corry (Leicester).

Australia: C Latham (Queensland); W Sailor (Queensland), M Turinui (New South Wales), M Giteau (ACT), L Tuqiri (New South Wales); E Flatley (Queensland; rep: M Rogers (New South Wales, 24), G Gregan (ACT, capt); W Young (ACT; rep: M Dunning (New South Wales, 62), J Paul (ACT), A Baxter (New South Wales), J Harrison (New South Wales), D Vickerman (New South Wales), G Smith (ACT), P Waugh (New South Wales), D Lyons (New South Wales; rep: S Hoiles (New South Wales, 74).

England: Moody, Lewsey, Cueto. Cons: Tindall (2).
Australia: Tries: Paul, Latham. Con: Flatley. Pen: Giteau (3)

The mood in the England dressing room is one of utter frustration. Josh Lewsey and I sit there, looking at each other, saying, "Well, we've come a long way in the last six months", but it is scant consolation. We still hate to lose.

I managed to score a try but to be honest that is forgotten as all I can focus on is the loss – anyway it was one of those where the pack drove me over, again. It's always good to score, but it doesn't mean much when we lose.

We let ourselves down in the first half but it's about ironing out those flaws now so they don't go into the Six Nations and beyond. England's recovery has begun, and it's up to us to take it on from here. We're disappointed we lost today, but there is still a lot of pride because of how many people we've proved wrong in this autumn series.

The most annoying thing is that the simple things we do so well, usually, just didn't click, but we have to be happy with the way we came back in that second half, to lead 19-15. I think most England fans would have taken two out of three from these Autumn internationals – especially after the way England played in the summer – but no-one in the squad was thinking like that. We believed we could take them all, complete the hat trick, but we lost because of a couple of stupid penalties towards the end – one given away by me – and the fact that we just couldn't get within striking range, although it is too simplistic to blame those factors alone.

The inquest will have to wait for another day. After the initial disappointment, we're feeling proud of what we've achieved after being written off by so many people. It's also time to get rid of any last vestiges of frustration by reminding Harry Ellis that he still hasn't had his initiation ceremony. He has to enjoy a drink with every one of his team-mates in the squad, and there are 21 of us. The Leicester lads start him off at the dinner with a few very large glasses of wine and by the time we leave for Kingston for the end of series party he's probably had eight or nine. Poor Harry doesn't cope too well with his ordeal and gets in a bit of a state, although he's probably doing better than me after my first cap. I say probably because I don't remember much of it.

When I got my first call-up, at 19, for a tour of New Zealand, I was still a student and didn't understand the etiquette. I was so excited I spent most of the time getting smashed, which didn't go down too well. Two years later, when I got my first cap proper, I didn't drink until the very last night of the tour when I had to take a drink with each member of the squad just like Harry.

I'd learnt my lesson on that tour and just kept my head down, sat in a corner and did as I was told... until that last night. Apparently the new team doctor had to wheel me up to my room in a wheelchair as I vomited all over myself. He tried to take my clothes off to clean me up and put me to bed and, as I vaguely slipped in and out of consciousness, I must have wondered just what the hell he was doing and I tried to swing for him. Class, Lewis!

Tuesday 30th

It's just three days since I played my third successive game for England but there's no time for a nice easy introduction back into club life. Two English sides have never been drawn against each other in the Heineken Cup until now; we are head-to-head with Wasps this Sunday. I'm not sure it gets much bigger than that. This is the Arsenal v Chelsea of the rugby code. The pressure is definitely on us this week, rather than Wasps, as we have already lost – to Biarritz – so we know that defeat will send us out of Europe.

Wellsy and the coaches quickly make me aware – as if I didn't already know – that it isn't just a case of walking back into this team, despite having been away with England. There is an injury doubt over Henry Tuilagi, but it is made pretty clear that if Henry is fit then he will play, as will Martin Corry, leaving it down to a straight fight between me and Neil Back for the final spot in the back row.

December

Wednesday 1st

Oh God. One of the biggest games in Leicester's calendar – in rugby union itself – and I'm running around the training ground shouting England calls and generally getting in the way. As you can imagine the abuse is flying thick and fast around me and deservedly so. In my defence, it's very hard to suddenly switch and adjust between club and country quickly. The good news (for me anyway) is that Henry doesn't make it, so both myself and Backy make the starting line-up. Sorry Henry.

Thursday 2nd

Disaster! Not much Christmas spirit in the Moody household today as we try to solve the mysterious case of *Who Broke The Christmas Angel?* There are basically two suspects – Mr L Moody (me) and Ms A Muggleton (the missus). The facts: we decided that today was the day to decorate the Moody household for Christmas (well, with an interior designer and a big kid under one roof, we were hardly going to leave it until Christmas Eve, were we?).

The tree is a strapping 6ft 6ins but I'm afraid it's about as real as Wellsy coming into training with a smile on his face. Anyway, we always enjoy the ritual of decorating it together – chucking on mountains of tinsel, gold, silver, purple, red and green shiny balls and little papier mache Santas and Ruldophs. Not really! Annie will kill me if when reads that. No, it's all very stylish of course. So, we're having a great giggle and add the piece de resistance – the aforementioned Christmas angel – which is placed on top with tender loving care. That's when it starts to go wrong.

One of us (I can't remember who, your Honour, honest) decides we need to move the tree – just a few inches – so the neighbours will be able to fully appreciate the lights and the cunning use of tinsel. Unfortunately, we make the huge error of believing that we can move it without first taking the decorations off. I am charged with holding the bottom of the tree and Annie the middle. And in the time it takes us to wiggle the tree five inches closer to the window we have a fallen angel – a smashed angel, in fact. Now, just because Annie was charged with looking after the middle of tree, I'm not suggesting for one minute that she was in charge of the angel's fate. Not for one minute. But obviously, it can't be the responsibility of the bloke holding the base of the tree, can it your Honour?

Saturday 4th

The guys are never, ever going to trust me to do anything ever again. Ever. It's the day before the game, so obviously it's cinema day and I rope in Leon and Damsy, (John Dams) one of our fitness guys.

Leon wants to see *The Forgotten* but I have already seen it before so I convince them to watch *Christmas with the Kranks* starring Tim Allen and Jamie Lee Curtis as a couple who decide not to celebrate Christmas as their daughter is away and then have to hurriedly create Christmas when she turns up unexpectedly. It sounds pretty bad from that description, but I like Jamie Lee Curtis and Dan Ackroyd (who's also in it) and I normally love Christmassy movies, so I thought it would be fun. I can confirm it is one of the worst movies ever and that I'll be buying Leon's popcorn until I've received a birthday telegram from the Queen.

I console myself with the thought that perhaps, like the team run, if the movie is rubbish the game will be great. Maybe if we win I'll have to find an awful movie for us to watch before every game? On the other hand that would be a terrible superstition to start! For one thing, Leon would probably kill me...

Sunday 5th

Wasps 31 – Leicester 37

Wasps: M van Gisbergen; J Lewsey, A Erinle, S Abbott, T Voyce; A King,
M Dawson; C Dowd, P Greening (rep: B Gotting, 59), W Green (rep:
A McKenzie, 65), S Shaw, R Birkett, J Worsley, J O'Connor, L Dallaglio

Leicester: G Murphy; L Lloyd (rep: A Tuilagi, 67), O Smith, D Gibson,
A Healey; A Goode, H Ellis (sin bin 24-34); G Rowntree, G Chuter, J White,
M Johnson, L Deacon, L Moody, N Back, M Corry

Wasps: Try: Lewsey. Con: Van Gisbergen. Pens: Van Gisbergen (8).
Leicester: Tries: Moody, Murphy, Corry. Cons: Goode (2). Pens: Goode (5).
Dropped goal: Goode.

All hail the Wigster! Graham Rowntree has today become the first-ever
English player to pass the 50-game mark in the Heineken Cup. It's an incredible
feat for anyone but for a prop, well I think it says all anyone needs to know
about Mr Rowntree. He's been kicked in the teeth by the England selectors a
couple of times over the years and was the unluckiest player in England not to
go to the 2003 World Cup. He was devastated by that, but he has never let any
of the knock-backs faze him – they've made him all the more determined.

The guy is a Leicester legend (the third member of the infamous 'ABC
Club') and against Wasps today he was immense. I know people talk about the
importance of the front five but it was simple today: unless we beat them in the
front five were we never going to win and with Wig and Whitey in such great
form the result was never in doubt, although we were disappointed with the
way we let them back into the match we started so well.

We were fantastic for the opening 20 minutes. I didn't have to wait too long
for the first try of the game, which was awarded to me after 73 seconds. For
once I wasn't just diving over the line under a pile of bodies. I scored after
Backy had grabbed an overthrown line out and, after the backs took over, I was
there to finish it all off.

That set the stage for us to storm into a 15-point lead – the key for us today
being our scrum which was way better than Wasps' and gave us the platform for

three early tries and for Goodey to kick his goals. Then the game deteriorated into a brawl of willpower and penalties. Everyone was giving each other lip and shouting at the ref to try and influence decisions. It was very niggly stuff, as you might expect from two sides who know each other so well and for whom there's so much at stake. But still, it was some game!

The match blew up a number of times, Cozza at one point getting Dallaglio around the throat in reaction to something that had been said. I don't give much back-chat (why, when I can let my tackling do the talking!) and neither does my old friend and England team-mate Joe Worsley. Very recently Joe and I had been plotting together to try to beat South Africa and now we are on opposite sides of the pitch. It's quite bizarre. You are trying to shoe someone out of the way in a ruck and then you realise it is your friend. You don't think about it during the game – it's only afterwards when you sit down together that you recall incidents and suggest he goes and gets another round in!

Being up against your mates is an added incentive and I always put in an extra one per cent to beat someone like Joe to the ball. Trouble is, it's cancelled out as he is doing the same!

Wasps host a short post-match reception and very generously give an opposition Man of the Match award to Whitey – something I've never seen before. That's a nice gesture, but I think the whole Leicester team deserve an award for putting up with the changing room they provided us. I know we are playing at a football ground and they may be only used to 11 players, but it was the smallest bloody room I have ever seen. The showers didn't work for about 20 minutes after the game either. The away changing rooms in most sports are rubbish, but this one was exceptionally bad. It was my first time at the Causeway stadium and I'd say it is just worse than Bath's Rec, where you normally have to get changed in the showers.

Tonight's celebrations are muted. Mostly because everyone is so knackered after such a gruelling game but also – although it was probably a great game to watch, being so close - we're all disappointed because we know we should have gone on and won by so much more. We also know we have a massive week ahead of us.

Jamie Hamilton gives me a lift back to Leicester and we head for Goodey's to crash in front of the TV with a couple of beers and several pizzas. Mission accomplished: well, part one, anyway. We have beaten Wasps once but it won't mean much if we can't do it again next weekend. Our early season defeat to Biarritz means we can't afford any more slip-ups if we are to make it into the quarter-finals.

Monday 6th

Am I bothered? No, but it is becoming quite clear that people don't have the slightest clue who I am. Annie and I are strutting our stuff on the red carpet at the world premiere of the film *Phantom of the Opera*, in Leicester Square and the crowd are doing their best. It's quite funny hearing them trying to place my face. "Rugby!" "Champions!" "World Cup..." people shout rather randomly as Annie sashays and I lumber down the carpet, seeing stars off the rugby pitch for once. No-one ever recognises me at events like this, which is absolutely fine by me. I'm not here to be seen; I just love the cinema. Not sure about Annie, though: like most girls she did take five hours to get ready (although of course she looks stunning in a black tuxedo thing).

I don't think any of the England lads are here but I do see Dougie Howlett, the Kiwi wing, and say hello. We see loads of celebs, like Andrew Lloyd Webber and Jennifer Ellison. Denise Van Outen is just in front of us and she's tiny! Unfortunately, I've got training tomorrow so I can't go to the after-show party. I'd love to go and see how smashed all these cool people get.

Tuesday 7th

Wellsy announces the team for the second part of our Wasps double-header and I'm in, which is great news on its own, but fantastic news as it will be my 100th start for the Tigers. It's a big milestone for me. Six months ago I couldn't look beyond one more game, let alone passing getting to a century and I've been stuck in the nineties for so long (yes, probably music-wise as well). I hope the next 100 comes a lot quicker – what with my shoulder injury, then the World Cup and then the foot injury, I've only played 15 matches for Tigers in the last two and a half seasons. People talk about rugby players playing too many games in the professional era, but with those stats behind me I can't play enough. I owe a big debt to this club. Besides, 100 starts is nothing compared to the likes of Wig, Johnno and Backy, all of whom have started over 300 matches. It's a nice feeling, but I'll wait until I get to their level, then I'll be impressed.

It's strange having to prepare for another game against Wasps so soon after beating them and it's incredible to think that we could beat the current

European champions and still get knocked out.

The coaches run us through the video of Sunday's game and pick out a few areas to concentrate on. Um, that's me, mostly, as I gave away a few penalties in the second half. It's a long time since I have played in a game where the referee was so strict. You literally couldn't step an inch over the line without him pinging you. That was a frustrating part of my game and so I am the star of today's video analysis.

I'm cringing a bit as I watch. I set myself really high standards and I know I'm still a few games off the level I'd like to be at; you always lose a bit of edge for a while after you've been injured. That said, things aren't going too badly: if you count my England games, I've scored five tries in my last eight matches. I've never had a run like that in my entire career.

We're all still really knackered from Sunday and a bit subdued in training: even the line-outs aren't going well and the contact work is sluggish. Today is meant to be our big contact session, but we've got so many injuries and knocks it's impossible, so we end up doing two-handed touch and some grip work. It is very rare that this happens at a club of our size and it is very frustrating. I hate going into a game without full training sessions, especially in defence.

Some players don't mind the odd grip session but if we batter each other in training, even for four or five minutes, it gives me the confidence that everyone is switched on for the game. Grip is basically a step up from touch – I guess you could say it's like giving a bloke a hard cuddle, by wrapping your arms around him to stop him breaking through, rather than just shouldering him to the floor.

We normally train for about an hour and 15 minutes, but it can be up to two hours, depending on how many calls etc there are to run through. Wednesdays are the worst: that's our pain day, the day the coaches run through defensive patterns and the like. We're supposed to start with touch, then move up to grip and spend the last ten minutes doing it full-on, but it always starts as grip and then we get frustrated if someone gets through, so we tend to go full-on, especially me. Bloody hurts when you get home though and seeing as Wasps is such a big game I'm not looking forward to tomorrow as much as I usually do.

Wednesday 8th

"One win over Wasps is worth nothing! One win over Wasps is worth nothing!"

As if we didn't know that, Wellsy and the coaches are screaming it at us what seems like every five seconds, but is probably more like... ooh, I dunno, at least ten. We are one defeat away from going out of the Heineken Cup and seeing Europe's biggest prize slip from our grasp. So we must drum it into ourselves to forget about last weekend. Lose this one and we needn't have bothered going through the pain and suffering that came with last weekend's hard-fought victory. We know it will be twice as hard this week. We all know that last season Wasps had the Celtic Warriors back-to-back. They lost the first game at home, won the second and went on to win the Heineken Cup.

Today's training revolves around unit skills – scrums and line outs. The coaches were pretty happy with our own ball against Wasps, but they were disappointed we didn't disrupt more of theirs so that is what we are concentrating on today. As we've had a lot of luck with the line-out against Wasps in the past, the talk today is about putting them under as much pressure as possible this Sunday. Wellsy reiterates how disappointed he was that we didn't do that last Sunday. I arrive home, after an hour and a half's intensive session, completely black and blue.

Thursday 9th

The Tigers announce that, after a series of long-term injuries, Steve Booth has parted company with the club. Steve made a huge impression here in the 2001–02 season, becoming the club's top scorer and sparking calls for him to be in the England squad. To be honest, though, it's not much of a surprise to any of the lads that the club won't be renewing his contract. It's a shame because he is a fantastic player, with awesome natural talent, but sadly I'm not sure he had the willpower to go with it. He finished with better than a try every three games for the Tigers though and I'd like to wish him all the best.

Saturday 11th

Wasps are a passionate side who will be out for revenge after losing at home, so we have been spending a lot of time this week working on our motivation, making sure we are right mentally. It would be easy to think that because we've beaten them once it will happen again, so the coaches want to make sure they banish any such thoughts from our minds. We know we need to be 100 times better than we were last Sunday and we know we must be more physical and totally dominate the match.

Sports psychology is coming more and more into the game. With England a lot of the guys work with kicking coach, Dave Alred, before big games, working on their preparation. You work out the challenges, write down the actions you want to achieve and then how best to perform them under pressure. Dave gets you to remember exactly how things were when you last performed well – making a note of your surroundings and feelings at the time, things like smells, noise and energy levels. It's always focusing on the positive, never dwelling on the negative. I know quite a few of the guys get a lot out of seeing him. I did it once, but it wasn't for me. I know this sounds daft but I look at it as if – for me personally – it would be a sign of me being mentally weak that I needed to go to him to talk myself up like that. I do go through it all in my own mind, envisaging games I've played well in and run through all the good things I did, but I just don't feel right going to see someone else to talk all that stuff through. Stupid really, but there you go.

Sunday 12th

Leicester 35 – Wasps 27

Leicester: G Murphy; L Lloyd, O Smith, D Gibson, A Healey; A Goode, H Ellis (rep: S Bemand, 75); G Rowntree, G Chuter, J White, M Johnson (capt), B Kay, L Moody, N Back, M Corry.

Wasps: M Van Gisbergen; J Lewsey, A Erinle (rep: R Hoadley 62), S Abbott, T Voyce; A King (rep: J Brooks 74), M Dawson (rep: H Biljon 66); C Dowd, B Gotting, W Green, S Shaw, R Birkett, J Worsley, J O'Connor, L Dallaglio (capt).

Leicester: Tries: Ellis, Chuter, Lloyd. Con: Goode. Pens: Goode (6).
Wasps: Tries: Voyce, Worsley, Green. Cons: Van Gisbergen (3) Pens: Van Gisbergen (2).

Yes! The best way to describe how I'm feeling on the final whistle is utter joy, as we complete the double over Wasps and give ourselves every chance of getting our season back on track by qualifying for the Heineken Cup quarter-finals. It's a great game and it's phenomenal to do the double over them.

But the euphoria disappears back in the dressing room. We really should have put 50 points on them and kept them to nil, but Wasps never gave in and while we raced into an early 19-0 lead thanks to Harry Ellis's try and Goodey's excellent goalkicking, again we lost our intensity, just as we did last week. That's twice in a week that we have failed to kill the game off. As I sit here in the dressing room I am more worried about what we haven't done rather than what we have.

Tuesday 14th

After two battering matches against Wasps I suppose it is inevitable that Wellsy will ring the changes for our forthcoming tie against Gloucester in the last 16 of the Powergen Cup. Rugby clubs don't take the mickey out of the competition as much as some of the bigger football clubs do with the League Cup, but many clubs will make changes this weekend as something has to give in a calendar that becomes more and more packed every season. The coaching staff were left with a difficult decision. Players need a rest and, perhaps more importantly with such a big squad as ours, quite a few players' contracts are on the line this season so they need the chance to prove themselves.

Wednesday 15th

I am sure Wellsy will be pleased with me today. I think I've mentioned before that he's a bit old school, likes the forwards to basically just beat the hell out of each other. We warm up this morning with a classic Wellsy drill: mauling. This involves one person having the ball and five or six lads piling in on top to try and get it. It's much more violent than a scrum and is just typical Wellsy. As a player he didn't want to be running with the ball, just making tackles and diving into rucks. He'd fly over the top, totally illegally, and always get penalised. In short, he was a nutter. That and the fact that he's developed massively as a coach, taken so many things on board while keeping that old-school edge, is probably why I get on with him so well!

Anyway, he's a hugely strong man, so he's got absolutely no excuses for what I'm about to tell you. We are in the middle of our last defence session before the game, a five-on-five drill, when one of our scrum-halves, Alex Wright, breaks across the field. As there isn't anyone else there I start legging it across the field to get to him – and, er, run straight into Wellsy who is standing in the middle of the field watching, as the coaches usually do, and he collapses in a heap on the ground. Now, look, I certainly didn't intend to poleaxe Wellsy; I genuinely didn't see him. Honestly. But if I had I'd have had to swerve round him and I wouldn't have got anywhere near Alex. Maybe I should pretend one of my contact lenses had fallen out...

Wellsy isn't the sort of bloke to hold a grudge and I'm relieved to discover that's true even of people who have almost just knocked him out. He announces the sweeping changes we've all been expecting and. luckily, I'm not one of the casualties – even if he is!

Backy, Johno and Wig get a rest, along with Geordan, Austin Healey, Daryl Gibson, Andy Goode, and Harry Ellis, which means that my old mate Ben Kay is made captain. It will be good for Johno to have a rest. Despite jetting off all over the world for his testimonial year, he has played every game of the season and he's been carrying a slight back injury for the last three or four weeks.

Not many sides could cope with leaving that many international caps out of their team – but although I'm the only one left from the back row that took on Wasps a few days ago, the team is hardly weakened by the introduction of Brett Deacon and Will Johnson.

The pressure is on: the Tigers have only lost five times in almost 40 previous cup ties, so we don't want to be the side that makes it six. Worse: after some Christmas shopping I arrive home to an empty house as Annie has gone to London to see her family who are over from New Zealand. Ah well, another chance to show off my salad-making skills.

Thursday 16th

"Hey Lewis," went the phone call. "Fancy coming to Johno's Christmas lunch at the Grosvenor Hotel in London, for his testimonial year?"

"Why not? That'd be great, cheers."

Pause.

"The only snag is that we are doing a nativity play on stage and we want you to be in it'."

Hmm, so they want me to play the donkey because Johno thinks I'm always making a prize ass of myself, running round like a headless chicken in training and it'll be really funny...

"So we'd like you to be a shepherd, if that's okay?'

Reee-sult! Towel round the head, hobble on with a crook (the wooden stick kind, I'm not casting aspersions on my team-mates, you understand) and the audience will think that I'm method acting, instead of noticing my dodgy knees, feet etc.

I haven't laughed so much in ages. Myself and Austin are shepherds. Leon, Geordan and Kyran Bracken are the wise men (I believe they call that casting against type), Nobby West is the Virgin Mary (ditto), Jase Leonard is the Angel (ha, somebody's been having fun with this), Benny Kay and Cozza are the innkeepers (now that's more like it) and Lol Dallaglio is Joseph (no comment).

Benny, Cozza and Jason are given some lines a few minutes before we go on. I start worrying when I see that, but thankfully all us shepherds have to do is shuffle across the stage and join the queue of people handing over presents to the baby Jesus, hidden from view in his enormous crib. After a while, however, the wise men decide it's a wise idea to start lobbing their presents into the crib – and it's not long before they're being hurled back, twice as fast. Well, Johno's so bloody competitive isn't he? Of course, he had to play Jesus, considering the career he's had!

It's ridiculous fun and the audience seem to love it almost as much as we do. I'm glad to be able to help out Johno – he's always been there for me with advice and I feel he's a real confidante – he was the first person I turned to when I was trying to decide whether to have a shoulder reconstruction and he was really helpful.

Friday 17th

I'm feeling very sheepish today as Wellsy is standing there feeling his side. At the time of the poleaxing he said he was ok, but he now admits that he went to see the physio and is feeling the effects. He mumbles something about not being ready for the tackle and that he was relaxed. Whatever, Wellsy!

We head off to a local hospital to do our bit at playing Father Christmas. It's clear most of the patients have no idea who we are (were they all in the crowd at Leicester Square?). It doesn't matter. They were probably hoping to see Posh and Becks, or someone properly famous, but I really enjoy these trips: handing out the presents and trying to put a smile on people's faces. I'll have to get Wellsy something nice to cheer him up – a zimmer frame, maybe!

Back at the house I stare, not for the first time, at the list of jobs Annie left me to do while she's away. Clean the oven, clear out the spare room, assemble the flat-pack chest of drawers we bought a few weeks ago, brush my teeth... Not many have been ticked off and instead of cracking into them I flop onto the couch and turn on the Discovery Channel.

Well, that way I might even discover how to put a flat-pack together. They're the bane of my life. I do try but my attempts are always horrendous. I have no idea, I'm completely clueless with stuff like that. I built a cupboard once and it looks like the Leaning Tower of Pisa, well it would if the Leaning Tower of Pisa had a door that doesn't open properly. I'm always having to call Dean the handyman ,who helped us renovate the cottage a few years ago, and say, "Um... can you come over and help me do this please?" He's like, "You're kidding!" Er, no. I might be built like a brick outhouse but I have absolutely no idea how to make one.

Saturday 18th

Leicester 13 – Gloucester 20

Leicester: S Vesty; A Tuilagi (rep: D Hipkiss, 80+3), L Lloyd, O Smith, T Varndell; R Broadfoot (rep: R Warren, 60), S Bemand; M Holford, G Chuter (rep: E Taukafa, 75), D Morris, J Hamilton, B Kay, B Deacon (sin-bin, 56-67), L Moody, W Johnson.

Gloucester: J Goodridge; M Garvey, N Mauger, H Paul, S Kiole; B Davies, A Gomarsall; C Bezuidenhout, M Davies, G Powell, A Eustace (rep: P Buxton, 50), A Brown, J Boer, A Hazell (rep: J Forrester, 62), A Balding.

Leicester: Try: Varndell. Con: Broadfoot. Pens: Broadfoot, Vesty.
Gloucester: Tries: penalty, Mauger. Cons: Paul (2). Pens: Paul (2)

Annie's still not back, which means I have the luxury of a full-on panic this morning. My routine on the morning of a game is always the same. A very light breakfast: Coco Pops or Special K and always some fruit. Then I go into my obsessive compulsive routine. I check my bag a million times. It doesn't matter how many times Annie reassures me, I have to check, check and check again. And again.

Much as I'm missing her, it's probably good for our relationship that she's not around to see my little routine too often. I'm like one of those holidaymakers who has to go back and check they turned the lights off, before reaching for their passport 64 times on the way to the airport. I never have forgotten anything before a game, but I know one day I will. Boots: two pairs (in case one splits)? Check. It's not like football, where they leave their boots at the club and the trainees clean them for them, you know. We even used to have to wash our own kit until about two years ago. Washbag, gum shields, half-dead poppy, contact lenses... I can sometimes go through three or four pairs of contacts in a game. It can be quite awkward if you get clattered and one goes flying out, as you have to wait until we're kicking at goal or there's a penalty or something before you can put another one in. That's very weird, because you're running around for maybe five minutes with one eye working and one not. You can't judge distances like that, so if you ever see me flying in for a tackle and missing completely that's my excuse.

Lots of the guys wear contacts and it can cause problems. I remember the Doc running on once after I'd been forced to play for a few minutes without one lens. I was desperate and really shouting at him to hurry up. He was really struggling to find my lens and spilling lenses all over the pitch. I ended up having to wear Wig's as he didn't seem to have mine on him. His are a slightly stronger prescription than mine, so that's another excuse for all the mistakes I made that day.

There are no excuses today: we put out a young team and lose. But there must be two moons in the sky this afternoon, because the referee gets it wrong and then apologises to us for his mistakes! His biggest was awarding them a penalty try, just before the hour mark. There was no way it was a penalty. They drove us over the line and we held them up, it's as simple as that. He said we collapsed it. For their second try they had knocked it on, by about five metres, so to say we were annoyed afterwards is an understatement. It is a credit to him that afterwards he apologises to Wellsy, though; a lot of referees wouldn't do that.

I don't think they ever looked like crossing our line. It seemed like we had the game sewn up. They had five attempts at driving a maul over and we stopped every one. Then they got a penalty try and a freak score against the run of play which was very, very frustrating.

Still, we had the better of them early on and there's a lot for us to be happy about. This Leicester team prides itself on its defence and if we are going to carry on that tradition then younger players coming through must keep up the standards, which they did today. The forwards had a fantastic game.

We were fielding a very young side and if nothing else the game allowed us a glimpse of the Tigers team of the future, summed up by a great try – the only one of the first half – from Tom Varndell, who in scoring beat one of Gloucester's young stars, Marcel Garvey. He's got electrifying pace and is definitely one to watch.

Gloucester were delighted, to say the least, to win at Welford Road. As we walked off I heard one of their forwards saying:

"I can't believe we have won at Leicester."

Believe it, mate, because it won't be happening again.

Monday 20th

Thud! I'm a bit hungover this morning as last night we had our Christmas dinner at Möbius, a trendy bar and restaurant in Leicester's West End. The social side at the club slipped a bit last season. I'm not sure whether it was because of us doing so badly, and the atmosphere being pretty bad, but there just weren't the team dinners and partners' events last season. Perhaps it also had something to do with the World Cup being right in the middle of the campaign.

When coach Paddy [Pat] Howard returned to Leicester in the summer, one of the first things he introduced was a new social committee as he feels it's crucial to team spirit... and of course he is right. He asked me if I would take on the job of being social events organiser and I roped in Danny Hipkiss to help me. One of our first big jobs was to re-introduce the partners and players' Christmas meal and last night around 50 turned up, including Paddy and some of the other coaches (quite a success I thought, especially as Annie made it back in time for the festivities)

We started with good intentions as we are still in full training and have a game at the end of this week, so I had to make do with drinking Kava – a traditional pacific drink made from roots of some kind – with a few of the Fijian lads. It looked like muddy water and tasted like muddy water, although the brothers seemed to enjoy it as they sat there all night drinking it. But, like every Christmas party, things degenerated quite quickly. Austin tried to punch me in the nuts about 20 times – well he was never going to land was he? Most people seemed to get very drunk indeed, and we got home about 3am.

Which is why I'm feeling like death this morning. It certainly sounds like Annie is playing Megadeath at full volume in our bedroom. I'll check in a minute, when I've forced my head off the pillow and out from under the duvet. I know rugby players have a reputation for big drinking but with so much training I seem to be a little out of practice.

Oh, she's not. Must be my head then. I crawl back under the duvet with a pint of water and some aspirin and tell myself that I wouldn't have bought any good Christmas presents anyway... or really benefited from the recovery session I was due to do.

I make it to the couch by lunchtime, and by 4pm manage to drag my sorry butt into town to pay a bill at the office of my financial adviser, Rob Bunting, which I've owed for about three months. He's the one who always tells me what an old rugby player I am and takes great delight in ramming home the point when he catches sight of my grey skin and the bags under my eyes.

Tuesday 21st

Thank God! The hangover from hell has gone to hell and I'm back in the land of the living. Well, until Wellsy sends me back to hell by telling me that I will only be on the bench when the club returns to Zurich Premiership action against Worcester this week.

"I want to give you a rest so you can get over your little niggles. We've got a lot of big games coming up," he says.

Fine, whatever. His decision, but I'm not happy about it.

I'm in by 11am for weights and a video run-through of the Gloucester match, followed by a skills session. I'm glad it's a pretty light day as my body is in pieces from the last two games (the booze has absolutely no bearing whatsoever on the way I feel, honest) and I'm really feeling every ache and bump during the skills session.

It's worth it all afterwards, though, when I sit down with the lads at our Christmas lunch, cooked by the two Jackies who look after us at Welford Road. It's great to kick back with the guys, pull a few crackers (not the two Jackies!) and eat some sweets. Turkey and stuffing is probably the favourite meal of the year for most of the lads and it isn't long before the Christmas songs are ringing out throughout the hall which is great for team morale.

After taking my fill of holly, ivy and brussels sprouts I head into town to meet

Danny Hipkiss for our ever-so-serious and intensely stuffy social committee meeting. Wig is supposed to be representing the older players on the committee, but he hasn't been – how shall I put this? – the most active of committee members this season, so Danny and I tend to leave him out and just tell him what we are doing. To be fair, he is getting on a bit, so probably needs those early nights.

Thursday 23rd

Only two days until Christmas. Yes! I love Christmas; I'm like a big kid about it and I have to admit that's big in the sense of size, not maturity. Danny and I decided we needed to sign up 'Secret Santa' for the occasion and I have to say the lads have really taken to him. Ben Kay gets Martin Johnson's autobiography (signed, of course) and Austin Healey gets Matt Dawson's autobiography (also signed – by Matt this time, funnily enough). Leon is Whitey's 'Secret Santa' and he's really got into the spirit of it, putting in loads of effort (hmmm... note to self: he has the makings of a Senior Entertainments Committee executive one day. If only I'd completed that business degree I could do a flowchart showing the benefits of having him on board, versus the cost implications of buying him a pint while discussing venues. Anyway, Whitey is a farmer so Leon searched high and low for something appropriate and eventually found a shepherd's crook (no, not the one I used in the nativity play). Whitey is delighted as he has apparently just bought some sheep so he may well get the chance to actually use his present one day, unlike poor Ben and Austin, ha ha!

I didn't actually get a present. (Boooo!). No, honestly, I don't mind, I'm just happy to see the looks of joy on my team-mates' faces and spread a little Christmas cheer. Yeah, right. they're all swines...

Friday 24th

Did I mention that I love Christmas? I am so excited today. Not only is it Christmas, but Annie and I have decided to host the family celebrations at our house for the first time. It's a bit nerve-wracking but I'm sure we'll cope. A significant step in the relationship, I think you'll agree.

As well as Annie's mum, her brother Jamie, his wife and their twins, Zak and Alex, we are being joined by her other brother Andy, her two step-sisters, Lana and Bryony, and their brother, John. My mum and dad are over from Jakarta, although as we have a houseful they have wisely and kindly decided to check into a nearby hotel. So that's just 13 of us then!

Annie and I decided that we would struggle to host everyone for a sit-down meal so we have adjourned for tonight's feast to The Castle pub, opposite where we live. It's one thing hosting Christmas, quite another cooking Christmas dinner for everyone. No-one seems to mind: the food's great and the alcohol's flowing freely enough to encourage people to put paper hats on their heads.

Andy (not me, honest) is the leader of a splinter group who can't wait until tomorrow and want to open one present tonight. In the end we open some games and then Andy, Jamie and I proceed to spend what could very possibly be hours playing Shock Doctor (and drinking). The game is a bit like Russian Roulette. Four people stick their finger in each of four different holes and then the game randomly picks someone to get an electric shock. Sounds fun? It's hilarious, especially if you don't get the electric shock! All the girls refuse to do it while the boys act like hard men, pretending it doesn't hurt... until we get a shock, at which point we squeal like babies.

The more intellectual members of the group (that'll be the girls then) play one of those name games where, for example, you have to name a fruit beginning with 'A' and you score a point if you give a unique answer. But the Shock Doctor rocks. I have no idea what time we get to bed, although I am dimly aware that my hair has, shall we say, slightly more body than usual.

Saturday 25th

When two families come together at Christmas the biggest problem is whose present-opening system you will employ and this is the cause of some heated discussion this morning. Having given in to the Muggletons' (Annie's family) idea of opening one present last night, I was hoping we could do it the Moody way this morning (ie, open all the presents at once after a late breakfast), but it is rejected in favour of the way they do it in Annie's family. Well, I suppose there are more of them than us.

Their way is sitting around while everyone watches you open your presents one at a time. Now, everyone seems to have about 40 presents and there are 13 of us, so I spend most of the morning watching other people open their presents and saying: "Wow, that's good" when all I want to do is open mine! When you're sitting on the floor, especially if you have an aching, breaking body like mine, it becomes something of a test of endurance. Is my attitude against the spirit of Christmas, I wonder? I can't complain: Annie came to my parents last year and we did it our way then so it's only fair to switch things around this time.

I got loads of cool stuff but the best present is from Annie – and I'm not just saying that because I'll be in trouble if I don't put that in print. She bought me guitar lessons, which is fantastic. I took up the guitar during the World Cup because there was nothing much else to do and it beat watching cable TV. Jonny Wilkinson and Matt Stevens are both awesome guitar players and have really helped me and Steve Thompson, who's also learning, when we get a bit stuck. I've been trying to learn *Nothing Else Matters* by Metallica for ages, but it's so hard. It doesn't help that it has a three-minute guitar intro. I must be mad trying to do that. Trying to sing and play guitar at the same time is like rubbing your tummy and patting your head – bloody impossible! I don't know how people do it. I'd love to get to the stage where I could pick up a guitar at a party and strum anything, but none of my family is at all musical, so I think it's going to be a slog. But now I've got the lessons, 2005 will be the year when I learn to play a bit better.

I got Annie some jewellery but we decide to open her presents upstairs as I don't want to appear flash in front of everyone else. There's no risqué underwear, well not this year anyway. Annie's brother John, who is 13, has made me an amazing present. He has carved the Leicester Tigers symbol out of stainless steel to create a really cool scuplture for me. My parents come through with a Mini-i-Pod and I'm also presented with a giant copy of my Timberland advert, which some people – I can't see it myself – suggest might be a little camp.

Annie lays on a huge buffet which we graze over for the whole day. And then, treat of treats, a massive cheeseboard. Cheese is without question my favourite food – Stilton especially, but I love all cheese – but it is so bad for me I don't have it as often as I would like, which is every day. If I see it on the dessert list I have to have it, but I have to restrict myself to just a tiny piece as it is the most fattening thing in the world. Today I make sure I tuck into the cheeseboard, as my special Christmas treat to myself. Oh God, this feels good. It tastes good. I can just about stop myself from grabbing big hunks and stuffing them down my throat! A perfect end to a perfect day.

Sunday 26th

Ouch! I was mucking about with Annie's brothers last night and accidentally twisted my wrist. We have the team run today, trying to shake off the excesses of yesterday before taking on Worcester tomorrow and the longer the session goes on, the more certain I am not going to be able to make the game. It hurts like hell. I finally tell Wellsy I won't be fit – as I was only selected for the bench it's not that big a deal for me or the club.

Once I get back from the team run it is time for the traditional Boxing Day walk in the park, an attempt to walk off some of the huge amount of cheese I consumed last night.

Still walking...

Monday 27th

Leicester 50 – Worcester 7

Leicester: G Murphy; S Rabeni (rep: D Hipkiss, 12min), O Smith (rep: M Cornwell, 52), D Gibson, S Vesty; A Goode, S Bemand (rep: H Ellis, 50); G Rowntree (rep: D Morris, 20), G Chuter (rep: J Buckland, 63), J White, M Johnson (rep: B Kay, 63), L Deacon, W Johnson, N Back (rep: B Deacon, 76), M Corry.

Worcester: T Delport; G Pieters, B Hinshelwood, G Trueman, P Sampson; J Brown (rep: T Hayes, 40), N Cole; A Windo (rep: L Fortey, 40), A van Neikerk (rep: C Hall, 65), C Horsman, T Collier (rep: P Murphy, 60), C Gillies, D Hickey (rep: S Vaili, 52), P Sanderson, B MacLeod-Henderson.

Leicester: Tries: Back, Penalty, Gibson, Goode, Murphy, Ellis, Hipkiss. Cons: Goode (6). Pen: Goode.
Worcester: Try: Trueman. Con: Hayes.

The postman delivers a slightly late, but very special Christmas card this morning. It's from Clive Woodward, who will be coaching the Lions next summer. It's in the form of six postcards and some pretty gay Lions wristbands, confirming that I'm being considered for the trip. They will remain in their packaging. Unfortunately, within ten minutes of meeting up with the rest of the lads, it becomes apparent that more than 100 players have also received the same package. So while it would obviously be a huge honour, I'm not counting my chickens as only 44 players will go. The only person wearing their wristband is Austin!

Geordy is on great form today, scoring a magnificent try as we run in seven against Worcester, although I'm stuck on the sidelines with this hand injury. I really didn't want to miss this one. For one thing the whole family have got tickets to the match and were hoping to see me play, rather than listening to my expert commentary and whingeing from the sidelines.

One piece of very bad news today is that Seru Rabeni has suffered a recurrence of his knee injury, which looks like it will rule him out for six weeks. On the plus side, the win against Worcester means we will end 2004 in a fantastic position – nine points clear at the top of the Zurich Premiership, continuing our recent run of stunning form. Happy days.

Tuesday 28th

My hopes of a quick and quiet recovery from my hand injury are dashed by Wellsy's decision to call me "a muppet" in the post-match press conference yesterday, and tell everyone I hurt my hand "opening Christmas presents".

I just didn't want him to mention my missus' brother, so it seems he embellished the story a bit and I'm really mad about it. It means that almost every journalist, radio reporter and TV person in Britain has been phoning me and my mobile has been jammed by mickey-taking messages from mates, asking me what presents I got.

"Did you get a Rubik's cube for Christmas?"

"I always said you couldn't fight your way out of a paper bag but I never knew you'd have trouble getting into one."

Etc, etc, etc.

I'm also not happy about being described as "accident-prone", but that's Wellsy for you. It was his idea of a joke, but it wasn't a very good one.

Still, Wellsy's words do lead to a rather a novel start to the day, to say the least, as he spent most of the morning apologising to me after I'd asked him what the hell it was all about and told him I thought he was bang out of order. He was a complete idiot for saying that in a press conference and he seems to accept that.

I like Wellsy a lot, but I have no intention of letting him off after he tried to embarrass me. My missus' brother may have exacerbated it a little (as did a builder friend of ours who's got such a strong handshake it almost brought me to my knees) but I've had this hand injury for some time – as Wellsy knows only too well – which is why, along with a couple of other niggles, he had originally named me on the bench for the game against Worcester.

Anyway, it's not the first time he's been out of order about me in the press. When I was coming back from my foot injury he suggested, via the press, that I might never play again, which isn't exactly what you want to read when you're really down and desperately trying to get back to full fitness. Sometimes you just have to say to him: "What are you doing? You can't say that!"

But he's a great coach. Very meticulous, very dedicated. Down to earth, too. We played together and have always greeted each other in that casual way: 'Alright, Wellsy you ****! [insert colourful swearword here], what's happening?' 'Hey, ****!, how are you?' It's a term of endearment between us, although he did say to me once, "Lewis, you can't call the head coach **** any more." Well, if he can call me "a muppet"...

It's ironic really: he doesn't drink that much (which is a shame as he's pretty entertaining once he's had a few) and he's not one for great speeches or being in the public eye. He's actually quite shy in public. When he was a player he was also a policeman, so he was always sloping off on the beat after a game, rather than coming out on the lash with us. We did manage to soften him up eventually, though.

Wednesday 29th

My England team-mate Will Greenwood is told, after a shoulder operation, that it will be three months before he plays again, raising doubts over his fitness for the New Zealand tour in May. I hope he makes it. He joined Leicester at the same time as me, roughly, and he has won everything except a Lions' Test place, a distinction denied him in South Africa in 1997 and again in Australia four years later by serious injuries. It's always frustrating to hear of another player going down like this. I have to remember to get in touch with Will, as I suffered the same injury a few seasons ago.

So many of the guys have had their shoulders done it is ridiculous. We call it the Zipper Club at Leicester, after the scar it creates on the shoulder. Me, Leon and Geordan had it done in consecutive years. Leon was first, the Geordan and I had mine the year after. It's quite a cool scar actually; I'm sure I could convince people I got it shark-wrestling or something. It really shows when it's cold: it goes a bit blue. It was a weird one though; there are so many stitches involved that for about a year afterwards it felt like I'd had someone else's skin grafted on.

Friday 31st

We are playing Gloucester in a couple of days so, even if it is New Year's Eve, I still have to stay sober. Which would be fine, except someone (not me) had decided that we had to dress up for a Murder Mystery New Year's Eve party round at our place.

And even more foolishly, someone (again not me!) decided that the boys would come as girls and the girls as boys. Now, it's ok to dress up in women's clothes if you are drunk, but I'm not sure it is the best idea if all you're allowed is a couple of glasses of Coke.

We've invited a few of the guys over, including Leon and Geordan and their partners, and I have to say that Leon and Geordy look absolutely stunning. Ha! Not. All the female characters are 1950s women. I'm Donna Matrix (geddit) and I would absolutely love wearing my very stretchy dress if I was drinking. But I'm not. And neither are Leon or Geordy. The girls are extremely sympathetic and down our share of the alcohol in some sort of twisted show of solidarity, which also involves giggling. A lot.

You normally find out if you are the murderer early on in these games but this version isn't as good. I turn out to be the murderer but don't discover this until right at the end. Not sure if that was my fault? It's so complicated it's ridiculous. It's much better when the murderer has to bluff their way through it after finding out at the start. You need a criminology degree to read half of the script and halfway through we all have no idea what anyone else has done.

So, we retreat to the back garden for the obligatory midnight fireworks. Ali, one of my old friends from Uni, is completely smashed and sticks all 20 fireworks in the ground. I decide we ought to do a test run on one of them and Ali lights it and takes cover behind a two-foot wall while I watch from the apparent safety of the back door. That's when we find out what the plastic poles left over in the bag are for!

The firework is wedged firmly in the ground and explodes all over Ali, who is by this stage almost wetting himself laughing, with a big bang. The doors and windows actually shake with the force of the explosion and I get covered with cardboard. Oh dear – maybe I am a muppet sometimes after all. Top night though.

January

Saturday 1st

What a way to bring in the New Year – training at Welford Road! It is lucky that we didn't have anything to drink last night as today would be a real struggle on the back of a hangover.

I always look forward to training, but today even I'm reluctant. It's one of those days where you have to dispense with the desire to look hard and just layer on the beanie, thermals and overjacket. As forwards, our training sessions are more heavy on the contact side than the backs – for them it's all kicking, sidesteps and handling – so we should be warmer than them, but today we're out in force in our full-length thermals and I'm still freezing. I'm sure the backs think we're a right bunch of gaylords, but I don't care. It's bloody cold and gone are the days when I dived into every muddy puddle with glee. I still love mud, mud, glorious mud, but now my body can't handle the extreme cold as well as when I was a kid and I try not to get wet and therefore cold. It plays havoc with your joints, I tell you.

Thing is, it's a job now. Back when I was a kid, we'd do rugby on Tuesdays and Thursdays at school and I couldn't wait for those days to come round. I still love training, but now I do it every day, twice a day, and I wake up in the morning stiff, battered and groaning from the session the day before. If it's freezing cold, muddy and snowing as well, I have to admit I am occasionally tempted to dive back under the duvet. But (like the professional sportsman I am!) I make it in and complete the session. I head straight for a nice, deep, hot bath when I get home though.

Today is also the old man's birthday, so I can't relax and soak for too long. He's coming over with my mum and auntie and uncle, who are my godparents, and so I reluctantly ease my aching body out of the bath and start the clean-up operation. The house is a complete tip after last night (there seem to be a lot of bits of cardboard around for some reason) so the tidying takes us about three hours. I always make sure dad gets two separate presents and that we don't just give him one joint one. He gets quite upset if you try and give him a combined Christmas and birthday present, so he's very happy with his new waxed jacket.

Sunday 2nd

Gloucester 13 – Leicester 28

Gloucester: J Goodridge; M Garvey (rep: J Bailey, 69), N Mauger, T Fanolua, S Kiole; H Paul, A Gomarsall; C Bezuidenhout (rep: T Sigley, 53), M Davies, P Vickery, A Eustace (rep: P Buxton, 67), A Brown, J Boer, A Hazell, A Balding (rep: J Forrester, 53).

Leicester: G Murphy (rep: S Vesty, 59); O Smith, L Lloyd (sin-bin, 57-67), D Gibson, T Varndell; A Goode (rep: M Cornwell, 80+3), H Ellis; D Morris, G Chuter (rep: J Buckland, 31-40+4, 41), J White, M Johnson, B Kay, L Moody, N Back, M Corry (rep: W Johnson, 23).

Gloucester: Tries: Mauger, Eustace. Pen: Paul.
Leicester: Tries: Lloyd, Smith, Gibson. Cons: Goode 2. Pens: Goode (2). Dropped goal: Goode (40+5).

I certainly hadn't planned to finish the game by towelling down one of my team-mates after he'd come out of the shower, but when duty calls! My old mate, Martin Corry, picked up a particularly nasty dislocated elbow during today's game and couldn't use his right arm, so I stepped up to the plate. I couldn't desert him in his hour of need – although it was a bit odd for both of us to say the least.

Trips to Kingsholm are always fiery encounters, but this injury was just one of those unlucky ones when you fall and land awkwardly. It's particularly unfortunate for Cozza because he is in such a good vein of form at the moment, and would have been one of the first names on the team sheet for the Six Nations. As soon as I saw him I knew his elbow was dislocated, his forearm was sticking out the side. Leon's reaction said it all. He went over to help pick him up, saw his elbow and winced, trying to look the other way. He signalled to the bench straightaway to get him off. The doctors put it back in immediately – apparently the elbow is one of the easiest bones to put back in when it is dislocated – and, ahem, I'm sure it wasn't too painful.

It was a great win today, payback for our recent cup defeat to them and ending a three-year wait for a win at Kingsholm, and it means we start 2005 with an eight-point gap over Wasps in second place.

Monday 3rd

We're the walking wounded today – I don't think I've ever been involved in a game where so many players have their calf muscles stamped on. We haven't had much luck this season and we have seen both Cozza and George Chuter banned (George for an eye-poking incident after the Citing Commission looked into it), so it was particularly frustrating to see that no action was taken against Phil Vickery, who appeared to stamp on Daryl Gibson's head. It is annoying when it's not picked up upon. Players just want consistency.

But you always expect a tough, fairly bitter game at Gloucester, because they hate losing at home so much. Their crowd is very vocal and they expect their team to be very physical.

Tuesday 4th

Cozza's injury means everyone is speculating that I might move back to the blindside for the opening match of the Six Nations against Wales in a month's time. It's not something that is uppermost in my mind; just staying fit would be an achievement, let alone getting selected for my first Six Nations game for two years.

But it is one of the topics of conversation at Newark Rugby Club, where I am this evening for a question and answer session – with Geordan – for their Under-14s and Under-16s. Dusty Hare and John Wells started their career at Newark, so they asked us to go over and help them out with their fundraising. I got to the stage after the World Cup where I was really bored of doing these types of things. There are only so many times you can tell people what it's like to win the World Cup before it gets boring (trust me), and I was getting a bit fed up of talking about it.

I think Johno's still living on it, but we always told the same stories, like the one about Jason Leonard peeing in a champagne bottle on top of one of the buses we toured London in for our civic reception. He'd had far too many cans of Tetley's and was desperate, but the worst thing was that he then shook up the bottle and sprayed it everywhere – mostly down the back of my trousers. I don't think the Queen was that impressed when we met her later, but the corgis loved it!

Anyway, these Q+As usually follow the same game plan and after an hour and a half of telling the lads what I do off the pitch (try to play guitar), what car I drive (Renault Megane – nothing very exciting) and who my best mate is (had to say Geordy, even though I hate him, as he is sitting next to me) we're done. Geordy and I have done quite a few of these over the years and have honed our "let's just take the mick out of each other" routine to perfection and it seems to go down well again tonight.

Geordy and I have a little bit of fun towards the end when we see Leon slink into the back of the room.

"Excuse me ladies and gents," I say, dramatically. "I'd just like to be the first to congratulate Leon on his engagement."

Cue wild applause and Leon making obscene gestures at me. You started it mate, remember a couple of years back when you told anyone who'd listen that me and Annie were engaged? Gotcha.

Thursday 6th

The story about my hand is going global. I am back playing now but someone shows me a copy of Sports Illustrated (yes the American one!) and I'm in it under 'THIS WEEK'S SIGN OF THE APOCALYPSE'. Can you believe it?

The article says: "English rugby star Lewis Moody missed the first game after the holidays because he said he'd hurt himself 'opening Christmas presents'."

The 'story' has apparently even made the press in Australia. I'm starting to see the funny side of it all now. The only thing that still annoys me is Wellsy calling me a muppet. That's the sort of thing he would say to me in front of the Leicester boys or when we are on our own. I can take it as a joke when he says it to me privately, but when something like that appears in the papers it can be taken out of context, which it has been. People do believe what they read in the papers and it can alter their view of you. I know it was said as a joke and actually quite funny, but the guys from *Soccer AM* have just rung up wanting to do something on it. Where will it all end?

Normally on a Tuesday we might do an easier session, such as tackle technique, which is only about 60 per cent of capacity, but given that we've got Sunday's massive game against Biarritz to prepare for, we endure one of the most intense defence sessions for a long, long time. It's two hours of full on one-on-one tackling, then two-on-two, followed by a full on session with the starting XV against those who have been left out. By the end of it I'm knackered.

I'm pleased though that the session's so demanding: Sunday is such a massive game for us: a side like Leicester simply cannot afford not to be in the last eight of Europe's top competition.

Saturday 8th

The nerves are starting to kick in. Although we've trained well all week and the lads are all fired up about the game, I can see it in their eyes – just a hint of the pressure.

The team run goes well enough (is that a bad omen?) and afterwards we all sit down to the now traditional chicken curry. I suppose it's a bit of a strange meal to have the day before a game when most people would think we'd be carbo-loading, but it's been the tradition at Leicester for as long as I can remember – and it does come with rice (we forego the poppadoms and Kingfisher though). So there you have it, the secret of our success – chicken curry (medium hot).

That, and the trip to the cinema of course. But before Geordy, Leon and I set off, we decide to go and watch our fitness adviser, John Dams, playing for his local club, Market Bosworth third team. He's always going on about how many tries he has scored the previous Saturday and how awesome he is at rugby.

The game is into the second half by the time we get there, but we're assured Damsy scored three tries in the first half. Mind you, the opposition look like they've either come from the office or off a building site and one bloke looks like he's pushing 50 for God's sake. John is actually rather good, but obviously I'd never tell the big mute that. It's about minus 20 degrees, so we don't hang around after the final whistle and finally hit the cinema. Foolishly we plump for *The Aviator*, which is good but incredibly long – not the best idea after such a heavy week.

I'm glad we're not going to a hotel tonight: I would much rather sleep in my own bed, get up and have breakfast when I want and get into my rhythm, rather than one that is dictated by the needs of a hotel.

Sunday 9th

Leicester 17 – Biarritz 21

Leicester: G Murphy; O Smith, L Lloyd, D Gibson, A Healey (rep: A Tuilagi, 68); A Goode, H Ellis (sin bin 54-64); D Morris (rep: G Rowntree, 52), G Chuter (rep: J Buckland, 76), J White, M Johnson, L Deacon, L Moody, N Back, W Johnson (rep: B Kay, 68).

Biarritz: N Brusque; P Bidabe, F Martin Arramburu, T Lacroix, J Marlu; D Traille, D Yachvili; P Balan (rep: B Lecouls, 52), B August (rep: J-M Gonzalez, 62), D Avril (rep: K Lealamanua, 52), J Thion, O Olibeau (rep: D Couzinet, 47), S Betsen, T Lievremont (rep: C Milheres, 79), I Harinordoquy.

Leicester: Tries: A Tuilagi, Ellis. Cons: Goode (2). Pen: Goode
Biarritz: Tries: Thion, Marlu, Con: Yachvili, Pens: Yachvili (2). DG: Traille

I have a funny feeling we're not quite right for this match as I look round at the guys in the dressing room. It's all gone quiet, legs are twitching nervously up and down, people are fiddling with bootlaces; the air is filled with nervous energy. You can almost see it. You can see it in some of the guys' eyes. I'm not really sure what it is, but you just get used to reading certain looks when you've played alongside people for so long and you think, "Uh-oh".

It had been such a good build-up to the match, but by half-time we are, incredibly, 18–0 down. I'm so frustrated and angry. I think we haven't realised what a big game this is and just how good the opposition are. Maybe the fact that we had such a good week worked against us; we thought we'd done our homework and would just be able to turn up for the result, rather than having to work hard to make it happen. Maybe we were just too cocky about our great home record. Maybe we've just had too gruelling a week.

Time and time again in the first half we let them off the hook, either turning the ball over or dropping a pass, and you can see everyone's heads dropping. It's like running through treacle when it's like this. Johno causes a ripple of discontent among our fans at the end of the first half when he turns down three easy points when we're given a penalty and asks Goodey to kick for touch. Andy kicks the ball dead in a move that just about sums up our half. I'm not at all surprised that Johno went for a line out as we need to score a try. He's known for going for the points in those situations but at 18-0 we need more than three and it's worth the risk.

We manage to claw it back in the second half – in fact we are virtually camped on their line for most of it – but it's too late and only Harry Ellis's late try, which gives us a bonus point, is the difference between us going out of Europe today and still having a fighting chance when we face Calvisano next week.

We can't win the pool now, but we could sneak in as one of the best runners-up, although that would mean we'd be away from home in the last eight which is very frustrating. Even more so is the fact that we now have to worry about other teams' results. Our future in this competition is now in the hands of other clubs, and even then we need to score four tries in a victory, and get the bonus, to have any chance.

After the game Geordy, his brother Ross and I are miserable hunched over our beers in a bar in the centre of Leicester, when this Leicester fan approaches.

"He's your agent, isn't he?" he says, pointing at Ross. "You're leaving he club."

Oh God, this is all we need.

"No, he's my brother," says Geordy.

"No, you're leaving. I can't believe it, you're going!" says the tired and emotional Leicester fan.

"We are not leaving, honestly," I say. "And he's not our agent. He's his brother."

"No, don't lie to me. You're going. I can tell!"

This goes on and on, but eventually he leaves us to our pints. Thank God. It's not been a great day at the office, and I really couldn't take it getting any worse.

The fan clearly doesn't believe us, though, and makes it all the way to the next table from where he sits and glares at us all night. We decide we've had enough and head home well before closing time. I'm tempted to lean across as we depart and whisper, "yeah, mate, you're right, we are going", but settle for a quiet exit and bed by about 11pm.

Monday 10th

I'm not sure if I will regret it but I have decided to settle down and watch the match against Biarritz, recorded on Sky Plus. I like to watch matches on my own as it is useless trying to concentrate if anyone else is there, especially team-mates, as they just chat through it, about the game or anything else that comes to mind. I like to see what I did right, and most importantly what I did wrong, and learn any lessons I can.

But just as I'm settling down on the sofa, Annie and her friend Heidi come in and start chatting, which sends me into the worst mood ever. I'm getting frustrated watching my own performance and Annie's asking me questions about the game, so I end up bickering with her. Several times.

I'm feeling guilty at being so grumpy, but somehow Annie seems to believe it's her fault so she cooks me dinner to make up for it. I would put her straight, but she's just served me up a huge dinner of chicken pie, followed by chocolate cake, so maybe I should pick fights more often!

I know what you're thinking: firstly, I'm in trouble when she reads this and secondly: chicken pie and chocolate cake – good God Lewis what are you doing? Don't England rugby players have to have every mouthful weighed, tasted and checked for calories before it enters their mouths? Well, actually I'm trying to put weight on at the moment, as I've dropped 5kgs since I've been back playing and I don't think it's helping me on the pitch. My body fat level is lower than it has ever been – at the moment it's 46 skinfolds, which is about nine per cent and I'm happier when it's about 53 skinfolds, more like ten per cent.

I think it's because when I was injured I made such a big effort to keep the weight off that those eating habits just stayed with me, although obviously I'm doing a load more exercise now. It's a bit of a culture shock to try and reverse my eating habits now – although it's a nice one. More pies please!

Tuesday 11th

My hand injury means I can't take part in certain training sessions, such as our weights routine. I see a wrist specialist this morning, but he just tells that I can carry on as I have been doing and that it will settle with time. Having this sort of injury is a nightmare as you can always play through it, but it really disrupts your training and match preparation.

After the weights session we have a review of the game, which involves a good look – at least from the forwards – at the line-outs and scrums from Sunday. Then something very strange happens. Wellsy gets us to play touch for the first ten minutes of our outdoor session. Has he gone soft on us?

I think he's using this much gentler warm-up as a morale booster as everyone is clearly feeling down about being so close to being out of Europe. We desperately need to beat Calvisano in our final match this weekend, to give ourselves a very outside chance of survival. We must win and we must win by scoring those four tries. Anything else and it doesn't matter what goes on elsewhere, we are out,

Wellsy announces a few changes for the game. Backy is given a badly needed rest, and I move across from the blindside to the openside; Louis Deacon is selected at eight, where he played nearly all his junior rugby, and Will Johnson moves from eight to blindside. Moving Louis to eight is a big call, as he doesn't normally play there, and we're all nearly as shocked as he is.

Wednesday 12th

As we are out of the Powergen Cup, the club have given us some time off next week, and I'm going to use mine by taking Annie to New York for some shopping and a little R&R. At least that's the plan, but I'm going nowhere unless I can renew my passport, which is about to run out.

You'd think as an England rugby player I'd have someone to do this for me, but no – and Annie isn't interested in joining me on the passport run. Gone are the days, of course, when you could just pop into a post office (are there any left?) and pick up a one-year passport. So to get a passport on the day I have to trek over to Peterborough and sit in a queue at the passport office for four hours. Thank God they haven't banned mobiles there, and I spend the next four hours catching up on calls I'm supposed to have made.

Actually, it's quite nice to have some time to myself – at home there's always someone calling or some job that needs doing (like another wonky wardrobe to put up) and, although I was dreading the queue, I end up relishing the space. When I was younger I hated being on my own and would often stay out late at night with my mates to avoid it, but now I look forward to it. Eventually my patience pays off and I have the ten year passport in my hand so I can start planning for my first trip to the Big Apple.

Tuesday 13th

A day of boring financial stuff: I've got to get my tax return in within two weeks so I spend most of the day running around, filling in forms and sorting out things for myself, Annie, my businesses (just a property one and one which handles my image rights) and her new business (Anneidi) which kicks off at the start of February, and meeting my accountant and my solicitor to put everything in order.

My current deal with Leicester ends in June so I call my dad, who always handles my contract negotiations, and arrange a meeting to discuss a new contract. The club normally talks to players much earlier in the season when their contract is to end but as I have been out for so long injured it wasn't in my or the club's interests to begin negotiations before now.

This is the first year my agent, Mark Spoors, a friend from university, is getting involved in the process, observing what happens. I don't get involved at this stage so after briefing dad, he and Mark head off to meet with Pat Howard, who is looking after the players' contracts this season. The club is in a strong position and so I aim to get a good, three-year deal.

In my early Leicester years I was aware that although we were winning trophies I was on half as much as I would have been at any other club. The club has a reputation of not paying their younger players very much, but now I'm looking for a reasonable salary.

That's all I'm looking for. Some people have very complicated negotiations, especially the foreign players who may want to include days off or travel home in their contracts, but I just want to know about my salary and length of contract. Oh, and whether they'll improve the quality of biscuits available after training!

I want to stay at Leicester but it isn't just a case of crossing the 'Ts' and dotting the 'Is'. I love the club, but on two occasions I have seriously contemplated leaving Leicester. The first was in 1997-98 when Harlequins made me a very good offer. John Gallagher was coach then and he wanted to get me down for a meeting, but once I had weighed it all up I thought the best thing for me to do was stay at Leicester for a few more years.

The other time was in the summer of 2001. I hadn't been playing much for Leicester anyway and then the club signed Josh Kronfeld – only one of the best number sevens in the world. I thought they were trying to tell me something. Who wouldn't? I was really upset. I didn't want to go, but I knew my chances of playing would be limited, so I asked Dean Richards, who was coach then, for a transfer.

Deano said he was happy for me to leave or at least go out on loan, but then I was selected to go on England's tour to Canada and I played awesomely. I don't know why – I think I felt a weight had been lifted from my shoulders. When I got back clubs were falling over themselves to offer me ridiculous sums of money to move. One club even told me to name my price. I was a bit freaked and told Deano I didn't really want to move, but could he give me a good reason to stay? He pointed out that I'd have the chance to learn from two of the best opensides in the world in Backy and Josh, so I decided to give it a go.

When I first met Josh I hated him. Well, I was only 20 and here was this legend coming to take my job away. I remember the first time we met we were in the gym doing pre-season fitness tests and I just thought, "I'll show him!" He did a load of chin-ups. I did a load of chin-ups. He did 20 weighted chin-ups with a 20kg disc. At that time I think I could manage ten reps with ten kilos, but because he'd done that, of course I decided, "Sod it, I'm doing 22kgs!" (much to the amusement and horror of fitness instructor John Duggan). Equally predictably, I managed two reps. Well, two and a half. I could see Josh looking at me, as if to say, "Just what are you doing?"

He was so fit. I wanted to beat him at everything. I tried to keep up with him at running, but I couldn't and got even more frustrated. And then the most annoying thing happened. I began to get on with him as a bloke, which really, really bugged me because I desperately wanted to hate him. He turned out to be a top man. He really talked me up before games and gave me loads of confidence, which was especially good of him because, ironically, he spent most of the season on the bench and I played the whole season. In fact I played some of the best rugby of my life.

Josh is a really, really nice bloke. He's the total opposite to Backy, on and off the pitch (although obviously I don't mean that Backy's a really, really horrible bloke). But whereas Backy's very serious, dedicated to rugby, has a one-track mind about it, Josh is the most chilled out bloke ever – your classic guitar-playing, hippy surf dude. He's quite outspoken too; back in his native New Zealand he's a massive celebrity, he's on telly left, right and centre. We became really good mates and I learnt a lot from him.

Friday 14th

Shoot me now! I don't want to, but I'm going to have to. Necessity means that I will have to be cheering for Wasps tomorrow, as the destiny of our Heineken Cup hopes lie in their hands. We need to beat Calvisano and hope Wasps beat Biarritz to give us any chance of qualifying. I, for one, am determined to fly into this game. It could be our last in Europe this season and I intend to play like it definitely is.

After the team run we hop on a short flight from East Midlands airport to Italy. Flying doesn't bother me. Alex Tuilagi and some of the other South Sea islanders could do without it, but they're fine once we are in the air. There are no Dennis Bergkamps in the Leicester or England squads, no-one who hates flying so much that they would rather go by road.

We're supposed to land in Brescia but it's so foggy we're diverted to Verona (that's a very unwelcome extra hour in the coach) and when we get there it doesn't seem an awful lot better. In fact, it's so bad that I can only see the runway about ten feet before we land, so we're worried the match might be called off.

The game has to kick off in the evening because it's on TV, which has led to a late switch of grounds – to Rovato – because Calvisano's home stadium doesn't have floodlights. This must be a nightmare for our fans, many of whom had booked to go to Calvisano. I really feel for them.

We finally make it, knackered, to the hotel at around 8pm, but I don't want to miss my traditional pre-match film so I end up watching a DVD, *HellBoy*, in the room I'm sharing with Geordan. Just before we turn in for the night we find out that Worcester's European Shield game at Rovato, against local club Leonessa, had to be abandoned after an hour because of fog, Worcester were awarded the game. Mmm... really looking forward to tomorrow now.

Saturday 15th

Calvisano 10 – Leicester 62

Calvisano: M Ravazzolo (P Viddari 70); L Nitoglia, M Murgier, C Zanoletti (G Raineri 71), N Mazzucato (A Tuta-Vodo 40); G Fraser, P Canavosio (P Griffen 40); G Bocca (D Davo 78), A Moretti, M Castrogiovanni (S Perugini 60), V Dernabo, M Ngauamo, R Mandelli, G Intoppa,

E Candiago (N Cattina 67)

Leicester: S Vesty (A Healey 56); G Murphy, O Smith, D Gibson
(M Cornwell 72), A Tuilagi; A Goode, H Ellis (S Bemand 66); G Rowntree
(J White 66, G Chuter (J Buckland 66), D Morris, M Johnson, B Kay,
W Johnson (N Back 57), L Moody, L Deacon (L Abraham 80)

Calvisano: Try: Nitoglia Con: Fraser Pen: Fraser
Leicester: Tries: Ellis, Tuilagi (2), Chuter (2), Murphy (2), Goode (2),
White. Cons: Goode (6)
Yellow cards: Calvisano: Nganamo (78min) Leicester: Moody (78)

I am so furious. Okay we won, but I'm still seething with anger at what happened.

Towards the end of the game their full-back poleaxed Scotty Bemand, as he was running through, with a 'clothes line' move that wouldn't have looked out of place in WWF wrestling. And then, when Scotty was on the floor, he just seemed to lose his cool and started throwing punches. I was closest so I ran over and gave him a couple of digs, but within a couple of seconds I was attacked from behind and gouged by one of their forwards. He stuck his finger right in the corner of my eye and I don't mind admitting that I lost it. I am in no doubt that he did it on purpose. Rugby is a physical sport and often fists fly in the heat of the moment, but I believe there is still a line and gouging crosses that line.

I turned on him and starting hitting him until some of the Leicester players pulled me off, and then I heard Martin Johnson shouting to Wellsy that he should take me off before I was sent off. He could see I'd lost it.

Obviously I was going nowhere, but I still hadn't calmed down and at the next scrum I grabbed the bloke who I thought had gouged me by the hair and started hitting him. When everything had calmed down I got sin-binned. As it turns out the guy I was hitting – Milton Nganamo – wasn't the one who gouged me. I'm not sure who it was, in fact. But anyway Nganam and I were both yellow carded.

I'm still so wound up by it all. Gouging is just not on and neither the touch judge nor the referee did anything to stop the initial incident, and that's when it got out of hand. When I see the red mist – which isn't that often – it's very difficult for me to control myself. It was a good job that I got sin-binned when

I did or I could have seen a red card.

I was prowling around on the touchline afterwards, still infuriated by what happened, feeling frustrated that I hadn't been able to sort it on the pitch and that there was unfinished business.

It ruined the after-match meal and even the drink we had out in Calvisano to celebrate. There were no lasting physical effects of the gouging but the incident ruined the night for me.

We're pretty happy with our performance and feel we've done all we could – we earned the bonus point by scoring more tries (ten) than anyone else in the competition and all we can do now is wait. At least we got the game out of the way – it was so foggy that I'm sure fans couldn't see what was going on the other side of the pitch and we were worried at one stage that the game would be called off and we'd have to wait 24 hours to replay it.

I finally cheer up (a bit) on discovering today is both my team-mates Mark Cornwell and Neil Back's birthday.s Backy is not the best at downing a pint in one so, knowing that, at the after-match reception we make him stand on a chair in the middle of the room and do exactly that. Unfortunately, they don't have a pint glass but, fortunately, they do have a massive glass boot, which we fill with beer (it takes around three pints) and give to Backy, with strict instructions that he's not getting off the chair until he's finished it. Fair play to him, we are almost asleep by the time he finishes and a fair few of the lads are looking a bit more stubbly than they were when he started, but he never gives in. Wish he would give over though, as there's some quality whingeing from him afterwards.

Sunday 16th

Johno is snoring away on the plane but he's the only one. The rest of us can't wait to find out if the other results have gone our way and we're through to the quarter-finals of the Heineken Cup. We need Perpignan to lose to Edinburgh, but it isn't really on: the Scottish district have failed to win a game all season in the Heineken Cup. And we need Newcastle to beat the Dragons, which is far more likely.

In desperation, Sam Rossiter-Stead (our communications manager) and Jo Hollis (our rugby manager) are dispatched to the front of the plane to see if the captain can radio ahead and find out the scores. They emerge from the cockpit triumphantly. Somehow, the Scots came up with the goods to win 40-17 and we are through (although I think we've now used up eight of our nine lives!). Yesssssss! Cue turbulence as 15 rather large blokes run up and down the plane doing high-fives and hugging each other in as manly a way as is possible when you're ecstatic.

We might have made it through to the quarter-finals, but for a few moments it looks as though we have lost our backs coach, Pat Howard, when we land back at East Midlands. Pat is an Aussie and his visa has run out. Eventually, after a lot of form filling, he's allowed back in on a tourist visa.

We land at 5pm and then I have to drive almost immediately – without even setting eyes on Annie – off to England training, which this week is with the Leeds Rhinos rugby league team. Should be interesting.

Monday 17th

Andy Goode breaks the land speed record this morning. He only gets the call to say he's in the Six Nations squad at 8.30 in the morning, but he's here for the first meeting at 10am, which shows you how keen he is. Goodey's arrival means we have a big crew of Tigers in our tank. I'm joined by Harry Ellis, Graham Rowntree, Julian White, George Chuter, Ben Kay, Goodey, Martin Corry, Louis Deacon, Will Skinner and Ollie Smith. Just another day at the office then. It's great having them all here.

Surprise, surprise, I am carrying one or two injuries from the weekend, not least a haematoma (blood clot to you and me) in my bicep, so the amount of training I can do this week is limited. However, it is important for me to turn up, attend the necessary meetings and take part where I can, even if it will be mostly just as a spectator.

Tuesday 18th

The training with the Leeds Rhinos is excellent. Andy Robinson suggests I would benefit from regular trips to train with the rugby league players and I would love to if it can be fitted in with my Leicester commitments. The main difference between union and league training is the lack of contact training the league boys do. They spend far more time on skills and I think we in union could learn a lot from that. Week in week out we spend too much time trying to knock seven bells out of each other in contact training, but during the season they don't do any contact work. The coach can see how they are performing without having to see them mash each other all the time.

There are obviously elements in union such as scrums, line-outs and mauls where we need the physical training, but too often this comes ahead of the skills side. I'm really enjoying this session but I can't ever see myself following players like Scott Gibbs, Scott Quinnell and Jonathan Davies and making the move from union to league. I enjoy union too much for that. I will, however, think of them, on a cold Leicester morning, when I am doing yet more mauling and contact training while they are out there doing one-handed off-loads, learning lines of running. We, or rather they, since I'm restricted to watching from the sidelines, end the session with a game of league against each other, involving a lot of touch rugby, and it looks very enjoyable. Then the league guys join in with a game of union. I'm not going to say who wins, it's bad enough that I'm admitting fraternising with 'the enemy'. Just think, a couple of decades ago just training with a league team would have seen you banned from union for life. How times change, thank God. This has been really useful and good fun – a great diversion from our usual training routine.

Unfortunately, back at our hotel, we've got the usual meetings to get through so there isn't enough time for a social with the league boys, but I'm sure we'll get round to that soon.

Wednesday 19th

Training finishes at 2.30pm, so I'm home nice and early to start packing for our trip to New York tomorrow. Annie's got her first big job on at work so she will be late back as she has to have the preliminary drawings finished before we leave tomorrow. Before deciding which pair of shoes she'd most like me to pack, I have just enough time to really put my foot in it by taking part in FHM's 'Bloke Test' feature, against Everton footballer James Beattie. Among other things, they ask me if I have ever made a home (porn) movie and instead of flatly denying it like any sensible person would, for some reason I splutter: "I don't know how to answer that", which means I will be caned in the magazine and again by the boys when it comes out. And no, Annie probably won't be too happy with me either.

Thursday 20th

New York, New York! Before we leave I manage to squeeze in a photo-shoot for British Airways, launching their new travel shop in Birmingham. The fee is two business class 'round the world' tickets and, while I am there, I also ask them to throw in an upgrade to 'world traveller' for today, which they do, giving us some vital extra legroom. We touch down at around 9pm and are blown away by the journey from the airport into Manhattan: there's a point where you can see the New York skyline from afar and it just looks so weird, huge and exciting. We're knackered so we decide to just chill out and have a meal in our hotel, the Plaza.

Friday 21st

I wake up around 4am – bloody jet lag – but I manage to grab a few more hours before having breakfast in our very posh hotel. We were prepared for the massive breakfasts but certainly not for the weather. It is about –10c and the wind chill factor is horrific so, unfortunately, we miss out on one of those horse and cart rides through Central Park. Wandering down Fifth Avenue we suddenly realise that all is not lost – the weather's a great excuse for Annie and I to pick up some new winter clothes.

I'm not a particular basketball fan, but Annie and I have got tickets to watch the Knicks play the Houston Rockets at Madison Square Garden and it's a pretty good game to watch as a neutral, to say the least. The Knicks completely blow it in the final minute and end up losing by one point. They steal the ball with 16 seconds to go and the player in possession dallies around with it, failing to shoot before the shot clock goes down. So the ball passes to Houston and, of course, they go down the other end to grab the last-second winner. The crowd goes absolutely mad. It's very exciting, but the best part of it for us was half-time as the entertainment was the Sugarhill Gang. It was awesome and both myself and Annie loved it.

Afterwards we're supposed to meet up with Austin Healey (who's also enjoying a short break) at Times Square but the weather takes a turn for the worse (if that's possible) and as the snow starts to fall, it gets so cold that we have to run from shop to shop, so we agree to call it a day and head back to our lovely warm hotel.

Saturday 22nd

Today was meant to be our mega sightseeing day, but as we venture out first thing to buy Annie some gloves and boots we are engulfed in a blizzard so we quickly head back to the hotel. Within five hours there's about five inches of snow, no visibility and everything has ground to a halt. We can't even use our tickets for the Empire State Building. We're determined, however, to honour our booking at a local Italian restaurant. Walking there is great fun; you can't tell where the road ends and the pavement (or rather sidewalk) starts. Should be even more fun on the way back after a glass or two of wine.

Sunday 23rd

Our flight's due to leave at 9am, but the news isn't good as we leave the hotel at 5.30am – apparently all flights have been cancelled due to the weather. We've got to give it a shot, though, as we've been told our flight should be okay. The snow's so bad there are no yellow cabs so we end up having to book a limo, the only thing we can get. The driver is a crazy Swedish bloke who is sliding all over the place, but gets us there in one piece (Can you imagine the headline in *Sports Illustrated* – 'British rugby star Lewis Moody injures himself in back of limo'!) only for us to be delayed ten hours at JFK. Luckily, when we won the World Cup British Airways presented us all with gold cards, which means Annie and I can use the lounge at the airport, which makes the delay a little more bearable. Annie's feeling pretty ill – nothing too serious, just a bit of flu, but not what you want when you're travelling – so it's great as it means she can lie down in comfort rather than put her back out by trying to lie on the plastic chairs.

Monday 24th

We finally touch down in London at 3am, get back to Leicester at 5am, and I have to be in Loughborough for a weights session at 10am. Not the best start to a day I've ever had. A real killer, in fact.

Andy Robinson tells us the team for the match against Wales, which comes as a bit of a shock, for two reasons. Firstly, we would normally be told a team in the week of a Test match – it's unheard of to tell us the team almost two weeks before the game. Secondly, there are a few new faces in the side, particularly a new centre partnership of Mat Tait and Jamie Noon. I had thought Ollie Smith would get his chance. Mat's very quiet, as most of the new youngsters are. I remember coming in all wide-eyed and just keeping my head down, doing exactly what I was told and only letting my personality show after I'd been with the squad for quite a while.

Robbo's obviously announced the team early to give all these new players the maximum time to work together. We normally reveal the team on the

Monday or Tuesday before a Test, so Wales would have plenty of time to adjust their side if they wanted to anyway and clearly he feels there's no point keeping everyone guessing for another week. It's not announced publicly, but it won't be long before the news spreads. Without Cozza – because of his dislocated elbow – the back row will be another new combination. I'm back on the blindside again, with Andy Hazell on the openside and Joe Worsley at eight. Hugh Vyvyan will provide bench cover.

It is annoying to have to change position again, as I've really enjoyed playing on the openside this year. Against Calvisano I thought I had one of my best games...but as the cliché goes I'd happily play anywhere for England (although I might question Robbo's sanity if he picked me in the front five).

Tuesday 25th

I still can't get over how many players have left the England team since the World Cup win, just 15 months ago. The return to the side of Ben Kay and Matt Dawson boosts our number and against Wales we will be joined by Jason Robinson, Josh Lewsey and Steve Thompson. But if someone had predicted that only five of the starting side from the World Cup final (I was a sub remember) would begin the Six Nations 15 months later, people would have said you were mad. On the current injured list, amongst others, are: Jonny Wilkinson, Mike Tindall, Cozza, James Simpson-Daniel, Stuart Abbott, Alex King, Matt Stevens, and Chris Jones.

So many of the team's key defenders over recent years are missing this time around, but our defence session still goes well as I still think the squad is well blessed with great defenders. Defence has been such a focus for England over recent years and I don't imagine anything will change this season. All the clubs in the Zurich Premiership run the same sort of 'up-and-out defence' apart from Wasps – who have more of an 'up-and-in defence' – so it is pretty easy to bring new players in. We certainly have the personnel to have another good season, defensively. We've never been a side to leak tries – against anyone – and I don't see any reason why that should change in 2005.

Once I get back to Leicester, Annie, Leon, Lisa, Damsy and I go to see one of the most depressing films ever – *Million Dollar Baby*. It is a genius film but it leaves you feeling really down. You are expecting a Rocky-type film, and then you are hit with the horror of her injury, which is not what you are expecting.

The girls are bawling their eyes out by the end.

Wednesday 26th

Back at Leicester it's another defence session as we begin the countdown to our trip to London to take on Harlequins. I manage to pull my hamstring during training, although I don't regard it as a serious injury. The Leicester medical team think it will settle down in a couple of days so I am still not ruling myself out of the match on Saturday.

In the evening we have a dinner at the Walkers Stadium – where it looks like we will be playing our home games next season – as part of Jamie Hamilton's testimonial. Most of the chat is about the England team and most of the Leicester boys can't believe that Ollie Smith hasn't been picked to play against Wales. Even Harry Ellis isn't involved this time, with Matt Dawson back in the team and Andy Gomarsall on the bench.

Pat Howard says he is mystified as to why the Leicester backs haven't had their chance to show what they can do for England this season. Pat says he had a big talk with Andy Robinson, pointing out that Leicester have scored more tries than any other side in the Premiership, yet the club is still under-represented for England in the backs. Even though Pat doesn't win the argument with Robbo, it is great to know that the Premiership coaches have a healthy, open dialogue with the England coach, as they are in a great position to know who is and isn't playing well.

The upside for the Tigers coaches is that when England play Wales Leicester are playing Bath, so they'll be able to select a couple of players including George Chuter, Ollie and Harry, who they thought would be on England duty.

Thursday 27th

The old man is almost permanently travelling with his job, as a development manager for a cement works, but mum is over here for a while, so I take the chance to catch up on the news over lunch in Leicester. Annie's company is really starting to take off and I'm very proud of her. She's already re-designed a couple of houses and is pitching for a couple of commercial jobs, so I spend most of the time boasting to mum about that.

I'm less full of it later when I go along to one of the guitar lessons Annie bought me as a Christmas present. I am now focusing on AC/DC, which means I can make a lot of bizarre loud noises, but not much else.

Friday 28th

I can't fail this fitness test, I just can't. I think I'm going to be fine, but as I get up to about 80 per cent speed I know I won't make the game as the hamstring tightens up. I'm hobbling about and I can't get anywhere near top speed. Having a match for England in eight days doesn't come into my thinking. If I was fit I would play for Leicester, no question. There is no way I would hold back from a Leicester match to make sure I could play for England – it just doesn't work that way, although I know it is a popular misconception.

Sometimes you have to play through injuries, and I have done so many times, but when it is a key muscle like a hamstring it is impossible. I know that if I can't reach 100 per cent speed in a controlled fitness test then it will never stand up to a match when there is more load going through the muscles because of the tackling, scrummaging and mauling. People may think that I'm missing the Harlequins game so I'm okay for England, but the reality is that if the England game had been this weekend there is no way I could have played. I'm feeling really down; I just want to be out there.

Saturday 29th

Leicester 32 – Harlequins 17

Leicester: G Murphy; J Holtby, L Lloyd, O Smith, A Healey (D Gibson 57); A Goode, H Ellis; G Rowntree (capt, J White 57), G Chuter, D Morris, L Deacon, B Kay, W Johnson, B Deacon (H Tuilagi 53), N Back.
Harlequins: G Duffy (T Williams 62); S Keogh, D James, M Deane, U Monye; J Staunton, S So'oialo; C Jones, A Tiatia, J Dawson (M Worsley 62), R Winters (S Miall 62), S Maling, N Easter, T Diprose (capt), L Sherriff.

Leicester: Tries: Healey, Tuilagi Cons: Goode (2) Pens: Goode (6)
Harlequins: Tries: Dawson, Monye. Cons: Staunton (2) Pen: Staunton
Yellow card: Leicester: Easter (50min)

England backs coach Joe Lydon is here today to have a close look at Leon Lloyd, Andy Goode and Ollie Smith, which gives them a bit of extra pressure, so although I would probably go along anyway, I really want to be make sure I'm there to give them some moral support – and hopefully bring them some good luck.

Before the game kicks off I am on duty in the corporate hospitality boxes. My hamstring only hurts when I run at full pace so as I am unlikely to have do that – unless some fans take exception to my recent performances. Former player Matt Poole and I visit the sponsors' hospitality boxes to shake a few hands. I don't mind doing this when I have just a short-term injury.

Leicester also have a corporate hospitality set-up at Twickenham and when I am playing for England I show my face around there as well. The supporters at Leicester are great and all of them ask after the injury. Matt and I do a few Q&As which I don't mind, although obviously I'd rather be preparing to take on the Quins. I haven't had much luck against them this year as I missed the first match because I was stuck on the bench after my foot injury. But when I do play against them I normally score a try so I'm sure they are glad to see the back of me this season.

I would never go into the dressing room before the match if I'm not playing as everyone is getting on with their routine and they don't want me around. But I make a point of popping in after the game to congratulate everyone. It's just part of supporting the guys. The boys are very frustrated with their performance. Leon is particularly annoyed as he thought he let his head go down after dropping an early pass from Goodey. I don't agree but he thinks he let himself down in front of Joe when there was an opportunity to stake his claim for an England place. He's hyper-critical of his own performance, but then I suppose we are all our own worst critics.

Sunday 30th

Everyone seems very interested in my health all of a sudden, but I am still very confident of being fit to face Wales. I tell a reporter from *The Sun* that I think, with some treatment this week and a couple of days' rest, I'll be there in Cardiff. I've already told England's medical staff about the injury so when I turn up at Pennyhill Park to meet the rest of the squad they have already planned my week, which basically involves spending a lot of time with Barney.

Monday 31st

I stop as a precaution when I reach 90 per cent of top speed during a hamstring run at Twickenham with Barney and Simon Kemp because I can feel the hamstring tightening and they recommend that I have an MRI scan to confirm their assessment of how bad the injury is. The scan rates a tear either as a grade one, two or three with three being a full tear of the muscle. If it's a three then I've had it for this week, and probably much longer, so I'm relieved to hear it's a grade one – nothing major – although I know that as every day that I can't run to 100per cent goes by I have less chance of me playing.

This week's rehab involves plenty of massage and muscle stimulation via a 'Complex' machine. This sends pulses via a pad to my thigh, while I lie back and think of England for half an hour. After this I work in the pool. We start with running in the water (or aqua jogging) for about 20 minutes and I build up my hamstring flexibility and strength by using a float so I can focus on my kicking. After this, I have the dubious pleasure of a full-on hamstring test. This involves a series of runs of up to four kilometres, at varying speeds, to test the muscle under fatigue conditions.

February

Tuesday 1st

We must sound like a group of very bad actors, learning their lines (very badly) for a very bad play. Myself, Danny Grewcock and James Forrester are in a room at the Pennyhill Park learning our calls for the match on Saturday.

I'm particularly keen that James joins us as Saturday could be his first cap. I've been looking out for him as he's in the most difficult position. He will be in the role of understudy on Saturday and has to cover as many as three positions off the bench. He could come on as openside, blindside or number eight and he has to be ready for all the calls that refer to these positions. Not surprisingly, he finds the session a bit mind-numbing, so I reassure him:

"Don't worry; if the worst comes to the worst just talk to Ben and he'll tell you exactly what you have to do!"

It must be quite daunting for James, being in an England Six Nations 22 for the first time, but he seems to be handling everything very well. The hardest thing about being an international rugby player is the calls, whether for line-outs, scrums, backs moves, defensive moves or penalties. I have a set to learn at Leicester and then a set to learn for England and it's a struggle to know which is which sometimes.

The ones we used with England in the autumn internationals are binned this week. Ben Kay was the line-out captain in the World Cup so it's down to him, Steve Borthwick (who did it during the autumn internationals), hooker Steve Thompson and our line-out coach Simon Hardy to come up with the new calls. Gone are the days when it was as simple as shouting a name and that meant the ball was going to the middle. Now every person in the line-out is affected by the calls and although I might not even be playing on Saturday I still get involved in learning them, as I hope to be involved in the Six Nations at some point, even if it is not against Wales.

It's crucial to change the calls as opposition teams will learn them. You'll often find that a TV microphone off the pitch, or the one that the referees wear, will pick up a call and broadcast it to the rest of the world. A call can be an arrangement of words, letters, numbers or whatever, which let everyone know where the throw is going and who it's going to. The idea is that it is complicated enough that opposition can't work out what you are going to do, but simple enough for us to learn.

Most sides try to work out the calls but the Italians present a different challenge as they just guess the calls or gamble on the throw. I would normally just run through the calls again and again with Grewy, but this time I make a point of involving James and Julian White as well. Grewy is a good mate and I'm often standing near Julian in the line-outs. It's crucial that all the calls are learnt parrot fashion. I hate – and I know other players do as well – going into a game when you are vague about one call or another. There is so much going on in a game that the calls must come instinctively to you or the line-out will look a complete mess.

At the start of each week team leaders are announced. This week Jamie Noon is the defence captain, Wig is the captain for scrums and Ben is confirmed as line-out captain again. It will be up to him to call particular line-outs against Wales, on Saturday. For Ben, apart from helping devise the line-out calls, it means many hours in front of the TV as he will be designated to watch hours and hours of videotape of both our line-out and the opposition one in action, and then report back to the rest of the forwards on strategies he thinks can help us. Lucky him.

I see that I am rated as 33-1 to be the tournament's top try-scorer, not something I am likely to achieve. At least Wally (Steve Thompson) is further down the list, at 50-1.

Sale's Chris Jones is added to the squad as England start training with a new back row, but I'm not bothered by that – I know it's a contingency plan and that if I recover I'll be back in. The coaching staff don't announce Chris' call-up and Robbo even claims publicly that I will "train fully in the next 24 hours". I hope he's right.

Today really is make or break for me: I've got to see some drastic improvement and I'm really beginning to worry that I won't make the game. I have a stretching session, another massage and a pool session at midday. At least this puts me out of the weekly media session. I quite like talking to the press, but after so long out injured I really hate being asked about bloody injuries all the time. It's even more frustrating when you don't know yourself how long it will be before you're fit. I do try to stay positive, but it's hard when people are always bringing up the subject.

Wednesday 2nd

I'm up at 7.30am for more rehab in a last-ditch attempt to be fit to face Wales, but it's not to be. The hamstring is still very tender and there is no way I'm going to be fit to play. I'm gutted, although there will be no announcement about me missing the match until Friday.

Many injured players would leave the England camp straightaway in such circumstances, but I have the match against France in ten days to focus on and it's far better for me to stay with England for the next couple of days; there's no better place to get treatment. At Leicester the medical team have 70 players to look after (and a big game against Bath to prepare everyone for), whereas here I can see Barney whenever I like and have the benefit of the latest technology. Alright, the real reason I'm still here is that it's the players' meal and this time it's at my favourite Italian – Number Ten in Virginia Water.

Friday 4th

Having travelled to Cardiff yesterday to continue my treatment (and also keep the Welsh guessing for as long as possible) I decide, after talking to the management, not to go and cheer on the boys, as it's deemed best if I get a day or so of complete rest after all that rehab. So I head off home.

Saturday 5th

It feels odd settling down to watch England play when I've just spent all week with these guys. Annie, Andy Goode's missus, Sonia, and I gather on the sofa to cheer on the boys on the TV, with Bath against Leicester to follow.

Annie is a pretty good rugby-on-TV companion, especially as she doesn't pretend to understand all that is going on and keeps me amused with some stupid questions. To be fair, her knowledge of the game has improved drastically and she'll often ask me why the ref's done this or given that and I have to be honest and tell her I haven't a clue.

Kicking off your Six Nations campaign in Cardiff is hardly anyone's idea of an easy start, but I am convinced we're going to win. Watching on TV gives you a distorted view: I tend to focus on my Leicester mates, rather than watching the game as a whole. I'm especially looking out for Wig, Harry, Whitey and Grewy as I want to see them turn in great performances. Mind you, it's hard to miss Grewy – he's yellow-carded in the first half. He stepped over a ruck and his boot caught Dwayne Peel's head as he went to pick up the ball. I don't think for one minute Grewy intended it. Why would he, right in front of the ref? Watching the slow-mo the referee couldn't help but give it as a penalty and send Danny to the sin-bin, but I think it was a genuine attempt by him to play the ball.

In the 70th minute we take the lead through Charlie Hodgson's penalty to make it 9-8 and I'm sure we've taken control and will kick more penalties to win the game. But the Welsh tactic of slowing the ball down and stopping our running game works very well and we never quite find our rhythm. Then, one decision later, Gavin Henson – the man of the hour – steps up to win the game to win the game for Wales.

Swearing, I switch channels to watch Leicester take on Bath. This is one of the greatest club rivalries in the world so it's going to be one hell of a game. Or maybe not. We're rubbish. Henry has a good game smashing people all over the pitch, but apart from him there isn't that much to watch. Neither side looks like winning and at 6-6, the final score is more reminiscent of a football match.

I can't believe I've sat down to watch two hugely anticipated games and only seen one try. And now it's 10pm so it's too late for me to go out and drown my sorrows. At least Sonia's happy, Andy got Man of the Match for Leicester.

Sunday 6th

Lonely day. I head down to Pennyhill Park early to start another week of rehab and it's deserted apart from Barncy and me.

Monday 7th

I feel very humble. Robbo had arranged for Jane Tomlinson, the woman who has battled cancer to achieve so much in recent years, to come in to talk to us. She's clearly very nervous, standing at the front of the room in front of a squad of rugby players, but in the 20 minutes she's talking for you could hear a pin drop in the room – every single one of the players is hanging on to her every word. She is an inspirational speaker, as well as an inspirational person. Some of the people in this room have achieved an awful lot in their sporting careers, but I'm not sure any of us will come within a mile of her achievements, no matter what we win. She has achieved so much, against massive odds, and I really enjoy listening to her talk about her experiences. At the end we're all fighting to speak to her, everyone waiting their turn to shake her hand.

The team for the France match will be announced tomorrow and after missing the Wales game I am taking nothing for granted. I feel positive – in the hamstring run I move up to around 80 per cent without feeling anything. A week ago I would have experienced some pain at this level. For the first time in around ten days I can work on my lower body with weights, which also gives me a big boost.

I still spend most of the day getting treatment. Playing through pain with some injuries is fine, but it isn't as simple as that with a muscle tear. The hamstring is one of those injuries where you can't fool yourself or anyone else. When you try to move up to full power if the hamstring isn't right it just won't go and you can't hide it from yourself or the coaches. The medical teams at Leicester and England know me well enough to know what 90 per cent of my speed looks like.

Tuesday 8th

I'm still not training properly yet and have to have a bit more rehab, so I watch from the sidelines as England start their week on the training pitch. Despite this, I'm delighted to discover I'm in the starting line-up against France. What's more, for the first time since I've been with England, I've been named as one of the team leaders – Robbo names seven or eight leaders for each game to attend sessions with team captain Jason Robinson and I'm a defence captain, along with Jamie Noon. It means I will have to liaise quite closely with the coaches and our defence coach, Phil Larder, will be asking me for input into the defence sessions: whether I think we've done enough, whether the sessions have been too hard, that sort of thing.

It might seem strange to outsiders that we have so many captains for a game, as though it might undermine that team captain's role, but it's something Clive Woodward introduced and it won us the World Cup so I think it works pretty well, especially when the calls are so complicated. The other captains for this week are Grewy and Ben Kay for line-outs, Wig for scrums and Cozza, Harry Ellis and Charlie Hodgson for attack.

It's our job to ensure that everyone is motivated and focused and I'm surprised to find I'm enjoying the extra responsibility as it's not something I look for. I'm not sure how motivational a speaker I am, I would rather lead by example than with words. But if there is something to be said then I will say it (and probably swear far too much while I'm doing it).

Today both Noonie and I are pretty happy with the way the session goes. The defence was fantastic against Wales, although we managed to miss one crucial line-out at the start of the game which led to Wales' try. I know Andy Robinson is not necessarily critical of hooker Steve Thompson on this occasion, even though it was overthrown. In today's rugby it is never as simple as blaming one person and it looked to me like the timing was off against Wales. Robbo did say that perhaps Steve was put under too much pressure at that line-out with a call that sent the ball to the back so early on, so that's something we're looking at.

There are so many reasons why a line-out can fail to find its jumper and to say it's down to the hooker alone (as some people have been doing) is rubbish, and shows a lack of understanding of the game. Of course it could be that the throw-in isn't right, but it could be that the lifters have not got the call or might not have done their job right, or the jumper might not have done his job or we haven't got the formation right. The permutations are endless. Sometimes you don't get them right and there is no point dwelling on that. We practise week in week out and make sure everyone has the calls. There is no blame culture in the England team as that is far too negative and unproductive. No-one is ever made a scapegoat.

Wednesday 9th

I am sharing with my Leicester team-mate Harry Ellis, who is very excited and nervous about his first start for England. When the team was announced on Monday night Andy Robinson clearly hadn't told him in advance as I heard him mumbling: "Oh my God, oh my God" three or four times to himself. He's calmed down since then, but I don't want to make him any more nervous than he already is so I am trying not to keep asking him if he's alright and he seems more confident and happy.

As am I. I'm still getting treatment for my hamstring injury but I can't see how it can possibly keep me out of another game.

Thursday 10th

My first training session as one of the defence captains and we're taking on the Royal Navy. We decide it's a bit late in the week for a full-on contact session so we have a 'grip' session. We're a pretty feisty, competitive bunch though, so our grip sessions always seem to turn into full contact ones. The trouble with grip is that the opposition are much more likely to run through your defensive line and this session starts really badly – before we know it two of the Navy players have come right through our line. I'm not having that. So I step in and say that is the last time that will happen. And if it means getting our shoulders in then that's what we'll have to do, as they are not coming through again. It works. They shall not and do not pass and it turns into an excellent session during which we turn them over a few times. In fact the session goes so well we bring it to a close after just 15 minutes. Job done.

I manage to get away before 4pm, much earlier than usual. I'm looking forward to just chilling out for a while, but Annie's still at work and seeing as I'm home first there's not much excuse for ignoring the pile of dirty dishes and washing. Cleaning is not something I enjoy and I don't find ironing therapeutic as some people do, but I hate coming back to find the house in a mess so I can't complain when the tidying has to be done. I suppose the job I hate the most is the dishwasher. Emptying or filling, it doesn't matter, it just annoys me. Often I just can't be bothered to empty the dishwasher before putting it on again, so we have the cleanest plates in Leicestershire.

Having a dishwasher is infinitely preferable to having to do it manually though. Geordy and I lived together for five years and I have to say he is the laziest man in the world. Luckily for him, he's also one of the nicest people you could ever meet. It wasn't quite *Men Behaving Badly,* but I did very little around the house and Geordy did even less. We were like an old married couple; I don't think you really know someone until you live with them. Geordy's very laid-back, which makes him very easy to get on with, except when there's housework to be done! I was always doing the washing up and hoovering. Although I suppose he did wash my sweaty socks and gear for me so he can't have been that bad.

Friday 11th

What a treat on my day off. No, not the interview I am doing with David Walsh of *The Sunday Times*, but the four-hour lunch I am having with my mum, Heather, as it is her birthday. We can't always see each other on special occasions like this, so I rush through the interview a little and head straight to Stones, a deli-restaurant in Leicester.

Mum was the person who always got up early to take me to training when I started playing rugby at Bracknell minis and she was the one to worry the most when the hits went in. I remember watching some videos of me playing at Bracknell and all you could hear was my mum screaming, every time I got anywhere near the ball. She's got better over the years, although she still gets a bit emotional.

I must admit I'm quite sad when it's time to make the long drive back to Pennyhill Park. I am very close to my mum and don't know how long it will be before I get to see her again, but we've had a fantastic afternoon.

Saturday 12th

In a real break with tradition Robbo brings in someone to present us with our jerseys the night before the match. I know the Wales team used people to present the team with their jerseys in the World Cup, choosing league legend Wally Lewis before they took us on in Brisbane in the quarter-finals. Usually we just arrive at the match and Reg (Dave Tennison) our kit man has put the shirts out on our pegs. But today Robbo has asked Jane Tomlinson back to do the honours which heightens the level of expectation for tomorrow's match. The only trouble is this means we have to look after them and bring them to the game ourselves. And, as we're not used to doing that, yes I am worried about forgetting mine.

Robbo reads out some good luck messages, one from the Leeds Rhinos rugby league side (signed by all their players). The boys really appreciate the gesture and it shows how the bond between both codes is growing.

I make my own break with tradition, opting for a DVD in my room rather than a trip to the cinema. Steve Thompson and I take a trip to the garage across the road for the necessary sweeties and popcorn and then settle down to watch Ray about the life of Ray Charles, which is awesome.

Sunday 13th

England 17 – France 18

England: J Robinson (Sale Sharks, captain); M Cueto (Sale Sharks; rep:
B Cohen, Northampton, 75), J Noon (Newcastle Falcons), O Barkley
(Bath), J Lewsey (London Wasps); C Hodgson (Sale Sharks), H Ellis
(Leicester; rep: M Dawson, London Wasps, 80); G Rowntree (Leicester),
S Thompson (Northampton), P Vickery (Gloucester), D Grewcock (Bath),
B Kay (Leicester), J Worsley (London Wasps), L Moody (Leicester), M Corry
(Leicester; rep:A Hazell, Gloucester, 66-72).

France:P Elhorga (Agen); C Dominici (Stade Francais), B Liebenberg
(Stade Francais), D Traille (Biarritz), J Marlu (Biarritz; rep: J-P
Grandclaude, Perpignan, 44); Y Delaigue (Castres; rep: F Michalak,
Toulouse, 72), D Yachvili (Biarritz); S Marconnet (Stade Francais), S Bruno
(Sale Sharks; rep: W Servat, Toulouse, 52), N Mas (Perpignan; rep:
O Milloud, Bourgoin, 52), F Pelous (Toulouse, captain; rep: G Lamboley,
Toulouse, 80+9), J Thion (Biarritz), S Betsen (Biarritz), J Bonnaire
(Bourgoin), S Chabal (Sale Sharks; rep: Y Nyanga, Beziers, 52).

England: Tries: Barkley and Lewsey. Cons: Hodgson (2). Pen: Hodgson.
France: Pens: Yachvili (6)

I can't believe it. That must be the most frustrating match I can remember in
a long time: 17-6 ahead at half time and they didn't threaten our defence all day,
but we still ended up losing 18-17. How? How the hell did we lose that?
France were surprisingly poor, I'm thinking, as I sit in the dressing room, trying
to make sense of what just happened. We should have won.

I'm pleased the hamstring stood the test. I didn't even need to have it strapped
and managed to get up to top speed from the kick-off. I felt super-charged
right from the start – I always really want to impress on everyone that I'm back
after I've been out injured. I ran as fast as I could after Charlie sent the ball
towards their 22. Chasing kick offs and restarts is something I love doing and
with Mike Tindall on the sidelines I can really go for it.

So how did we lose? From the kick-off I got to Chabal and Cozza killed off their full-back and our game plan was working, in that we managed to put them on the back foot right from that first minute. Game-wise it went pretty well for me. I didn't get as much hand on ball as I would have liked, but I chased down a lot of kicks and kick-offs and made a few yards when I got the ball in the first half.

The defence went very well, especially with the turnovers we created. They simply never looked like scoring, but still beat us with those six penalties, two given against me towards the end, which I was disappointed about as they weren't from rucks. During the first half particularly it was a very thin line between whether we were penalised or they were. It seemed to be them more than us in the first half and after the break the roles were reversed. It's a complete waste of time to blame the ref, though. You have to play the ref and we didn't.

We know the laws. But rugby is not an exact science, especially at the breakdown, and when there is a ruck. It is not just a matter of staying within the law, every player tries to do that, you have to play the referee and give him what he wants.

It's a sapping defeat, but there's no point in stewing over it – we haven't got the time to be negative with games coming so thick and fast at this stage, so I head for the showers and start focussing on the next game.

Monday 14th

I am romantic, honestly, but I won't be named Boyfriend of the Year 2005. I know it's Valentine's Day, but Annie and I have offered to babysit for our friends Debbie and Michael. It's partly Annie's fault because she arranged the babysitting some time ago, when I thought I would still be with England. Then the coaches said we could have the day off – doh! At least we're making sure our friends can have a nice night – we've both been so busy lately that it'll just be nice to spend an evening together, even if it isn't that romantic.

I managed to get Annie a card but not a present, so I'll take her out for a meal on Wednesday to make up for it. Hers is the only card I get and mine is the only one Annie is admitting to receiving. Note to self: "Have a word with postman about non-delivery of cards."

Tuesday 15th

I'm back at Leicester today and have to admit I'm not that excited at the prospect. Firstly, I know that because of being away on international duty

I'll probably be relegated to the bench. Secondly, my contract's still being negotiated and I'd really like to have it all done and dusted. Basically, we went to them with an offer, they have countered that with a slightly different offer, we went back to them with a second offer and now we are awaiting a response.

I can't see me leaving Leicester but I don't want the club to know that, especially at this delicate stage in the negotiations. You don't want to show your hand; you want them to think that, at any stage, you could decide to go elsewhere. Rugby League's Andy Farrell is with us this week, so maybe the club are going to sign him for the back row. Even if that's not a direct threat to my position, the club has to abide by a £2 million salary cap, under union rules, so any increase to the overall wage bill could impact on Leicester's negotiations with current players like myself.

Wellsy announces the team for Saturday's match against Newcastle and confirms that I'm joining Geordy, Leon and Harry on the bench. Ben Kay doesn't even make it that far: he's given a complete rest. Cozza, who has just returned from his dislocated elbow injury, is the only England player who starts for Leicester as he needs to get games under his belt.

The last time I was told I was on the bench I was really angry and gave Wellsy loads of abuse, but this time I try to keep calm. The fact that I know it is coming makes it easier to take – and I know it's the right thing to do. We have been training for this game all week and there are others in the squad who need to get a few games. For example, it is great to see Seru Rabeni joining us on the bench for his first appearance since picking up a knee injury against Worcester at the end of December.

I spend the afternoon getting back in Annie's good books by picking up a huge bouquet of flowers and telling her what a wonderful Christmas present she got me. My guitar lessons are going pretty well. I'm learning AC/DC's *Back in Black*, slowly but surely, and my guitar teacher's pleased with my progress with what he describes as "a very difficult song to play". I bet he says that to all the would-be rock stars!

Thursday 17th

Although I'm only on the bench for Saturday I still have to try and forget all my England line-out calls and replace them in my brain with Leicester ones. I spend the whole day clearing England out of my brain and then at 7pm it's straight back in there. The text is simple and to the point: "Congratulations. You have been selected for the England squad to play Ireland".

The even better news is that my good friend, Andy Goode, received one of those texts for the first time, along with Chuts (George Chuter) and Ollie. The bad news is that where Andy lives, in new town Linford, is a bit of a no-go zone for mobile phones so I can't get through to him to congratulate him.

I'm especially pleased for Andy as the newspapers have been linking Jaco van der Westhuyzen with a return to the Tigers, following a year playing in Japan. I'm worried about where he'd fit in: Andy has been exceptional for Leicester this season and I'm delighted he's finally got the call. He seems to have been on the scene for so long and has done so much that people tend to forget he's still only 24.

As for myself, I would have been shocked not to get a text, but after the defeat to France and giving away two penalties I had a few doubts. I always feel my place is under threat when we have lost a game.

Leon and I have bought a plot of land locally with permission to build two small houses, which we plan to either sell or rent out, so we have a quick meeting with the architects, before I head home to complete chaos. Annie's brother, Jamie and his wife, Sarah, have brought my lovely godchildren, twins Alex and Zak, over to see us. The twins are now three so they're into everything and chattering away. They're great fun – although they've got a lot more energy than me!

Friday 18th

I'm sad to find out that my room-mate Julian White isn't in the squad for the Ireland game. He injured his neck against Wales, but I didn't realise it was that serious. We will really miss him in Dublin. Whitey is an awesome scrummager and I really enjoy playing with him as his spirit is infectious. We both respond well to a bit of a gee-up from the other.

Annie is having a load of her girlfriends and clients round tonight, to introduce them to her new company. It sounds like an interior designer's version of an Ann Summers party to me. Sounds great in theory, but I make a hasty exit for the cinema, to watch *Sideways*. Goodey and his missus, Geordan and his and Leon join me and I'm glad Annie had other plans, as the film is based on two guys on a stag week, where one decides to have as much sex as possible and bed almost every woman he sees. It's the sort of movie where you are almost guaranteed to row with your missus at the end. Goodey and Geordan are squirming in their seats as their better halves give them knowing looks.

Leon and I make a swift detour to Nando's on the way home and arrive back at base just in time to find Annie clearing up after the party. Perfect timing.

Saturday 19th

Leicester 83 – Newcastle 10

Leicester: S Vesty (rep: G Murphy, 70); L Lloyd, O Smith (rep: S Rabeni, 40), D Gibson, A Healey; A Goode, S Bemand (rep: H Ellis, 70); G Rowntree (rep: J Rawson, 51), G Chuter (rep: J Buckland, 51), D Morris, M Johnson, L Deacon (rep: W Johnson, 55), H Tuilagi (rep: L Moody, 55), N Back, M Corry.

Newcastle: T Flood; T May, M Tait, M Mayerholfler, M Stephenson (rep: O Phillips, 61); M Wilkinson, J Grindal (rep: L Dickson, 50); I Peel (rep: J Isaacson, 24-28, 40), M Thompson (rep: A Long ,40), M Ward, L Gross (rep: C Hamilton, 50), G Parling, M McCarthy, C Harris, S Sititi (rep: P Dowson, 61).

Leicester: Tries: Smith (2), Lloyd (2), Back (2), Healey, Gibson, Tuilagi, W Johnson, Murphy. Cons: Goode (11). Pens: Goode (2).
Newcastle: Try: Mayerhofler. Con: May. Pen: May.

It's been a while since I have been among the subs and I am quite relaxed, but focused. Emotions-wise, it's the opposite of playing: it's only once the game starts that your nerves start to jangle as a sub, as you have no idea when you are going to get on and have to be prepared to do so at any moment.

Newcastle start well, scoring the first try and heading into a 7-3 lead, and I'm looking forward to getting on for a little bit in the second half. I keep warming up ready for the inevitable call. Seru Rabeni comes off the bench and marks his return with a try and by the time I get on, with 25 minutes to go, Newcastle are collapsing, big-time. In the second half they completely capitulate. How can a side fall apart like that? Ollie Smith, in particular, is on fire and there's even time for Geordy to score a try when he replaces Sam Vesty with ten minutes left.

It ends up being Leicester's biggest ever league victory – in fact only two clubs have scored more points since the league structure kicked off in the late 1980s. It's an incredible day and the changing room is buzzing afterwards.

Annie, Leon and his missus Lisa, Geordy, Goodey and I head to Mobius to celebrate. Not too much though – I'm back with England again tomorrow.

Sunday 20th

At around 5pm – just before I am about to leave home to join up with the England squad – I start to feel some pain in my finger. I have a small cut there and it is now red, hot and throbbing like a small heartbeat, so I ring England doctor Simon Kemp, just to let him know that I think I will need him to have a look at the finger and probably give me some antibiotics as well. I'm sure it will be fine and Kempy thinks so too. Fingers crossed – well, I would if I could!

You do tend to get a bit gnarled after a few years in the game. My thumbs won't bend properly now and I can't fully straighten some of my fingers. At least I don't have to wear splints overnight to straighten them like some of the guys do. They take off the splints during the day, obviously, and by nightfall their fingers are flopping down uselessly again. Joe Worsley has dislocated his finger a ridiculous amount of times and the joint is completely buggered now, it's just a massive lump. In fact, I'm sure we've had smaller turkeys for Christmas. It really is a ridiculous sport when you think about it – endless stitches and scars – and I'm relatively unscathed. At least the only thing stopping me playing the guitar well is me!

Monday 21st

Today it dawns on me that this cut I have on my finger is a little more serious than I first thought. I am in a whole new world of pain.

I cut the finger against France, just over a week ago and although some of the England management are angry that I played for Leicester on Saturday, I think they've misunderstood the situation. I think they're just frustrated at having another player missing as they build up to a Test match. I don't remember exactly how I cut it, but it was probably a stray boot at a ruck as it is that sort of shape. It's the sort of run of the mill injury I pick up all the time, so I certainly wasn't worried about it last week.

It wasn't infected and it certainly wasn't sore. I have played with a lot worse before, like 20 stitches, so a small cut on the end of my finger was hardly a reason to drop out of the Newcastle match. It was my choice to come off the bench; there was no pressure from Wellsy as we were well ahead in the game. Everyone presumes the infection came from the Welford Road mud but the cut was covered so who knows? Probably, but it could have come from anywhere. I've just been unlucky, I suppose.

The cut is just below the nail and the infection has spread down my finger and into my hand today. Kempy tells me that we have to see a hand specialist as soon as possible. The only problem is that it is 5pm and the hand specialist closes at 6pm. Luckily he is a rugby fan and agrees to stay open a little longer so he can have a look at my finger at around 7.30pm. He decides to drain it. I didn't realise a finger could hold that much puss. Ouch!

Tuesday 22nd

Oh great. The hand specialist I see this morning is keen to explain all the options to me, but the one that kinda sticks in my mind is his suggestion that if I carry on training and playing this week, and the infection gets worse, that I might lose the finger completely. I'm shocked but I don't really believe that could happen. At least he's not one of those doctors who umms and ahhhs. What you want is a doctor who explains all the options and every scenario so you can make a proper decision.

It's a difficult one to call, but me being me, I feel sure I can get through the pain and make the match. After missing the Wales game with a hamstring injury and having so much time off, I'm intent on playing against Ireland and the thought of losing my finger seems too remote not to at least try and get fit.

Wednesday 23rd

Falling asleep on the sofa in the team room at 2.30am with my finger in an ice bucket isn't exactly how I had planned to continue my preparation for England's game in Dublin, but that is where I end up.

The painkillers wore off at around 1am and from then on I was in agony and not even close to getting any sleep. So, as I didn't want to wake up my room-mate Ollie – especially as this is his first week in the England squad for a while – my only option was to wander from our room to the team room. I did think about waking the doc up, I know he wouldn't have minded, but I just put my finger in ice in the hope of numbing the pain enough to allow me to get some sleep. After about an hour of lying there I fell asleep for about an hour and an half and then I went back to my room to try and get a little more.

We go back to see the hand specialist and he says that to have any chance of making it I need to go into hospital for a couple of days and move from taking my antibiotics as tablets to going onto an antibiotic drip. I agree, as it's obvious now that I'm not going to make Sunday's game with normal treatment, so it looks like I'm off to hospital.

Thursday 24th

I've already had enough of daytime TV and I've only been in the hospital for a day. I am in the King Edward VII hospital bored out of my mind, unable to do anything apart from watch *This Morning* and eat. Annie and my godparents have offered to come and visit me, but there's no point (anyway, I'm afraid Annie would just turn up and take the mick out of me). I've got to be re-attached to this drip every two hours so I can't do anything, apart from wander round the hospital every now and then, but even getting lost in the corridors doesn't help the tedium. I'm not a big TV watcher at the best of times, but knowing that the England team are about to fly to Dublin makes it doubly hard.

A couple of nurses and some South Africans recognise me on one of my ward rounds, but that's the sum excitement of my day. Robbo has informed the press of my injury, as we knew it would get out before too long, and there's a sudden deluge of texts and messages. One of the first is from Geordy, swiftly followed by several from his brothers, all alleging that I'm so scared of facing Ireland that I made up a finger injury and then checked myself into hospital. I'm so going to get fit and kick your ass mate!

Friday 25th

The specialist is still a bit worried about me playing, but the finger looks much better and, after a long discussion about the risks, Kempy says the final decision has to be mine. Five minutes later my bags are packed. I think specialists – especially those who don't come from a sporting background – will always come down on the side of caution, which is fair enough.

I'm 'Norman No Mates' at Heathrow as I have to fly over to Dublin on my own to link up with the rest of the England squad. It's a very odd feeling: I've never gone to an away game on my own. The lads keep me amused by sending me silly text messages saying that Snoop Dogg is staying in the same hotel as us. Yeah, right. He's obviously a big rugby fan...

The cab driver from Dublin airport is obviously made up to see me. Well to see me with my arm in a sling, to be more precise.

"They all think you are going to play, but I can tell them that you won't!" he says, cheerfully.

I'm trying to tell him that the sling's just to keep my thumb elevated and that I'm down to play, but he's having none of it. I suppose it does look a bit odd, less than 48 hours before a Test match.

Even odder, I find out the boys have been telling the truth about Snoop Dogg. He's here for the Irish Music Awards apparently and everyone's seen him around. Well with a posse of about 100 I suppose it's hard to miss him. It's a shame I didn't bring my guitar – I'm sure the finger would be up for a quick jam.

Joe Worsley has returned to the cinema gang, so along with Wally we head off to watch *Coach Carter*. It stars Samuel L Jackson so it's got to be pretty good – and it is. It's about a high school basketball coach who stops the kids playing because their grades aren't good enough and it's excellent, although it does come with a heavy layer of cheese.

Saturday 26th

I know that I don't have to take part in today's team run but that's not how I see it. The coaches tell me I don't need to do it in order to be picked, but as far as I am concerned it's vital that I make it. Psychologically, I wouldn't feel confident going into a match where I had not trained with the team all week and then failed to make the team run as well. The one thing I don't want to do is take the field and only last 15 minutes, that would be unfair on everyone, so it is a huge relief to complete it. I now know I can get through the match.

I feel for Andy Hazell and Chris Jones, because my arrival means that Andy drops to the bench and poor Chris moves out of the 22, so he has had a really pointless trip to Dublin. I had to do it when I was younger – with Backy – so I know how difficult it is for those guys who have stood in for you all week and then don't get to play. I feel a bit out of order, so I make a point of going up to Andy but he knows how it is, and is gracious about it, although I still feel

I need to apologise for not being around all week. I know how frustrating that can be and fair play to Andy for being so good about it.

After lunch, the hunt for Snoop Dogg continues but apart from spotting some of his entourage, and a few more women around the hotel (and a few more fur coats) than normal, there's no sign of him. Perhaps we are out and about a little too early for him.

Although we went to the cinema yesterday we still kept up our ritual of going the night before a game. So we're back at the UCI to see *Spanglish*, but as we were tucking into the sweets and Tango last night we try to be a bit more sensible tonight and – in a complete break with tradition – I have a pack of Minstrels and a bottle of water. Spanglish would be a great film to watch with the missus, but she's not here so Wally makes a great stand in... up to a point.

Annie's coming over tomorrow for the post-match dinner but she's obviously a little more worried about me than normal, so I make sure I keep in touch with her by text (that's fun with bandaged fingers!) and phone just to reassure her that all is well. I actually don't know if it will be but the time to think about that is after the match.

After all I have gone through this week to make it this far I go to sleep determined to enjoy tomorrow. I can't wait to get out there.

Sunday 27th

Ireland 19 – England 13

Ireland: G Murphy (Leicester); G Dempsey (Leinster Lions), B O'Driscoll (Leinster Lions, captain), S Horgan (Leinster Lions), D Hickie (Leinster Lions); R O'Gara (Munster), P Stringer (Munster); R Corrigan (Leinster Lions; rep: M Horan, Munster, 70), S Byrne (Leinster Lions), J Hayes (Munster), P O'Connell (Munster), M O'Kelly (Leinster Lions), S Easterby (Llanelli Scarlets), J O'Connor (London Wasps), A Foley (Munster).

England: J Robinson (Sale Sharks, captain); M Cueto (Sale Sharks), J Noon (Newcastle Falcons), O Barkley (Bath), J Lewsey (London Wasps); C Hodgson (Sale Sharks), H Ellis (Leicester; rep: M Dawson, London Wasps, 73); G Rowntree (Leicester), S Thompson (Northampton),

M Stevens (Bath), D Grewcock (Bath), B Kay (Leicester), J Worsley (London Wasps), L Moody (Leicester), M Corry (Leicester).

Ireland: Try: O'Driscoll. Con: O'Gara. Pens: O'Gara (2). Dropped goals: O'Gara (2)
England: Try: Corry. Con: Hodgson. Pen: Hodgson. Dropped goal: Hodgson.

I have to sleep with my arm in the sling, sticking up in the air to keep the finger raised, but surprisingly I enjoy a pretty good night's sleep. I lie in until 9.30am, as it has been a week of fairly early starts and I want to conserve as much energy as possible. And as we don't share rooms at this stage of a competition, I don't have anyone jumping on my head to wake me up, which is nice.

Breakfast is porridge and some fruit to keep me going through the morning, as I know we'll have a light pasta meal (spaghetti bolognese in my case) before we leave for the match.

Our hotel is only about five minutes' drive from Lansdowne Road which makes a pleasant change: the journey from Pennyhill Park to Twickenham can take ages, depending on the traffic. Before we can get our bags on the bus at 1.15pm we have one final run through our line-out drills, at the back of the hotel, just to make sure everyone is up to speed with every call. This is something we do every week but I am particularly grateful after all the training I have missed this week. Our attempts to find Snoop Dogg so he could act as opposition failed.

We're remarkably quiet on the bus. I normally am. I like to whack my i-Pod earphones in as soon as we get on the bus and lose myself in my own little world. I listen to rousing rock stuff – Eminem, Guns n Rose, Rage Against The Machine, that sort of stuff – and I don't remove the earphones until I'm safely inside the stadium. I try not to look at the crowds or catch anyone's eye. I don't want anything to break my concentration or set the nerves off, so I tend to keep my head down and block off the shouts of support (or boos from the opposition fans).

Not this time though. For a start, it's not worth getting out the headphones for a journey that we could probably have walked just as quick, but this may be the last time we play at Lansdowne Road as it's being redeveloped at the end of the season. I love it – although I guess it's time it was brought into the 21st Century. It's a grand old thing, unlike almost any other stadium I've played at with England. It's very old-fashioned and atmospheric, with huge terraces, a railway line that runs under one of the stands, and a quirky old pub in one of the corners that is quite cool. For once I break with my routine and drink in the surroundings.

I'll miss it, but while it's being redeveloped we'll be playing at the Gaelic football stadium, Croke Park, the next time England are in town. I've never been there but I have seen it on television, and with a 100,000 capacity it looks equally impressive.

Our shirts are on the pegs when we get to the changing room so we know where we are sitting. As usual, I get changed between Danny Grewcock and Ben Cohen, before heading onto the pitch for a warm-up with the ball.

I'm pretty sure that Matt Stevens and Belly (Duncan Bell) are out there with me but I couldn't swear to it. I go into blinkers-on mentality: keep myself to myself, take in some of the atmosphere and start to focus on the game, going through my little routines.

The nerves jangle for far longer at a game in Dublin, because you have to line up for two Irish anthems as well as our one. Great songs, I'm sure, but they seem to drag on for ever. I always feel immense pride when I'm standing on the pitch and I hear *God Save The Queen*, (although I don't really find it that stirring or emotional, I'd prefer *Land of Hope and Glory* or *Rule Britannia!*) but to be honest, the players just want to get all the formalities over and done with and get on with the game. You're so pumped up at that stage that you're like a greyhound being taunted by the hare. The minutes tick by and then, unusually, both teams are presented to the Irish president, Mary McAleese, which is nice, I suppose, but after all I've been through to make it this far, I just can't wait to get at them.

I don't hear a word Josh says when we all get together for the pre-game huddle as I am in my own zone, which I suppose is a good sign, in that I am focused on winning that first kick-off.

I'm presuming – as Geordan will have told them all about my work from the kick offs – that I will be knocked out of the way of the ball, as I'm going through to their 22. But it doesn't happen: they allow me to get into their 22 before the ball comes down and put in the hit I wanted to. All I wanted to do was smash the living hell out of the person who caught the ball, and take out some of the frustrations I've felt this week.

In the second half I manage to grab one re-start kick from right under their noses, which gives me great pleasure, although I am annoyed to drop another one. It is difficult to catch restarts as the ball is always going away from you and you have to take it from over your shoulder. Many sides don't even chase those 22 drop outs when they are long, as the odds are so stacked against you succeeding, but I focus on it for that very reason and the fact that when I succeed it gives the team a great boost and turns us from being in a defensive position to an attacking one.

We're having plenty of pressure, but Ireland are very good at slowing the ball down and the longer the game goes on, the more frustrating it becomes. The painkillers and the adrenaline mean that I hardly feel the finger, but none of that matters because we don't get the win we came for and the 19-13 defeat equals England's worst run in the Five and Six Nations for 18 years.

Back in the dressing room we're all pretty upset about the way the game was refereed. We lost the penalty count 10-4, but it is up to us to adjust our play to the referee and give him whatever he wants. The annoying thing about this referee, Jonathan Kaplan, was that he refused to talk to us about the decisions he was making. Many referees will explain their decisions. You can ask, "Why did you ping me there?", and he will explain so you can avoid doing it again. That wasn't possible with this guy. He was getting more and more annoyed with people talking to him and told us he didn't want anyone talking to him apart from the captain. Still, we had enough opportunities to win the game.

Geordan is one of the first people to find me after the match; well, I had managed to knee him in the back during the game. He dropped down on the ball and I knew (as he does it all the time at Leicester) that he would try to jump back up again so I accelerated towards him and as he turned round he either slipped or dived at my feet, my knee going into his back – accidentally of course. He knew instantly it was me. I thought it was quite funny, but Geordy seems intent on getting as much drama out of it as he can and doesn't stop bloody whingeing about his "poor back" all night.

You wouldn't take the mick out of a mate straight after a victory as you know how much the other one is hurting, but I know full well the banter will start flowing in the days to come. Geordy will be lording it over me for ages. For now it's all smiles (and moans about bad backs) as Annie joins us for a black-tie dinner for both teams. We're on a table with Frankie Sheahan, among others. Again. He always seems to be on my table at these do's and I'm delighted to see him again; he's great company and we got completely smashed together at a previous game. We talk about anything but the game – it's a little too raw at this stage – although there's no animosity. It can be awkward sometimes as one side's on a high and the other dejected and you're sharing a table, but tonight's fine and both sides know they played pretty well.

So I tell Frankie about how close I came to jamming with Snoop Dogg and we have a few beers and a laugh and eventually head back to the hotel at about 1am. God, it's good to see Annie again.

Monday 28th

We arrive back at Pennyhill at around 3pm and I drop Wally off at Northampton before heading home for a quick change and then out to Stanley's casino in Leicester with my former college flatmate, Ali Smith. I'm not a regular casino visitor but this has been in the diary for a long time and it will be the perfect way to take my mind off the game yesterday. It ends up driving you mad if all you think about is rugby.

I haven't seen Ali for a while as the last six weeks have been almost solid Six Nations, so it's good to catch up with him. Poker is my game but they're not playing it tonight so I resort to throwing my money away on the roulette wheel. I always put my chips on the same numbers, including my team number, seven, and I always get the same result. To give you a rough idea of how good those are, rearrange these words into a sentence: Lot. It. Good. Of. Fat. Me. Does.

March

Tuesday 1st

We don't have a game this week as it is the semi-finals of the Powergen Cup and we obviously bit the dust earlier in the competition. Normally, if I don't have a game at the weekend I would try to take a trip somewhere and make the most of an easy week, but with Annie's business (Anneidi Interior Design, available for houses, bars, restaurants etc) starting to take off and the Six Nations starting again next week I decide to embark on a chill-out week – with a small amount of rugby training – before meeting up with England again on Sunday.

So, after a quick weights and running session, I head off go-karting with Danny Hipkiss and Will Skinner. I refuse to reveal who won as it would be big-headed of me. Oh alright then...! It was so wet we were sliding and skidding at every corner but on the last lap they slowed down, for some unknown reason, and I went through to take it and claim the victory. Disappointingly Danny and Will hadn't brought any champagne to shower me with.

My guitar lesson goes equally well: I have now moved on to *Nothing Else* Matters by Metallica. I absolutely love rock music, although this song is proving to be a bit of a sod to learn. Afterwards Annie and I are knackered, so we head off to The Castle for some decent pub grub and hit the sack by around 9.30pm.

Wednesday 2nd

"It's Ladies Night and the feeling's right!" Yes it is Ladies Night and ohhh, what a night we have in store at Leicester this evening. The event is part of Johno's testimonial year. Basically all us players are being auctioned off at a women-only dinner and we then have to wait on them hand and foot, with all the money going to charity.

The 'ladies' (not sure that's the correct term for some of them!) are a mixture of players' wives and girlfriends and supporters. Thankfully we don't have to dress up in loincloths or anything like that. The girls are a decent bunch and although they end up completely smashed they're pretty well behaved. One of them kept calling herself my mother and saying she's going to look after me!

It's a great night – until the 'entertainment' starts. A few of the guys, led by Harry Ellis and Will Skinner, take to the stage to perform a little sketch. It's not just that the acting is woeful, or that the microphones aren't working, but when I tell you that one of the characters was Goldfinger and he had a gold dildo you can probably understand how gut-wrenchingly, bottom-clenchingly bad it is.

Everyone looks pleadingly at Annie – she didn't get involved this time, but the last time we had one of these Ladies Nights she choreographed a *Full Monty* strip routine for the boys, which went well. We're all wishing she'd had some input into tonight's performance. Annie's got a few tricks of the trade up her sleeve – her step-mother is the singer/songwriter Judie Tzuke, they own their own record label and her sister works in the music industry – so one day if my guitar lessons go well you never know!

Thank God for the Samoans: they save the day by doing a haka and treating us to some brilliant tribal singing.

Thursday 3rd

I gather I am 12-1 with William Hill to take over the England captaincy, after we find out that Jason Robinson will miss the rest of the Six Nations with a thumb injury. However, I don't think it will be me so I haven't encouraged any of my mates to head down to the bookies. It's good to make the list though. Looking at the squad it probably comes down to either of my Leicester team mates, Martin Corry or Ben Kay. Cozza was at the ladies night until about midnight and he certainly wasn't letting on if he knew anything.

A couple of hours later I find out that he's a bloody good actor. Leon calls me to share the good news that he's in the 30-man England squad and then tells me that Cozza is captain, which is also magnificent news. I'm really chuffed for them both. I had been about to ask Leon to do me a favour while I went away with England, but I'm delighted he won't be able to as he'll be with me next week.

"Just act as keen as you can at training," I tell him.

Leon has been there before so he knows the craic, but it will be hard for him to break into the 22 as the squad is so settled, so I just want to remind him to bring his best keen head for the week and make an impact. He has to train as hard as he can and make himself noticed and get involved, giving feedback at sessions, whenever he can. It'll be great to have him around.

Cozza and Johno have been training partners at Leicester for years so I suppose it's inevitable that people will compare them as captains. They are quite similar in many ways – genuine leaders – and I'm really pleased for Cozza. But I'd just like to stress what a great job Jason did, in very difficult circumstances. He always leads by example, just like Johno. People say it's hard to captain the side from the full-back position, but in theory it gives him more scope to follow the game, so it was never a problem. It would be wrong to blame him, or any other individual, for the three defeats we suffered.

Once Leon gets off the phone, the text duly arrives congratulating me on making the 30 for the Italy match with an instruction to read the email which sets out the plan for the week, and tells you when you have to turn up.

It's good news all round today as I get a visit from an old friend of mine, Simon Feek, who's now living in Liverpool. He's back in town for a couple of weeks with his girlfriend Melanie. We've known each other since we were nine so we are like brothers and we've seen each other through good times and bad. It's great to catch up. Leon, Goodey and their partners turn up to celebrate their England call-ups and we are also celebrating the proper launch of Annie's company, so a few shandies are followed by a few glasses of champagne and by the end of it, well, I'm pretty drunk.

Friday 4th

Saracens, Northampton and Harlequins have all expressed an interest in signing me, but although they've offered a bigger salary I think I am getting close to signing again for Leicester. I'm prepared to sign for Leicester for less, but I don't want it to be too much less.

I have been considering the offers though. You are only in this sport for a short period of time, so it would be stupid of me to have rejected those three clubs out of hand. It was only right for me to listen to what they had to say. I suppose the move to London was the least likely and Northampton the most likely, and if Leicester had tried to call my bluff I would definitely have looked elsewhere.

But fortunately they have come up with a deal that is close to what we wanted and the contract is all but sorted. It's probably about £20,000 a year less than I've been offered elsewhere, but it's a weight off my mind to finally have it done and dusted.

I finish Friday off with, surprise, surprise, a trip to the cinema to see a film I've been looking forward to for some time - *Hotel Rwanda*. It is a very emotional film, very much like *Schindler's List*, revolving around a man who tries to help people flee the genocide in Rwanda. Ultimately it's a very uplifting story that makes me realise that I worry about all sorts of things in my life that just aren't important compared to what some other people have to go through.

Saturday 5th

As it is the North v South match at Twickenham today and the Powergen Cup semis tomorrow, neither of which I am involved in, I have the strange experience of a Saturday off. I'm not quite sure what to do as I haven't been saving up all the DIY jobs in the house.

I end up having something of a busman's holiday as I watch the North v South game on the television at home, in between tidying the house. It's disappointing to see the North get a real hammering. Due to other commitments they weren't able to field their best players, while the South turned up with a raft of great players. I would have loved to have taken part, but even if I had been asked (none of the England players were), considering what happened to me last week I would probably have had to pull out.

This evening Leon, his missus Lisa and I meet up with Tom Tierney, who used to play scrum-half for the Tigers. His team, Connacht, didn't have a game today either, so he took the opportunity to pay a visit to his old mates. We all go out for a meal and I end up getting quite smashed. How does that work, then?

Sunday 6th

I am so pleased Leon is in the England squad. Yeah, yeah, I'm delighted for him, of course, but even more pleased for me, as he can give me a lift down to

I began rehearsing for Johno's testimonial aged 5, with a performance at the Newbold Primary School nativity play. Notice the fruit pastilles on the crown!

Aged 6 on holiday in Portugal, having taken up rugby a year earlier I was already touting for my first sponsorship deal.

LEICESTER MERCURY

LEICESTER MERCURY

(*Above*) Back in action: Just being on the pitch against Northampton A was incredible after 11 months out

(*Right*) I remember making this tackle against Sale, it took everything I had to get him into touch.

(*Left*) I can't think why Vulkan, who make supports for sports injuries, chose to sponsor me?

Just look at me go. No-one can get near me!

I was fighting for breath on my return to the England team against Canada.

(*Below*) Josh Lewsey takes all the glory for my try against Australia, as I lie winded and in agony under a pile of bodies after landing on the ball

(*Top*) My England buddy Joe Worsley can't stop me diving over the line early on in our Heineken Cup win away at Wasps. I remember smashing my fist in the ground after touching down, we were so pumped up for this one!

(*Above*) I really enjoy the community stuff with Leicester, just seeing the kids' faces is brilliant, they love it!

I thought the audition for
Blake's Seven went well,
but I never heard back!

Any excuse to dress up and I'm there. This was Austin Healey's wife Louise's 30th birthday party, with me as a member of Kiss and Annie as Austin Powers.

(*Below*) It's a tragedy! At the Bee Gees concert at Wembley a few years ago with my mates Oscar, Jim, Guzzy and Jim.

(*Top*) I decided not to go for a seventies wig when we were awarded our MBE's at the Palace... I didn't want to scare the corgis! That's Annie on the left and mum and dad on the right

(*Above*) Board meetings at Anneidi Design Ltd are fairly informal affairs. Annie's business partner, Heidi, is on the left.

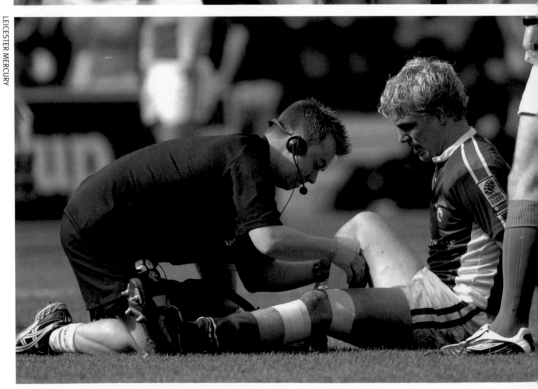

(*Top left*) Geordy had been getting grief off his Irish team-mates for weeks, so beating Leinster in the Heineken Cup was extra special for him.

(*Above*) I've always been quite shy and retiring!

(*Bottom left*) Leicester physio Brooksy ticks off another ligament on the Moody body. He's strapped up most of them now!

(*Left*) Here I am beating the vertically-challenged Matt Dawson to a high ball in the Zurich Premiership Final at Twickenham... not too difficult considering!

(*Left*) I am incredibly proud to have worn the famous Lions jersey.

(*Right*) A bunch of turkeys... and some dead birds! Julian White, Neil Back, Graham Rowntree and I get the chance to see some of the spectacular NZ countryside, and hunt for our dinner at the same time.

(Bottom *right*) We all piled into the dressing room to help the Midweek Massive celebrate their final win of the tour, against Auckland.

(*Below*) Lions v Argentina at Cardiff. A nice gentle warm-up game to kick off the tour!

In action against the All Blacks in the
Second Test, here I'm just brushing past
Keven Mealamu and Richie McCaw.

Me and Annie on holiday in Spain... the morning after the deed was done.

Pennyhill and I can sleep off my hangover in the car. It is the first time since 2002 we've been able to do this.

We didn't ask to share a room, but I usually get put with someone from Leicester and it turns out we're in together. And we've only been in there five minutes before Leon's bed collapses. I can confirm that he has put on a bit of weight since the last time he was in the England squad.

There's always something with us. We used to room together when we played for England under-21s. We were always mucking around, throwing each other on the bed. One time I tipped him off my bed, so he WWF-wrestled me into the corridor and barged me into the wall. I did it back and he cut his head on the corner of the wall and it quickly degenerated from us laughing hilariously into a full-scale fight where we'd pinned each other up against the wall. We were fine with each other five minutes later.

We're a little bit more mature these days, although we have the odd food fight in the tea-room after training (Leon's got a bit of a trigger temper, but he's a lot better these days – or at least he will be until he reads this, when the red mist will probably descend again!).

Leon is still a complete stirrer. If we're sitting down talking after lunch and another player comes up, he'll go:

"Say it to his face, Lewis, go on you have to say it to his face!"

There is no way of getting out of it and reassuring the poor guy that I haven't said anything at all, that actually we were talking about the time I pulled Leon's hood over his head to stop him throwing his dinner at me and that Leon's just winding him up. He's very funny but he does make life awkward for you at times.

Not tonight though. We're both still knackered from last night so after getting room service to deliver two of the hotel's excellent club sandwiches we're in bed about 11.30pm. Of course, unlike Leon my bed's not actually on the floor.

Monday 7th

Robbo decides to bring Iain Balshaw into the side for the Italy game to replace Jason Robinson. I'm surprised with that selection as Balsh will be picking up his first cap for more than a year. I thought Robbo would move Josh Lewsey to full-back and bring Ollie Smith on to the wing, with Leon or James Simpson-Daniel coming on to the bench. Balsh is a great player and I know he is getting back to his best, so I'm not worried about him. Perhaps, significantly, Balsh is now captain of Leeds.

After three successive Six Nations defeats the mood in the squad is one of 'any win will do'. I know we have a great record against Italy, never losing to them and putting 80 points on them a few seasons ago, but I can honestly say that I – and everyone else in the squad I speak to – would settle for a one-point win on Saturday. We simply have to win or we could face the Six Nations wooden spoon, just 18 months after England won the World Cup.

Training is disrupted a little by the fact that Bath, Gloucester, Leeds and London Irish played the Powergen Cup semi-finals yesterday, so their players are unable to start the week with a bang. The schedule that the top players face at the moment is nothing short of ridiculous. How can they think it is right to play the cup semi-finals between key internationals for the England team (especially when the one between Bath and Gloucester went into extra time)? It's so difficult to go from such a big game as a cup semi-final straight back into an international. It's exhausting, physically and mentally.

The international periods we have at the moment, such as the autumn internationals or the Six Nations, should be confined to internationals, with no club games in-between. All the other club games should be organised around those periods, so when you are back with your club you are really back with your club and not around for just a few days before going back to England. We are pretty lucky at Leicester in that our squad is big enough, and we have enough good young players coming through, that the coaches can rest their international players at the right times. Many other Premiership clubs do not have that luxury.

Tuesday 8th

Charlie Hodgson has been getting some amazingly harsh criticism in this Six Nations wich I think is unfounded. I just have so much respect for Charlie and Jonny, or anyone who has to kick the goals. They're at the sharp end and under huge personal pressure. I know I'd never be able to do it. I've seen Charlie kick consistently well in the Premiership, so there's no doubt he can do the job.

Wally has also come in for a lot of stick after our defeats. He and Charlie have the pressure jobs, they are the guys who are isolated on the pitch –Wally for line-out throws and Charlie for his kicking. It doesn't matter how well you play, if you miss a kick or mess up a line-out to lose the game then that is what is remembered.

Wally is one of those very thick-skinned characters and he makes sure most of the stick just bounces off. He always gets abuse, but he will always be the first to put his hand up and say if he hasn't played well.

Charlie is pretty quiet and he seems to take it on the chin but I am very impressed with the way he seems to be handling it. I haven't seen any evidence of the criticism affecting his performances and I can't be confident I would react in the same way if that level of stick came my way. It must affect him, but he is clearly able to make sure he doesn't take it on to the pitch, which is remarkable.

The key with England is that you are not alone. Everyone sticks together. You don't need to put your arm around someone, however, they just get on with it. We all have to deal with pressure of some sort at some point in our careers but in a team game like rugby a defeat is very rarely the fault of one player. People have short memories, don't they? I can remember going through precisely this with Leicester after our second Heineken Cup win. Suddenly we were mid-table, struggling to qualify for Europe. It happens. The important thing is reacting in the right way. The bad times are going to come, because that's the nature of what we're involved in.

Wednesday 9th

Before we leave for the team meal tonight – which as we're preparing for battle is fittingly in an Italian restaurant in Sandhurst, home of the military training school it suddenly dawns on me how much influence the Leicester Tigers are having on the England team. It hits home at the leaders' meeting, which always takes place just before the meal, with Robbo. This is a chance for the England coaches to check all is going well and that the players have no major concerns. This week Cozza is obviously skipper, but then you have Wig leading the scrums, Ben Kay the line-outs, Harry Ellis the attack and me the defence. It's the Leicester mafia!

There are no egos amongst the Leicester players, we all get on really well and all the young players have come up through the age-group sides with each other. We don't go round in a big group and certainly there's no danger that a clique might develop, but it makes for a great atmosphere in the England squad, probably one of the best we've ever had. Well, apart from Leon being here, of course. Actually, he's not any more. Sadly he doesn't make the final

22 so he leaves this evening, but he's happy with the way the week's gone. He'll be back.

Thursday 10th

I treat myself to a nice long lie-in, getting up about 11am for a photoshoot with the *Leicester Mercury* which is doing an article on Annie's company.

My Lions contract has to be in by tomorrow so, along with a number of the other England boys, I spend the afternoon rushing around trying to get it finished on time. Just getting the contract doesn't mean I will be on the tour as I think more than 100 players received these contracts and there are only 44 places in the squad. It's a bit awkward talking to my fellow England players about it as you're not quite sure who's got one and who hasn't!

There are no sticking points; for me it is just a question of going through reams of paper. I'm not worried about the money, I was just happy to get a contract, sign it and send it off. I regard Leicester as my salary and anything else above that is a bonus, whether it comes from England or the Lions, so I don't haggle; I just sign it and send it off.

Friday 11th

Where is Ben Cohen when you need him? Ben always drives us to the cinema but is out of the squad after breaking his cheekbone in the North v South game last week. So Wally is driving Goodey, Harry and I to the cinema in Reading and we, in turn, are driving him mad. Unfortunately when Ben drives we take absolutely no notice of the way he goes so all we can manage is to give Wally loads of abuse when he gets lost. Not for the first time, Wally ignores all the flak, and comes through for his team-mates: he gets us there about two minutes before the film starts.

We're back in time for Cozza's first team talk. It's a bit bizarre when one of your mates becomes the captain of England, but he's made of the right stuff. There are so many similarities between him and Johno. Neither are overly outspoken, but they know how to get their point across if they feel it necessary. The great thing about Cozza was that he was no different this week than any other. All that changed was that he had a bit more to say.

Cozza took control very well this week. The sessions became his sessions and when he felt we'd done enough he'd call it, especially when we were doing well. He called an end to the team run after about 20 minutes. Normally they last around 40 minutes, but it had been going so well, it was good to quit while we were ahead. There's no point pushing it, once you've got it. His team talk is typical Cozza, very forthright.

"It's a case of fronting up now," he says, "we need to go forward from here as if it was a new day."

Saturday 12th

England 39 – Italy 7

England: I Balshaw (Leeds); M Cueto (Sale), J Noon (Newcastle, rep: O Smith, Leicester, 69), O Barkley (Bath), J Lewsey (Wasps); C Hodgson (Sale, A Goode, Leicester, 79), H Ellis (Leicester, rep: M Dawson, Wasps, 51); G Rowntree (Leicester, rep: D Bell, Bath, 79), S Thompson (Northampton, rep: A Titterrell, Sale, 69), M Stevens (Bath), D Grewcock (Bath, rep: S Borthwick, Bath, 65), B Kay (Leicester), J Worsley (Wasps, rep: A Hazell, Gloucester,79), L Moody (Leicester), M Corry (Leicester, capt).

Italy: G Peens (L'Aquila); R Pedrazzi (Viadana), M Barbini (Petrarca, rep: W Pozzebon, Treviso, 34-37 & h-time), A Masi (Viadana), L Nitoglia (Calvisano); L Orquera (Petrarca), A Troncon (Treviso); A Lo Cicero (L'Aquila), F Ongaro (Treviso, rep: G Intoppa, Calvisano, 24, rep: M Castrogiovanni (Calvisano, 60), S Perugini (Calvisano, M Savi (Viadana, 45), C Del Fava (Parma, rep: S Dellape, Agen, 54), M Bortolami (Narbonne, capt), A Persico (Agen), D Dal Maso (Treviso, rep: S Orlando, Treviso, h-time), S Parisse (Treviso).

England: Tries: Cueto (3), Thompson, Balshaw, Hazell. Cons: Hodgson (2), Goode; Pens: Hodgson
Italy: Try: Troncon. Con: Peens

That was exactly what we needed. We scored six tries but it could have been 15 as we broke our Six Nations duck and ensured we won't finish bottom of the table. This was our 11th win in a row against Italy and it couldn't have come at a better time.

Mark Cueto led the way with a hat-trick. He now has seven tries in seven Tests, an incredible record. He is a top lad and I'm delighted to see him have so much success. Cozza was his usual self and it was great to see him kick off his reign as England captain with a win. It was business as usual with Cozza, nothing flamboyant, just hard yards. I hope people don't underestimate what a good job he did. Of course we were expected to beat Italy, and beat Italy well. But that level of expectation brings pressure as even a slim victory would have been failure in the eyes of some. We could easily have faltered against the Italians. Cozza played a huge part in making sure that didn't happen.

The game did end in something of a surreal way as Italy suffered so many injuries we were forced to have uncontested scrums for much of the second half, which ruined it a bit as we lost the opportunity to turn the ball over or put much pressure on them. Luckily we had won the game by then though. Prop Duncan Bell came on in the 79th minute to uncontested scrums, which must have been very strange for him. Even if he had wanted to he couldn't push.

My great mate Andy Goode won his first cap, as a late replacement for Charlie Hodgson, but not too late to kick a conversion – after scuffing a couple of touch finders – before the final whistle blew. I was so happy to see Goodey finally pull on that England jersey, in front of his family, as he has been written off so many times in what is still a relatively short career.

Even though we are all chuffed for Goodey it doesn't mean he – or Belly, who also got his first cap – will escape the ritual humiliation of having to sing for us on the bus, as we leave the ground. Goodey had made up a song to the tune of *Wonderwall* and got shouted down quite quickly, as did Belly who sang *The Greatest Song in the World,* which was actually very good. I think he could have gone on for about an hour, but this is not something they are supposed to enjoy.

One ritual humiliation Goodey did miss was the traditional first-cap drink with the whole squad. Somehow he had arranged to go home... but his time will come!

Sunday 13th

Mum is heading back to Indonesia soon so I take the chance of a day off to meet her, my nan and grandad for lunch. This trip is my mum's last before she and dad come back for good, at the end of July.

I manage to catch the second half of the Scotland v Wales game on TV. We're playing the Scots on Saturday and I'm keen to see what their patterns are, although obviously we'll get the video from the England management in the next couple of days. Scotland make a very strong comeback, as they have been doing in games recently, and we will have to be wary of the way they will come back at us in the second half on Saturday.

Another big game today is Newcastle's trip to Quins where Jonny Wilkinson is trying to get himself fit, both for the match against Scotland and the Lions tour. Jonny is a good friend and our paths from the World Cup are pretty similar. We both came back injured, so I understand some of what he is going through. Unfortunately the news from Quins today isn't good as he has gone down injured again. He's certainly had it pretty hard over the last 16 months, but he's mentally very strong and I have no doubt he'll back in an England and a Lions shirt before we know it.

Monday 14th

I awake to the bad news that Wellsy will leave Leicester at the end of the season to take up a role with the RFU national academy. He left a message on my phone saying he wanted me to know before it got in the media. Wellsy has been a great servant for Leicester and a great coach, so from a playing and personal perspective I think the club have made a big mistake in letting him go.

Wellsy was in his last season as a player at Leicester when I made my debut for them, so we have been through a lot together as fellow players and as coach and player. He has to be the coach I've learnt most from. In the first couple of years, he really picked on me and Geordan – whatever went wrong was always our fault. I think it was because we were young, but I suppose there's an element of taking it out on the people you are closest to. I get on really well with him. I don't think you can, or should, ever become really close mates with your coach – after all, he's going to be the one dropping you as well as picking you – but we've always had a good relationship. Well, except for when he told the press I was a muppet!

The Leicester players are all shocked and sit down to discuss his departure. When I finally get hold of Wellsy he says that he will tell me exactly what happened once the season's over. He's very disappointed. Wellsy is a great coach and is so dedicated to his job. His research was incredible; he brought the technique of video analysis to Leicester. He'd spend hours and hours watching tapes of line-outs just so that the Tigers could get the slightest advantage in a game. He knew what to do and how to prepare people for games and there's no question Leicester will miss him next season.

Leicester went through a fabulous time at the turn of the century and then we had a poor season, followed by this year where Wellsy has led a resurgence of the Tigers, leaving us in the hunt for two trophies. If you were making a list of Premiership coaches most likely to leave he wouldn't have been on it.

He had done all the graft, even though Dean (Richards) was the face of the club for years. He hasn't changed his role since he and Dean took over, or since Dean left, and he's a top man too. Under that grumpy, miserable exterior Wellsy is a nice guy and quite entertaining at times.

It seems that he had to make a decision before it was made for him, before he was pushed, and with the RFU offer on the table I can fully understand why he took it. As a coach or player you always look for security and he was offered that elsewhere and not given it at Leicester. It is clear that players like Backy and Johno are being groomed for his role at the club, sooner rather than later, so maybe Wellsy could see the writing on the wall?

Within a few hours Leicester have confirmed the coaching team for next season. Pat Howard takes over as head coach, Richard Cockerill as forwards coach and Neil Back as technical director, responsible for defence, analysis, and individual player development.

Tuesday 15th

A very solemn day today as rugby and our preparations for Saturday's game become a very distant second to some very sad news. After training Robbo asks to see all the Leicester players to let us know that one of our young props, Matt Hampson, suffered a serious neck injury while preparing for an England under-21 game and there's a fear he might be paralysed – he has to undergo an operation to stabilise the fracture in his neck. We all know Matt very well and everyone's thoughts are with him and his family. It is a difficult thing to know how to feel as it is such a tragedy.

Bad injuries like this occur in rugby from time to time and it seems the longer you play the closer you become to someone who has been hurt like this. A few years ago it happened to a friend of a friend and now to a guy we all know and like at Leicester. Matt played in my comeback from injury game last

October for the A team. It is harder in many ways for the props like Wig as they know that Matt was doing something they do every day.

In the short term we try to get focussed on fundraising for a trust fund which we are sure will be set up for Matt. That starts with the decision that we will all give our match shirts from Saturday's game to him.

Wednesday 16th

You don't expect to have your nearest and dearest come at you with a knife, but I suppose I might have deserved it as I had sneaked back home tonight to surprise Annie.

I knew what time she was due in so I sat in the dark, waiting for her. Unfortunately it backfired spectacularly when she discovered the alarm was off and, fearing we were being burgled, went straight for the kitchen knife draw, before discovering me sitting on the sofa, smiling sweetly at her. She's was not impressed:

"You're lucky you weren't hiding behind a door or I might have stabbed you!"

"Yes, darling. Sorry," I say, secretly thinking, "Or you might just have dropped it on your foot."

Thursday 17th

After scaring Annie last night I decide to take the day off from pranks and just chill out, trying to think of anything but the up and coming match against Scotland. So me, Leon, Damsy and Jamie Hamilton spend the day in Leicester, mooching around the shops and getting our Starbucks hit.

In a Leicester week I would normally fill my day off with things to do, like photoshoots for sponsors or a spot of business. But there comes a time when you need to clear the day so you can do nothing. Even on Sundays we don't have a lie-in as we always have to do a recovery session first thing. Having a relaxing day off in an international week is crucial for me.

One bit of good news coming out of Leicester today is Daryl Gibson's decision to sign a new two-year contract with the club, which will see him remain at Leicester until the end of the 2006/07 season. A former All Black, Daryl is the sort of experienced player I am sure the club will look to, to captain the side when the internationals are on next season. He's suited to that role, he's a very forthright player.

Friday 18th

Cozza's second team run as England captain goes as well as his first. He really is settling into this captaincy lark. Normally the coaches set the agenda but Robbo says he wants it to come from the players this time, so before the team run is over we sit in the Twickenham dressing room for a meeting.

Robbo wants the leaders like me, Charlie and Harry to address the players about our particular area, so the focus is more player-driven. Cozza introduces us – almost like he was chairing the meeting – and then wraps everything up at the end. Talking like this is not something I revel in or particularly enjoy, but I have to get on with it. I can appreciate what Robbo is trying to achieve. I talk about the level of physicality we need against Scotland. From a defence point of view there are only a few things you can get across; I just make damn sure that everyone knows we want to batter them.

Sadly, one of the unsung heroes of the England and Leicester team, my mate Wig, has pulled his quad muscle in the team run and is ruled out of the game. Duncan Bell is brought in for his first start and Mike Worsley takes up a place on the bench.

After the abuse he got last week Wally is refusing to drive to the cinema this week, and I can't say I blame him. We manage to talk Goodey into getting behind the wheel to take us to Reading to see *Hitch,* starring Will Smith, and we're all concentrating really hard on where we're going this time, so we make it there in time to buy plenty of popcorn. The film, about a 'date doctor' who finds eligible women for his male clients, is pretty good, light-hearted fun.

It's the perfect end to a pretty good day when we get back to the hotel to discover that Michael Wright, the top man who looks after us there, has made sure to save us some of the chocolate biscuits. He can do anything that man: find you a harpist for a wedding; arrange a helicopter trip to the races or even stop a couple of dozen hungry rugby players from demolishing the entire plate of biscuits. Legend.

Saturday 19th

England 43 – Scotland 22

England: I Balshaw (Leeds, rep: O Smith, Leicester, 32); M Cueto (Sale), J Noon (Newcastle), O Barkley (Bath), J Lewsey (Wasps); C Hodgson (Sale, rep: A Goode, Leicester, 76), H Ellis (Leicester, rep: M Dawson, Wasps, 64); M Stevens (Bath), S Thompson (Northampton, rep: A Titterrell, Sale, 72), D Bell (Bath, rep: M Worsley, Harlequins, 52), D Grewcock (Bath), B Kay (Leicester, rep: B Kay, Leicester, 14), J Worsley (Wasps), L Moody (Leicester, rep: A Hazell, h-time), M Corry (Leicester, capt).

Scotland: C Paterson (Edinburgh); R Lamont (Glasgow), A Craig (Glasgow), H Southwell (Edinburgh), S Lamont (Glasgow); G Ross (Leeds), M Blair (Edinburgh); T Smith (Northampton, rep: B Douglas, Borders, 23), G Bulloch (Glasgow, capt), G Kerr (Leeds), N Hines (Edinburgh), S Murray (Edinburgh, rep: S Grimes, Newcastle, 33), J White (Sale), A Hogg (Edinburgh, rep: J Petrie, Glasgow, 63), S Taylor (Edinburgh).

England: Tries: Noon (3), J Worsley, Lewsey, Ellis, Cueto. Cons: Hodgson (4). Scotland: Tries: S Lamont, Craig, Taylor. Cons: Paterson (2). Pen: Paterson.

Wow! That is the worst pain I have ever felt. Just before the end of the first half I chased a 22 drop-out. Earlier in the match I had caught one, off-loaded to Joe and we had gone tearing off down the field, so I was feeling pretty confident and went to do the same thing again. Everything was going well when I went up in the air and even better when I caught the ball, but then it happened. Jason White's knee went driving into an area where knees should never go and I convulsed into the foetal position long before I hit the deck, writhing in agony. I'm struggling to even begin to describe the pain It was like someone putting a blowtorch to my nuts. I have been clattered in the groin a few times before, but nothing like this. I was running flat-out when Jason jumped towards me so you can get an idea of the force of the impact.

My head was spinning and the pain was excruciating. Getting up simply wasn't an option – even though everyone else was trying to help me up – but I was sure I'd be okay to carry on because the pain of being hit in the nuts usually subsides in a few minutes. Not this time. In the end I had to get the doc and Phil Pask, one of our physios, to help me off the pitch as my legs had gone and I couldn't put any pressure down on the left hand side of my body. I felt like I had been hit with a sledgehammer.

Luckily it was half-time so we didn't need to make an immediate decision about me carrying on, so I went straight to the medical room where the doc examined me. He thought the pain was just a result of severe bruising and helped me to the dressing room to sit in my cubicle. I put my new shirt on ready for the second half but as the minutes went by I realised it was not getting any better. I couldn't even lift my left leg, let alone get out of my cubicle, let alone play another half of rugby. The doc told Robbo that I needed to be replaced and I ended up watching the second half on the side of the pitch with a load of ice taped to my groin.

On the field we certainly finished the Six Nations with a flourish, scoring seven tries, including a hat-trick for Jamie Noon.

After the match Cozza goes into the Scotland dressing room to let them know that we won't be able to do the traditional swapping of shirts with them this time as we're donating them to the Matt Hampson Trust Fund. The Scots of course understand and even tell Cozza that we can have their shirts as well. Quality.

At the after-match reception I bump into Jason White. I know it was an accident – he was looking at the ball – and we end up laughing about it. Well he's laughing anyway, I'm still in bloody agony.

We finish off the Six Nations with a large amount of alcohol in a bar in central London, arranged by Matt Dawson. All our partners are there, as well as my old Canadian friend Simon and his girlfriend, and finally we get our chance to all have a drink with new cap, Goodey, before heading back to Pennyhill at 3am. We're all pretty smashed, but does the drinking stop? Does it hell. We carry on, but somehow we manage to get Goodey's missus, Sonia, more smashed than him.

Sunday 20th

Why, why, why do I ever listen to Geordy? He was involved in Ireland's defeat to Wales yesterday in the Grand Slam decider at the Millennium Stadium and after much persuasion and despite a raging hangover, I agree to head across to Cardiff to meet him and cheer him up.

I know it sounds easy to say now, but I was one of the people who tipped Wales (and Ireland) to do well in this Six Nations, so it is no surprise to me that they have picked up the Grand Slam this time around. They have been in good form for 18 months, starting at the World Cup and again in last autumn's matches where they came so close to beating South Africa and New Zealand. They play the sort of exciting rugby that every team aspires to.

I think the crucial moments for them came in the second half of their game against France, when they had lost their captain, Gareth Thomas, and were behind. Back they came and, fittingly, Martyn Williams scored two tries on his way to being named the RBS Six Nations Man of the Tournament. That French game turned the tide. They knew once they had come back to win in Paris they could beat anyone. I have always admired Martyn and maybe I'll get the chance to see how good he is, up close, if both of us get selected on the Lions tour. I'm sure he will make it – hope I do.

So anyway, I order a taxi from Pennyhill Park to Reading station but, once in the cab, decide I really can't be bothered with the hassle of getting the train in my condition so I ask the cab driver to take me all the way to Cardiff. He thinks it's Christmas and promptly charges me £150 for the trip.

Leon, Adam Balding, Damsy and a few of the other guys we know also head to Cardiff to meet us and we proceed to go on an all-day drinking session, flitting between Newport and Cardiff and finally settling – with me still hobbling a little – at the Walkabout in Newport.

Brian Hall, who used to own a Walkabout in Leicester, is our host for the day but I think he soon wishes he hadn't invited us. We stay drinking with him until five in the morning, spending most of our time behind the bar, squirting lemonade at unsuspecting Newport drinkers. Brian very kindly gives us walkie-talkies so we can speak to all the bar staff whenever we want. Luckily for us, or Brian, or both, we don't realise until too late that at the back of the bar there is an entrance to a massive nightclub. Ah well, next time.

Monday 21st

This morning the newspapers are full of stories of Clive Woodward moving to Southampton and it seems my old England coach (and hopefully future Lions coach) will become the first person to make the move from rugby to football. It is going to be very hard but if anyone can cross the divide, Clive can.

Clive is a man who is driven by challenges, which is why he has taken on the Lions and why he stayed with England as long as he did. He's great at managing teams and resources and making sure they have the very best facilities possible. If he is put in a position where he is organising or overseeing a football team, rather than having any technical input, then he can achieve great things. Then he will want to go and coach but a coaching role is probably a long way away.

The crucial thing, and I'm sure he understands this completely, is that he needs to make slow progress behind the scenes before moving anywhere near a coaching job. If Alex Ferguson came into rugby as a manager, away from the playing side, he would immediately get respect, but not, perhaps, if he came in as a coach.

Tuesday 22nd

The Super 12 is now in full swing down under and I keep on top of the action from Australia, South Africa and especially New Zealand whenever I can. Geordy played rugby in New Zealand for a while some years ago and I considered playing in Australia when Bob Dwyer was coach at Leicester, but he thought I would get better coaching in England, so I stayed.

I've always said I wouldn't mind finishing off my playing days in a nice sunny environment, chilling out and playing a reasonably easy level of rugby, but now I feel I'd prefer to stay and finish my career at Leicester. There are, however, a lot of new guys coming through so I may yet go 'down under' at some point.

After this contract, the next one will probably be my last. I'd love to stay on as I think the atmosphere at Leicester is brilliant and crucial to the club's success. It is a club driven by the players and very many former players, from chief executive Peter Wheeler to the current coaches, are heavily involved. The club's loyalty to their former players and the way they promote from within are just two of the reasons I could see myself staying at Welford Road beyond my next contract. Leicester have a club called the Troglodytes, which is the old players' association. They have their own bar, which is subsidised and run by them. The former players serve behind the bar and it is just shows how Leicester look after their own.

Wednesday 23rd

Injuries picked up in the Six Nations mean that we can't call on Wig or Ben Kay this week, while I'm confirmed on the bench after that kick in the goolies at the weekend. On the positive side, Whitey is back for the first time since our opening loss to Wales in early February.

Sadly, we hear some very bad news about another prop, Trevor Woodman. At the age of 28 he finds himself out of work, having had his contract terminated by Sale due to a serious back injury suffered in a gym weights session last September. Trevor isn't someone I know particularly well, but I can imagine how desperately disappointing it is for him. I gather that he is going to return to Gloucester and give it one more go with his physio. I hope he knows he has all the Tigers behind him.

Thursday 24th

Saracens today confirm that they have won the race to sign rugby league legend Andy Farrell, who is moving from Wigan to rugby union, it seems with the next World Cup in mind. He'd been at Leicester a few weeks ago, but I think ultimately it came down to the salary he was looking for and the club keeping within the salary cap.

I wish him all the best, but there's no question it will be tough for Andy. When others like Jason Robinson and Henry Paul made the move to union they were in their mid-20s, but Andy is 29 and, while we all know what a great league player he is, making the switch (in time for the 2007 World Cup) will be hard. I'm sure he'll do well but there's no question it is a risk on his part, especially after the reputation he has built up in league. That will be on the line in union. He might just step in and be fantastic, but he'll need a good team around him to learn all the new rules and tactics in union.

If Andy does break into the England team quickly we discover today that he'll kick off his Six Nations career at home to Wales, as that is England's first game in 2006. What a cracker! England v Wales at Twickenham is always a special game, but with them as reigning Grand Slam champions it should be a magnificent occasion.

Friday 25th

I hear that the RFU are thinking of revamping the Powergen Cup for next season and, from what I hear, I really hope it won't happen. It seems the plan is to restructure our only domestic cup competition, making it for just the Premiership clubs and the four Welsh regions. What a nightmare. It would completely ruin England's cup competition and I can't believe they are even talking about it.

I've never won the Powergen Cup, but to end the opportunity of small clubs like Pertemps Bees (who beat Wasps two seasons ago) playing the Premiership sides is simply wrong. Can you imagine the national outcry if they decided the FA Cup was only for the Premier League sides? No-one would stand for it. It is where the underdogs have their day and for people to come along and say we are not doing that any more is wrong. I'd be gutted if I was playing for a club outside the Premiership. If they are serious about promoting rugby in England they need to look after the junior clubs. This certainly isn't the way to do it.

I would favour a system like the FA Cup where every club in England gets a chance to play in the competition, but when the Premiership clubs come in (in the sixth round) they should always be drawn away from home. So if we drew Exeter we would have to play at their ground. That way they'd have a better chance of beating us and would hopefully get a big pay day for themselves

Saturday 26th

I wouldn't call it fraternising with the enemy, but as I am in Leeds I take the chance to catch up with my former Leicester team-mate, Craig McMullen, who is on the bench for Leeds tomorrow. He's a top lad. He's had quite a few clubs since he was at Leicester. He's one of those laid-back, chilled out people who travelled over from Australia.

There is a rumour that Serge Betsen is coming to Leicester in a move that would obviously have massive repercussions for me. The club have hinted that unless I sign my contract they might sign Serge, but I'm not really buying that line. I don't believe for one minute that he would leave Biarritz – where he is a successful businessman – and play for Leicester. Well, unless they offered him silly money, which I don't think they would; Leicester don't pay that much. I think it is a ploy on his part to get a better contract in France.

Sunday 27th

Leeds 23 – Leicester 22

Leeds: T Biggs; A Snyman, P Christophers (rep: D Albanese, 58), C Bell, D Rees; G Ross, A Dickens (rep: M McMillan, 58); M Shelley, M Regan, G Kerr (rep: M Holt, 78), S Hooper (capt), T Palmer, S Morgan (rep: J Dunbar, 50), R Parks, A Popham

Leicester: G Murphy; L Lloyd, O Smith (rep: A Tuilagi, 60), D Gibson, A Healey; A Goode, H Ellis (rep: S Bemand, 80); D Morris, G Chuter, J

White, M Johnson (capt), L Deacon, W Johnson (reps: M Holford, 4-13;
L Moody, 49), N Back (rep: H Tuilagi, 65), M Corry (rep: Moody, 21-30).

Leeds: Try: Biggs; Pens: Ross (6).
Leicester: Try: Lloyd; Con: Goode; Pens: Goode 4; Drop goal: Goode

Leeds are bottom of the table and fighting for their lives at Headingley today
and inflict only our third league defeat of the season upon us. If they'd lost to
us they would have almost certainly gone down. Having said that it was a game
we should have won, only coming up short by a point in the end. We had a
number of kicks and drop-goal attempts at the end of the game and if any of
them had gone over we'd have won.

There were a few tasty off the ball incidents in the game, most notably Mark
'Ronnie' Regan knee-dropping Leon in the face right at the start of the game.
Leon is one of those players who holds a grudge and he finally hunted him
down in injury time, catching him with a huge cheap shot. But they came off
winking at each other as they knew it was even stevens on this occasion. Ronnie
was happy, they had won and Leon was pleased he had got his own back. That
sort of thing is part of the sport, as long as its not injury-threatening.

Under the new play-off system it's quite hard for the teams at the top of the
table to keep their motivation as the regular season ends. We are on course to
finish top of the table but, unlike in football, finishing top actually means
nothing. It does entitle you to go straight to Twickenham to contest the Zurich
Final, but that is about it. I have never been a fan of the system. If you play a
season for nine months of the year and then at the end of it you have a one-off
game to decide the champions it goes against the whole concept of it being a
league. The league championship should not depend on one game which you
could lose by the bounce of the ball or by a referee's decision. We have seen
sides play average rugby for the first six months and then put together a run to
get into the top three and the play-offs and emerge as champions of England
because they have hit form at the right time. Surely that can't be right?

After the game I take the chance to catch up with Mullers again and we are
joined by another former Tiger who is also at Leeds, Tim Stimpson. He was
fantastic for the Tigers when he was with us, breaking almost every record in
the book with his kicking when we were winning titles and European cups. He
was awesome and I don't think he ever got enough praise for what he did for

Leicester during his stay at the club. The way he performed in both Heineken Cup Finals we won was immense. The kicks he had to get were in such difficult places and he was under so much pressure, but he reacted as if he was on the training field. He is a very off-the-wall character and Tim and I have come through many tight situations together and have a strong friendship. It is weird because I haven't seen him for eight or nine months, but it is as if time has stood still. It feels like only yesterday that we were out on the training field together.

Monday 28th

It's a Bank Holiday for everyone else, but not us professional rugby players. For us, the biggest consequence of the holiday is that there is no chef at the training ground so it means piling into the nearby village of Oadby to try and grab some lunch. Johno, Leon, Cozza, Backy and myself are a little slower off the mark than everyone else, who must have known what was coming. Around 30 hungry players descending on a village that small means the places fill up pretty quickly, so the five of us have to make do with a Wetherspoon's pub, as all the other cafes are rammed out by the rest of the lads. It takes us about an hour to get our food and by the time it arrives there are only 50 minutes to go before the team meeting so we break all previous records for downing spag bol. Despite all this stress, we have a pretty good training session – so maybe one of our new superstitions should be Wetherspoon's spag bol every day of the week.

I have a niggling knee injury that is still hanging around from the Six Nations, so after training I head off to see the physio and he thinks that I may have pinched a piece of cartilage on the knee. Once that is over I take part in a 'fitness blitz' session, as I was only on the bench at the weekend. Alex Tuilagi and myself take part in the session, which includes a lot of cardiovascular work, all at a very high intensity. For example, one test we do consists of 12 x 15-second sprints with 15 seconds rest in between. It's knackering but it works.

Amazingly, I still haven't signed my new contract. It's all agreed but we are still finalising those last few details. It is not worrying me too much but we do need to get it sorted before the summer, whether I go to Canada with England or to New Zealand with the Lions. There is always that endless, on-going process of changing the odd word around. To me it means nothing but to my dad and my agent it means a big delay. There seems to be no such thing as a standard contract in rugby so we go back and forth on every point once the general parameters have been agreed. Apparently a few paragraphs we took out at the last stage, about my image rights, have been put back in. Is this deliberate or have Leicester just made a mistake? I'm happy to leave all the nitty-gritty to my dad.

Tuesday 29th

Look, the reason that Austin Healey beat me in the go-karting today was that his kart had two engines, as did Danny Hipkiss's. The rest of us just had one. I am gutted. Even with that advantage I still thought I would be able to force them off the track.

It is Austin's second big win of the day as he also wins *Soccer AM's* crossbar challenge. He went on the programme a few weeks ago and challenged them to come up to Leicester. We wouldn't have accepted if we thought there was any chance Austin would actually hit the crossbar with a football, from the halfway line, as we had to try and do. Incredibly he was the first person to have a go. Up he stepped and just hit it. No-one could believe it. It couldn't have happened to a worse person. We won't talk about my effort, as it was horrendous. I missed by about 100 metres, the only compensation being that it was closer than Johno's attempt.

It is accepted that the Leeds defeat was a bit of a shambles, so rather than just have a few people grumbling we decide to have a players' meeting so we can sort a few things out and air any grievances. It goes well and everyone accepts the need to step up a gear in training and be more committed this week for us to have any hope of beating Leinster this weekend. Geordan says he's been taking a lot of stick off the Leinster boys this week and he's not prepared to let a bad attitude or two come between him and beating them. He wants to stick their comments right up them and hammers home the point that this is a one-off opportunity; there are no second chances, like there are in the league. It's a great rallying call and we all feel very positive. We haven't done anything fundamentally wrong this season and there's no need to panic and change anything. Okay, we lost a match but we are still top of the league and in the Heineken Cup. The will to win at Leicester is far more important than anything else.

It was winger John Holtby's birthday last week so it's high time we show him the time of his life...and take him to Pizza Express. It's becoming the place to go for Leicester Tigers' birthday parties as we can't go too mad in the week of a game. I normally have pepperoni but this time I decide to be a bit healthier. I love anchovies so I end up having ham, Greek cheese and anchovies. A strange combination, I know, but it's pretty good. No dough balls to start but obviously I steal a few from some unhealthy person to go with my salad.

Wednesday 30th

Ever since we squeezed into the quarter-finals I've been looking forward to this game against Leinster. Unfortunately, with the way Henry has been playing, I know my place in the side is far from assured. What you may or may not have done before counts for nothing as we move towards the most important game of our season so I am very nervous and when Wellsy finally tells me I'm in, it's a massive relief. Sam Vesty is selected ahead of Austin Healey. He's in great form this season and deserves the chance but it is harsh on Austin as he's a great player and has always played well in Europe.

I think yesterday's meeting really had the desired effect as we have a very intense defence session. The focus we had been missing is back and we are really getting stuck into our training this week. We also do some handling drills with Pat and finish the session off with ten minutes at full-on intensity, which is enough to get anyone going. The team who will be playing defence takes on the guys who aren't playing. Yup, that's right, the guys who won the places get kicked to pieces by the guys who were dropped. Great idea. It can get a bit out of hand sometimes. As I am in and Henry is out I don't really fancy having him running at me a few days before a big match. Thankfully, he doesn't take it personally and I'm just as bruised as I normally would be after this type of session, but I must say that I'm glad that I'll never go up against Henry in a match. Leinster certainly haven't got any runners as powerful as him.

To recover from the defence session I take Annie into town for a romantic meal at The Opera House restaurant. It's not quite black tie but it is pretty posh. It is really nice to spoil ourselves as I've been away with England so much recently and will be away again this weekend in Dublin.

Thursday 31st

It's our day off, so I head for the golf course with Ali, Leon, Geordan and Damsy. We were going to play a proper round but by the time we get there it's raining and getting on a bit, so we settle for hitting about 100 balls on the driving range. I'm no Geordan Murphy or Austin Healey, but I'm not too bad at golf. I play off about 24, but 18 if I am having a good day. I used to play quite a lot and got down to about 14, but now I seem to be restricted to around two or three rounds a year and it takes me a long time to get into it these days.

I'm a very optimistic golfer. I am one of those guys who tries to smash it one hundred miles off the tee but normally ends up walking one hundred miles in the other direction to get the ball. Annie has played a little bit. I tried to give her a lesson once and she says I lost my patience. It's a charge I vehemently deny. She wouldn't take the advice so we had to stop. She wanted to do it her way, which was basically hockey. We've never played a round together.

Geordan is the best out of us but Ali normally wins as he is Mr Consistent and never tries to hit the ball too far. Leon went through a period of being really good when he played three or four times a week, but now he has gone backwards through lack of practice. Me and Damsy have a competition to see who can chip it and drive it closest to the hole, and who can hit it furthest just with our left hand. I win, although I still get loads of grief as I managed to hit a ball the wrong way, it went behind me back inside the hut, ricocheting all over the place. Oops.

When I get home Annie's sitting there having her hair cut by a friend of hers and she talks me into having mine done at the same time. Just a trim, please.

April

Friday 1st

Funny, isn't it? Former Tiger Matt Poole doesn't play for us any more but he still gets the best seat on the plane – he's always in the front row with all that lovely extra legroom. Why?

Could it be something to do with the fact that he organises our away trips for Tigers Events, a company run by the club. They have chartered a plane to take us, and some of the supporters and club members, from East Midlands airport to Dublin. While the taller people get the aisle seats and the giants like Johno and Ben Kay are guaranteed a place by the emergency exits, it's pot luck for the rest of us. I'm next to Scott Bemand and Geordan and luckily we're not too far away to fire loads of abuse at Matt.

"Got a big game this week, Pooley?

"You should have a lie-down, mate; conserve your energy for the big game!"

I feel a bit guilty as he does work hard, but if he hogs the front seat he deserves some abuse.

Once settled into our hotel Geordy, Leon, Vesty, Ollie, Damsy and I go to see the film *Constantine*, which is about Heaven and Hell. It's pretty good but they could have put a lot more meaning into the characters.

April

Saturday 2nd

Leinster 13 – Leicester 29

Leinster: G Dempsey; S Horgan, B O'Driscoll, F Contepomi (rep: G D'Arcy, 53), D Hickie; D Holwell, G Easterby; R Corrigan (capt), S Byrne, R Nebbett, M O'Kelly, L Cullen, C Potts (rep: V Costello, 49), K Gleeson (rep: S Jennings, 59), E Miller.

Leicester: S Vesty (rep: A Healey, 77); G Murphy, O Smith, D Gibson, L Lloyd; A Goode, H Ellis (rep: S Bemand, 35-40); G Rowntree, G Chuter, D Morris, M Johnson (capt), L Deacon, L Moody, N Back, M Corry.

Leinster: Try: Horgan. Con:Holwell. Pens Holwell (2).
Leicester: Tries: Smith, Gibson. Cons: Goode (2) Pens: Goode (4). Drop goal: Goode.

We're all pretty tense in the coach en route to the ground. As usual, I'm keeping my head down, trying to keep my focus, when the lads burst out laughing. We're stopped in front of a pub with loads of Leinster fans outside and there's two guys in the middle of them all, dancing away like loons: it is Tom Varndell from our academy and one of his team-mates. They look hilarious and the tension suddenly melts away.

Well, nearly all away. It's very quiet in the changing room and I'm a little bit worried: this is normally a bad sign. This quarter-final is a big, big game for us. If we win today we'll become the first English side ever to win a Heineken Cup quarter-final on the road. It seems amazing no other English side has done it in ten years of the Heineken Cup, but it shows how tough a competition this is.

To do so, however, we need to step it up a gear. All week we've been reading about how good the Leinster backs are. But from the moment we step out onto the pitch, I can sense the release in the guys around me and it goes like a dream. In the pre match huddle it's clear that everyone really wants this game. We are left out on the pitch on our own for about three minutes before Leinster come out, which gives me good vibes.

I manage to catch the first kick-off, which I hope puts us on the front foot.

It's certainly a big confidence boost for me, as I feel I've had a real stop-start season. We make a couple of mistakes, but no-one's head drops and we just pile on the pressure even more. It feels great. Everything just feels right. We're dominating their pack, our backs are going well and everyone's fighting hard for each other, taking the 'shoeing' that comes our way without complaining. We figure out the ref, Joel Jutge, too. We know he doesn't like people backchatting him or trying to talk to him in any shape or form, so we just take whatever he says and walk away.

We don't walk away from the alcohol afterwards though. This is one of the most satisfying victories of my entire career, and certainly beats anything so far this season. To go back to Lansdowne Road and win after losing there with England so recently makes it all the sweeter. And now we can look forward to top seeds Toulouse in the semis.

Geordan has arranged for us to have a few free beers and I think today we really deserve them. It's a great chance to let our hair down as an entire squad – it's very rare we all get to go out together, as people have families and have to get back for their kids, or always seem to have some family do or friend's birthday to go to back in Leicester. So we hit the bars until about 11pm before going to a nightclub, myself Geordan, Leon, Austin and a couple of the others finishing off a great night in the hotel bar drinking until about 7am. I'm going to pay for it tomorrow (today!) but I couldn't care less. What a great day.

Monday 4th

Despite doing nothing but sleep yesterday I am still struggling this morning. Whose stupid idea was it to stay up until the early hours – well, breakfast-time, really - of Sunday morning celebrating our victory? It certainly wasn't mine; it must have been Geordy's. That's it, it's all Geordy's fault.

Luckily, Wellsy's very sympathetic to our plight and has only laid on a two-hour fitness session involving loads of running. Alright, it's not two hours, but it certainly feels like it. We play a bit of touch rugby, which is the norm once you get to this stage of the season as there is no need to batter yourself every day. We play Fijian two-touch rugby, which means if you are touched two times the ball passes to the other side, but if you are touched once you can't score and have to pass to someone else.

It's a great session as everyone is still buzzing about Saturday. In the 2003 Heineken Cup we lost in the quarter-finals and in 2004 we didn't even get out of the pool, so it is a massive boost to be back in the last four again.

Geordy and I head into town to continue the recovery from our hangovers by chilling out in Starbucks and I eventually drag my sorry ass home in time to tidy up a bit before Annie gets back.

Annie is turning into a bit of a Nigella Lawson and she lays on a superb meal this evening – chicken stuffed with stilton and a fabulous salad with couscous. No more pies and chocolate cake for me. I have put on around 3kgs since Christmas so now I am back up to my fighting weight.

Tuesday 5th

One of the strange things about the Heineken Cup is that the draw for the semi-finals takes place on the same day as the draw for the quarter-finals. So for a while now we have known that our prize for beating Leinster would be a 'home' tie against the winners of the Toulouse v Munster game. By 'home' I mean your home country not you're your home ground, but today we discover the fantastic news that our semi-final is against Toulouse and will be played at Leicester City's Walkers Stadium. Great news but this will put a little bit more pressure on us to play well.

Unfortunately we also find out that we won't, as planned, be playing all our matches at the Walkers Stadium next season, although I expect we'll be in there for 2006-07. I am pretty disappointed; it is always good to play in front of bigger crowds and the Walkers holds 32,500, compared to Welford Road's 16,000. As it is a new stadium the facilities are excellent and everything seems twice the size – the changing rooms are like a cavernous hotel.

I know our supporters love Welford Road, but hopefully the semi-final will give them a taste for the Walkers and allow the club a dry run, so if things need to be changed for when we come in full-time they can be. It will take some getting used to: Welford Road is always very noisy and intimidating, but the stands at the Walkers are quite far from the pitch in certain places so the atmosphere might not be quite as good until the fans work out the acoustics.

Wednesday 6th

Cozza manages to whack me in the knee during a three-on-three tackling drill, so Wellsy suggests I take it easy for the rest of the session.

Tonight Andy Goode deservedly picks up the Players' Player of the Season award at our sponsors' dinner and Tom Varndell gets the Players' Young

Player of the Season award. I didn't vote – I think I must have been away with England when it was done – although if I had I would definitely have picked those two.

Goodey is currently the top points-scorer in the Zurich Premiership with 207 points in just 14 matches (40 points ahead of Charlie Hodgson) and he's poised to become the top scorer in the Heineken Cup when we take on Toulouse. He's in the form of his life, and must have a big shot at being named in the Lions party next Monday.

I'm on a table with Leon and my sponsors, Owen Brown, the marquee people, who are big Tigers fans. They're nice guys and have sponsored me for quite a few years now, but while they're all enjoying the hospitality I have to remember I've got a game in two days time so I call it a night about 11.30pm.

Thursday 7th

The whole squad is suffering from the hangover of the Leinster match. Not the physical one, but it's hard to up the pace again, keep the focus, after such a great victory and training isn't going too well.

But there are plenty of motivating factors: Sale are one of just three clubs to beat us in the Premiership this season, as we lost 19-26 to them in September. Also, due to the way the season is structured now, we know that a win on Saturday will guarantee our place in the Heineken Cup next season, as we will be assured of at least third place, which is a very satisfying position to be in with three games to go.

It was Goodey's birthday last Sunday so Annie and I have him and Sonia over tonight for a belated celebration. Annie picked up a recipe from Geordan's missus so rolls out a magnificent chocolate cake for him, as a surprise. He is 25, but we put 26 candles on the cake just to wind him up. Goodey's fantastic, a great mate, but it really winds me up that he can eat whatever he wants and still maintain that 'perfect 10' figure. He's naturally so fit. The sod.

Friday 8th

The Lions squad will be announced in a few days time but everyone's cool, no-one's really talking about it. Apart from Austin Healey, obviously. I find him holding court in the dressing room:

"None of you lot will be going! You've got no chance. No way, mate..."

He then proceeds to tell everyone exactly how he'd get the side playing... oh and some other stuff. No-one's listening mate!

Austin is the club's practical joker. He does all the Deep Heat in your pants and cutting up socks stuff. A while ago he found out that I'm scared of spiders. Well, not scared exactly, I just don't like them very much. So, of course, the next day there are spiders in my shoes, in my bag, my locker, being thrown at me... I think it's fair to say that I've conquered my fear now! Which is good as now I can help stitch up the next bloke, like Will Skinner.

Austin's always taking the mick, but he's easily wound up too. He's got a right temper: him and Goodey have the most heated arguments ever. They start off as banter, then progress to childish name-calling and gradually escalate into full-on warfare. All over nothing. They're both very confident and like to be the centre of attention. Neither of them like being put down so if they feel someone's having a go they'll never stop. Goodey's terrible: if he thinks he's being attacked he'll resort the harshest personal abuse, before backing off and saying he was just joking when he sees he's really affected the other person.

Anyway, I'm not being drawn into Austin's mad ramblings. I would regard being selected for the Lions as a huge honour, due to the large number of eligible players. I would be devastated not to get in. Back in December we received those wristbands, and over the months since then Clive has sent us a series of motivational postcards. "Be Ready! Are you READY?", that sort of thing. When we won the World Cup it was all about making 100 things one per cent better, and it seems he's using the same philosophy with the Lions. Those reminders keep you focused.

I received a letter earlier in the week telling me that if picked I would get a text message at noon on Monday, when the squad is announced at a press conference at Heathrow. It may seem a strange way to do it (Clive has some great ideas but the texts always seem a bit bloody odd to us!), but that is how it was done for the World Cup and I guess Clive likes to do things differently.

After training Leon, Pat Howard, Geordy and I take Pete Lloyd into Leicester for a bite to eat. Pete has been an unofficial scout for Leicester for years and is the reason that a fair few of us are at the club. He had a big hand in Leon joining us from Barkers Butts and he really pushed me and talked me up in my early days at the club. He's a lovely bloke, about 70-odd now, and it's always great to see him at the Friday team runs – he's become really firm friends with Martin Johnson and Neil Back over the years. He hasn't seen my new house yet so I give him the tour before dropping him back at Geordy's.

Saturday 9th

Leicester 45 – Sale 15

Leicester: G Murphy; A Tuilagi, L Lloyd (rep: O Smith, 55), D Gibson (rep: S Vesty, 74), T Varndell; A Goode, S Bemand (rep: H Ellis, 74); G Rowntree, G Chuter (rep: J Buckland, 78), D Morris, M Johnson (capt), L Deacon, W Johnson (reps: H Tuilagi, 48; J Rawson, 65), L Moody, M Corry.

Sale: J Robinson (capt); M Cueto, C Rhys Jones, R Todd (rep: J Payne, 68), S Hanley; M Hercus (rep: D Blair, 58), B Redpath (rep: S Martens, 58); A Sheridan, A Titterrell (rep: S Bruno, 58), B Stewart (rep: S Turner, 52), C Jones (rep: P Anglesea, 81), D Schofield, J White, M Lund, S Chabal (rep: I Fernandez Lobbe, 58).

Leicester 45: Leicester: Tries Moody, Lloyd, Goode, M Johnson, A Tuilagi, Varndell. Cons: Goode (6). Drop goal: Goode.
Sale 15: Tries Cueto (2). Con: Hercus. Pen: Hercus.

The lack of edge that was evident in the team run yesterday rears its ugly head again at the start of the match, and once again we're slow out of the blocks. We concede the first try and they're in the lead for 25 minutes, but I score from a pushover try and that seems to set us off. I love scoring tries. If nothing else it means I'll get slightly less abuse from people like Leon who love to remind me how long it has been since my last one.

From that moment on, everything seems to go for us in this game. Every pass goes to hand and every move seems to come off. I think beating Leinster has given us confidence and a bit of an edge, even when we conceded that first try we knew we would come back, dominate and go on to win the game.

Goodey turns in a magnificent performance and many of us believe he's done enough to win a place on the Lions tour. His tactical kicking and all-round play drove Sale backwards. He scored a try, then created another for Alesana Tuilagi with a sharp break and also kicked seven conversions and a drop goal.

We shoot off straight after the game as Geordy and I have decided to give the girls a bit of a treat and take them to a magnificent 11th Century country house hotel, Stapleford Park, near Melton Mowbray, for a night and day of pampering. It's an awesome place and after a stunning meal we retire to the lounge (as I believe they say), just chilling out until about 2am.

Sunday 10th

Geordy and I start the day with a recovery session in the pool at Stapleford Park, followed by nine holes of golf, while the girls hit the treatment rooms – and our wallets. Four hours later we're all glowing and chilled – especially as the club have pretty much given me the whole of next week off as a precaution to make sure my knee is right for the Toulouse game in just over two weeks' time.

Monday 11th

I head to London for a Lions fitness test, knowing that the squad is due to be announced at Midday.

It's 11.55am. My mum always said that a watched pan never boils and I'm beginning to realise that a stared-at mobile never buzzes. Especially when you're waiting for a text to say whether or not you're in the Lions squad.

11.59am. Maybe it's not working. Ah well, one minute to noon... my clock could be fast.

12.02pm. What's going on? An hour ago I was having a final fitness test, which went well and made me think I'm in the frame.

12.10pm. I'm having lunch in Oxford Street. The food has arrived. Oh good, at least something has.

12.18pm. Texts aren't the most reliable of mediums, but I'm starting to get worried now.

12.24pm. Definitely going to have to phone my supplier. This phone's rubbish.

12.27pm. Bloody technology. Only texts I am getting are from mates asking me if I got in?

12.30pm. I love Geordy! He's seen the squad on the news. "Congrats mate! I'm in too!"

12.31pm Still no text from Clive but at least I can stick my phone back in my pocket.

12.37pm. Oh no I can't. Goodey didn't make the cut. I'm really surprised by that – he's been in such great form this season. Trouble is, I think up until the last few months he hadn't even contemplated winning a place but, after being sent a contract and reading loads of stuff in the press, even he'd really started to believe that he would be going, so he's even more disappointed. It will be scant consolation to him, but I'm sure he will now go with England to the Churchill Cup, where he has a great chance of being the starting outside-half, rather than a bench man.

I will be joined in New Zealand by seven other Leicester players (although I'm surprised Harry Ellis isn't one of them either) and, unusually, Clive has left the door open for Jonny Wilkinson, Tinds (Mike Tindall) and Vicks (Phil Vickery) to be added to the list of 44 should they prove their fitness before the end of the season. Which is fair enough, there are still a number of games left and players may well finish the season strongly.

After lunch I meet an old friend from the Tigers, Huw Owen, who is now working in London, and then I spend most of the journey back to Leicester speaking to my parents and friends who ring to congratulate me on the Lions call-up. I say everyone, but there's still no text!

In the evening the club ask me if I'll go down to Welford Road to chat to our fans and keep their spirits up: there's a massive queue for tickets for the Heineken Cup semi-final with Toulouse. I'm happy to oblige and I bump into a few, familiar, friendly faces. I can also share my good news with them as, at 7pm, the Lions text finally arrives. Only seven hours late! There's a great buzz around the ground about the Toulouse game and it feels great to see so many happy, smiling fans.

Tuesday 12th

I have a couple of meetings to drum up support for Annie's new business, Anneidi. The first is with our architect, Malcolm Fox-Arnold (who's also an ex-Tigers man), and then I sit down with the Tigers chief exec Pete Wheeler. God, our ex-players are a talented lot, and I'm not just saying that because they both gave me quite a few contacts and ideas.

Brace (as we call Pete Wheeler) captained England and the Lions and people who saw him tell me he was one of the game's greatest. At Leicester you get used to seeing people like Pete, who are legends of the game, just strolling around. You'll stroll in and see Dusty Hare (25 caps for England) sitting in the office doing paperwork or Paul Dodge (32 caps for England) training the academy players. Dodgey is the quietest, most unassuming man I have ever met. You'd have no idea how great a player he was. He played for Leicester when he was 16, was capped for England when he was 19, captained England and went on to play for the Lions.

That's another reason why I love Leicester so much and would find it so difficult to leave here. There's a real sense of community, of the club still belonging to its former players and decisions being taken with an understanding of what it's like to be a current player. It is weird at first, seeing all these legends, but you get used to it – I suppose because there are so many of them around and because they are just down-to-earth everyday guys, with no ego at all.

Wednesday 13th

I'm delighted to hear that Irish referee Alain Rolland will be in charge of the Toulouse game a week on Sunday. Alain is a former player and has refereed me many times before, at club and Test level. I like him as a ref as he allows a lot more competition than most for the ball at the breakdown. He won't just blow his whistle all the time, he likes to keep the game flowing. He's a very good communicator so I know exactly what I can do with him. I know when I can compete – and for how long – and when I can't.

I think it helps that he is an ex-player and while I know the RFU is constantly on the look-out for players to become referees there is absolutely not a hope in the world that I would ever want to become one. I would rather be punched by Johno again!

Tonight I discovered that there is a difference between methylated spirit and white spirit; a big and important difference: one burns, the other doesn't. Leon decided to have a cheese fondue night so Damsy and I piled over his place. The three of us spent about an hour trying to work out how to light the fondue stove, and, after discovering we had no methylated spirit, we tried to get it going – with no luck at all – with white spirit.

I was getting really frustrated with all that lovely cheese going begging and was just on the verge of suggesting whisky (or any other spirit) when Leon somehow managed to get it to take and I stopped salivating and started tucking in. Cheese is to me what doughnuts are to Homer Simpson, so I have a wonderful night, topped off with a trip to the cinema to see *Bullet Boy*, kind of a UK *Boyz in the Hood*. Their hood was in London, and I began to wish I was wearing one so I could fall asleep unnoticed.

Thursday 14th

The Lions pre-tour publicity starts in earnest today. I'm off to a photoshoot in Droitwich for one of my sponsors, Gilbert, with fellow Lions Steve Thompson, Cozza and Michael Owen. And Damsy, who is either a bit bored or after some freebies.

Today is just a question of wearing shorts, pads, that sort of thing, as my footwear is supplied by Nike. Photoshoots like this will come thick and fast from now on and the club is starting to organise dinners and personal appearances. It's not too bad, and certainly not as bad as it was for the World Cup, when I could have attended events every hour of every day if I'd wanted to. It's over quite quickly and Damsy gets his freebies.

After being stuck in traffic for hours, it's fantastic to head off to the Italian restaurant, Zizzi, with the missus. I haven't really had time to eat all day and I'm starving, absolutely ravenous. I forego the anchovies and order a massive Calzone pizza filled with chicken, meatballs, bolognese and about 101 other things. It hits the spot quicker than you can say cheese fondue.

Friday 15th

I still haven't put pen to paper on my new contract with Leicester and I want to get it signed before I go away with the Lions at the end of May. Leicester are notoriously bad at actually sorting contracts. When I was first at the club – when Deano Richards was in charge – I don't think I ever signed a contract. It was always that sort of arrangement, a gentleman's agreement.

I have, however, got a contract for the two properties Leon and I are building in Lincoln. We bought up an old garage in the heart of Lincoln and are converting it into two semis, both two-up, two-down, which we hope to sell to first-time buyers. So as it's my day off, I drive over to see the plot, and how the builders are getting on. They are making great progress: the first floor is in and the roof is going on next week.

Saturday 16th

After the team run, we adjourn to watch the Powergen Cup Final as Mullers (Craig McMullen), the former Leicester player, is playing for Leeds against Bath. He's on the bench but comes on after 30 minutes to help the underdogs to a 20-12 victory over Bath. Well done mate! It wasn't a particularly exciting final, but then they rarely are. After seeing Mullers lift the trophy it's our weekly cinema trip, this time off to see Nicole Kidman's new film *The Interpreter,* the one that was partly filmed in the United Nations building. It's a well-done thriller, but the ending's a bit disappointing.

Sunday 17th

Saracens 19 – Leicester 17

Saracens: M Bartholomeusz (rep: N Little, 62); B Johnston, K Sorrell, D Harris, T Vaikona; T Castaignede, K Bracken (rep: M Rauluni, 58); K Yates (rep: N Lloyd, 83), R Ibanez (rep: M Cairns, 58), B Broster, S Raiwalui (rep: I Fullarton, 73), K Chesney, R Hill (rep: B Russell, 29-36), D Seymour (rep: B Russell, 45), H Vyvyan (capt).

Leicester: S Vesty; G Murphy, M Cornwell, D Gibson, A Tuilagi (rep: T Varndell, 70); A Goode, H Ellis (rep: S Bemand, 70); G Rowntree, G Chuter (rep: J Buckland, 74), J White, M Johnson (capt), L Deacon (rep: L Moody, 12), W Johnson, N Back (rep: H Tuilagi, 79), M Corry.

Saracens: Try: Castaignede. Con: Castaignede. Pens: Castaignede (4). Leicester: Try: Chuter; Pens Goode (4).

The plan is for me to play around 15 minutes today as I am still struggling with this knee injury. However that plan doesn't include Louis Deacon fracturing his eye socket in the first few minutes.

Obviously my problems in having to play almost a whole game pale into insignificance compared to Deacs, who could now be out for ages and the injury will probably lead to him missing England's tour to North America this summer and the possibility of a first cap.

Saracens definitely targeted us today, trying to wind us up from the start but, as Wellsy said afterwards, we do it, so we need to be able to handle it when it comes our way. It was a very niggly game, culminating in a red card for Cozza and a yellow for Johno.

We'd been penalised constantly for taking the mauls down, but they had been doing exactly the same. One of our guys did and got a good shoeing – as he should – and then Richard Hill did the same, at which point Cozza reacted and caught him in the face. I was very surprised to see Chris White hold up the red card but that is what was recommended by his touch judge, so he had no option. I would have thought it was more of a yellow card offence as I don't believe there was any intention to do that kind of damage to Hilly. I was surprised he didn't give a yellow card and say 'if there is any more it will be red'. It happened in the 27th minute after all.

We were very disappointed with our performance. We never got going and were unable to put any of our patterns into play. Towards the end I must admit I lost track of the score. When we were 19-17 down I thought we were ahead and that Goodey was trying those drop goals to stretch our lead, not take us into the lead. One of Goodey's efforts went so high there was no way of telling if it had gone over and even when Chris White consulted the video replay it proved inconclusive. I thought it was good but it was so hard to tell and I can understand why it was disallowed. Goodey was pretty sure it had gone over but even with 14-men we should have beaten them so there's no way we are blaming that drop goal decision.

It's Saracens' first win in ten attempts against us, and to complete a thoroughly bad day at the office we are knocked off the top of the table by Wasps.

Monday 18th

Today, for the first time, my Lions call-up seems real. Clive has called a two-day meeting of the whole squad, players and management at our UK base, the Vale of Glamorgan Hotel near Cardiff, so everyone can get to know each other.

I can only stay until 2pm as I need some treatment on my knee after yesterday's game, but I feel it's important to be here, even briefly. I gather that after I left there was a series of team bonding exercises, including players doing a few sketches on stage – but I really did need that treatment, honest.

It was good to meet the lads, especially as there are so many from Scotland, Wales and Ireland who I don't know (although I'm rubbish at remembering who I've played against unless they've tried to gouge my eye out!) although I'd prefer to spend our precious time out on the training field, learning the calls.

Back at Leicester the knee specialist decides just to keep monitoring the injury. I'm in a dilemma: I don't know whether I want to have it scanned and find something I don't want to see, or have it scanned and find out there's a little tear which they can do something about. In the end I go along with the specialist's view, although I am a bit worried as it's not been right for a while now. But at this stage of the season, so long as there is no major structural damage, you have to just play on. I'm desperate to make the Toulouse game.

Tuesday 19th

As we all expected, Cozza is banned today, after being sent off against Saracens on Sunday, but Johno has his appeal next Tuesday so he will definitely play this weekend. Cozza has already apologised to the team – although no-one's blaming him – and, as he said himself, it was not as if it was his first offence. It says it all about Cozza as a bloke that he felt the need to apologise, as we have all been there before. He feels he's let us down, which isn't the case.

The team will be announced tomorrow but Wellsy has already told me the back row, with strict instructions for me to keep it under my hat, as he doesn't want people to know before they are told by him. With Cozza out, I'll be playing, as will Henry.

Wednesday 20th

Training consists of a team skills session. As Henry is playing eight he won't be jumping in the line out, and I'm at six, so I'm practising being a line-out target, a pretty big change for me. Henry is good at a lot of things but he is not particularly good in the air as he weighs about 85 stone!

Annie has been in Spain for a few days, buying some furniture for our apartment, so after a quick meal at Nando's with the lads I head off to the airport to pick her up.

It's Geordan's birthday, so later a group of us are off to Italian restaurant San Carlos in Leicester. It's pretty much a boys night out although Geordan's missus, Lucie, is there along with Will Johnson's girlfriend. On the way we pass a Chinese herbal shop and can't resist buying Geordy a little something. We've already got him a PSP, the new hand held Playstation, but I like to think that our bonus gift, 'Mr Dragon, Chinese super Viagra', goes down (or rather up) just as well!

Thursday 21st

The team is formally announced today and Louis Deacon gets the nod, despite the fact that he cracked his cheekbone against Saracens. It is an injury you can play with, you just have to be careful about is blowing your nose. Do that and whole face swells up. I had the same injury a couple of years ago. I got up, thought I was fine, went to clear my throat and my whole face filled with air, which was a bit of a shock.

It's Johno's final testimonial dinner tonight and so many people are paying tribute to his career that you can see it starting to get to him a little. Johno talks really well about how much playing at Leicester has meant to him, listing loads of players and coaches he's worked with, desperate not to miss anyone out. He's very eloquent on the subject of how much he will miss the game once he finally retires and is getting quite choked up as it finally sinks in that he won't be playing at Welford Road next season. We'll miss you too mate.

The big moment of the night is yet to come though. No, not the fabulous funky soul singer Kid Creole but the audience's chance to see me and Nobby (Dorian West) starring as his backing group, 'the Coconuts'. We went early to rehearse with the band, but luckily the evening is running late so we get to wriggle out of it – well, we've got a big game Saturday and need our sleep don't we? I am, however, a little upset that a lifetime's dream, to be a Coconut, has been smashed.

Friday 22nd

Victoria Park in Leicester is the scene of one of the most audacious of mankind's attempts to launch himself into space. Forget the Shuttle, forget Richard Branson in his hot-air balloon; this is hardcore. Our brave would-be astronaut, Jamie Hamilton, is strapped onto a skateboard and holding onto a five-metre kite for dear life, but despite possibly breaking the land-speed record, we fail to have lift-off. Unfortunately I have a knee injury so am reduced to laughing hysterically from the safety of a park bench as Damsy then has a go. He fails to fully understand the principle of strapping yourself onto the board, which results in him cartwheeling around the park, hitting every bump, as the kite drags him along. Amazingly he survives.

Saturday 23rd

Guess what film we're seeing tonight? *Guess Who* with Bernie Mac. I like him, so I've been looking forward to it, but unfortunately it turns out to be one of those films where the trailer contains all the funny bits.

Sunday 24th

Leicester 19 – Toulouse 27

Leicester: G Murphy; A Healey, O Smith, D Gibson, L Lloyd (rep: T Varndell, 77); A Goode, H Ellis (rep: S Bemand, 68); G Rowntree (rep: D Morris, 20), G Chuter, J White, M Johnson, L Deacon, L Moody (rep: B Kay, 41), N Back, H Tuilagi (rep: W Johnson, 68).

Toulouse:C Poitrenaud (rep: G Thomas, 68); V Clerc, Y Jauzion (rep: B Baby, 77), F Fritz, C Heymans; F Michalak, J-B Elissalde (rep: J-F Dubois, 80); J-B Poux (rep: D Human, 55), W Servat (rep: Y Bru, 44), O Hasan, T Brennan, R Millo-Chluski, J Bouilhou (rep: I Maka, 8), F Maka (rep: C Labit, 72), G Lamboley.

Leicester: Try: Varndell. Con: Goode. Pens: Goode (4).
Toulouse: Tries: F Maka, Elissalde, Michalak. Cons: Elissalde (3). Pens: Elissalde (2).

What a frustrating, disappointing, miserable, utterly depressing afternoon. We make an awful start to it and get too far behind, too early on. As Leon and I are running a planned move off a ruck in the 10th minute, someone runs in and hits me on the side of the knee, partially tearing the medial ligaments and ensuring I'm not going to last much longer. I can run in straight lines but as soon as I try and turn or twist it gives way. I get the physios on quickly to strap it up and try to carry on as best I can. I could take contact like that 100 times and have no adverse affects...but today of all days. I had the same injury once before, when I was 19, so I know it's going to mean three or four weeks out – effectively the end of my season with Leicester.

I am therefore keen to keep going through the pain to do what I can to help the team. I want to stay on but it means I can't really run properly or chase kicks so I am reduced to hitting rucks and defending. By half-time I realise it's getting worse so I reluctantly make the decision not to go out for the second half.

It's even more painful watching from the bench. We get our act together and so many times we seem to be one pass away from scoring the vital try. The only time they score is either when we turn the ball over or when we kick it down their throats and they run it back at us.

I like Allain Rolland as a referee, but I thought he had a bit of a shocker in this game. You can't blame him for the fact that we won't be going to Edinburgh next month to take on Stade Francais in the final, but there seemed to be a number of questionable decisions. From our first kick off I was taken out off the ball and although Allain held his hand out, indicating he was going to give a penalty, he quickly withdrew it as if he'd changed his mind, while a pass in the move that led to their second half try was clearly forward. That's not why we lost, we played poorly, but it doesn't mean we can't be frustrated with his performance.

Losing in the semi-final is the absolute worst way to do it. I'm gutted. I head back to Welford Road for a few drinks with Annie, her brother and a couple of his mates, swiftly followed by an early night.

Monday 25th

I would rate myself as 50:50 for the game against Wasps this week, but before I can think about that match it's time to turn my attention to our A team in which I started my comeback last October.

More than 11,000 people are at Welford Road to see them beat Wasps 29-22, which adds to their 35-19 first leg win and gives them the A team championship. Well done lads. Alex Tuilagi puts the match beyond doubt with two tries in the right hand corner, after 48 and 65 minutes, and Roger Warren scores 14 points which takes him to the top of the Zurich A League scorers chart. Hopefully we can now do the double with the Zurich title.

Tonight is also significant because we've organised a collection for Matt Hampson, our A team prop who suffered that serious neck injury after a scrum collapsed when he was on England Under-21 duty. Myself and quite a few of the first-team lads carry buckets around the pitch perimeter at half-time and get a good response. Most of the boys have visited Matt in hospital since his injury and the bucket collection is our way of letting him know that we are still thinking about him.

Johno has his yellow card from the Saracens game rescinded, ensuring he can play in the rest of our games this season. We have some big matches coming up and it is only fitting that Johno will now be there. I'm not surprised it was cancelled. I think to have deprived Johno of one or two games at the end of his career would have been a travesty. Yes, punches were exchanged, but it could easily have been dealt with by a warning.

Tuesday 26th

Once again I start my day with some physio. Today it's a massage with ice, followed by some ultrasound. I am a popular boy today as I get messages from Clive Woodward, Phil Larder and Andy Robinson, checking on my fitness after my rather public knee injury at the weekend. I am able to report that the medics have diagnosed a grade two tear of my medial ligament so, although it is very doubtful I will now make it on Saturday, it is nothing too long-term and shouldn't affect the Lions tour.

This is some consolation, but not much. First we under-perform in the biggest match of our season and now I find out I'll definitely miss our last league match of the campaign and possibly the Zurich Final, two weeks later. I've had better days.

I decide to give the video of the Toulouse game a miss and huddle in front of the TV with Geordy and GG (Glenn Gelderbloom), a former Leicester player who is in town at the moment. We play Mario Cart and some Jonah Lomu rugby on the Playstation, just to take my mind off my knee injury, and it works a treat, with the bonus that England win the World Cup (again!), although this time there's no need for a parade through central London and another MBE. Just as well really as Gelderbloom is South African, so he wouldn't qualify for a trip to the Palace.

Wednesday 27th

We are off to London to watch Geordan's girlfriend, Lucie Silvas, in concert at the Shepherd's Bush Empire. Lucie's career has taken off in an amazing way in recent months, with two top ten hits. My knee injury means that I need to sit down for most of the concert – no reflection on Lucie's abilities. I was up there dancing with the best of them, if only in spirit. Anyway, Annie turned out to be an able dancing deputy.

Thursday 28th

It's time to draw the curtains in the Moody-Muggleton household and take the telephone off the hook so Annie and I can indulge ourselves in a night of trash TV. We've got Sky Plus at home and with us being so busy in recent weeks the episodes of *Desperate Housewives* have been racking up on the hard drive...until now, when we settle down on the sofa, popcorn in hand. Obviously Annie is the one who wants to watch all these episodes of *Desperate Housewives* and I am just keeping her company.

I usually watch something like the Discovery Channel (no, honestly) because I am away so often it is difficult to get stuck into any of the soaps and I'm not that big a telly-watcher anyway. I also like *MTV's Cribs* and those Japanese game shows you can find when you are flicking through the channels. One of my favourites is *Takeshi Castle* on Bravo, where the contestants have to run an assault course and batter the hell out of each other. One day I could imagine myself hurtling over those obstacles. Another fave is *Extreme Dodgeball* – a game they have launched in America (only in America!) on the back of the film. I might ask Geordy and Leon whether they fancy getting a Leicester Tigers team together and going over to show them how it's done.

Friday 29th

I'm having more physio while the boys go through the team run before our final game of the season against Wasps. We have a great record against Wasps so let's hope it continues so we can finish the season on top of the table. As I'm not playing tomorrow I think I'll save my usual cinema trip until I'm back in the side, because even for a self-confessed film addict like me, there are only so many films out there I want to see and I don't want to be left with the equivalent of Christmas with the Kranks if I'm lucky enough to be involved in the Zurich Final in two weeks!

I've been in a knee brace all this week but thankfully that comes off today, so at least now I don't look as bad as I feel. Being miserable doesn't stop me tucking into one of Lucie's famous roast dinners, with Geordy, who thankfully stayed out of the kitchen. We talk about Wednesday's concert and Geordy's move to the wing tomorrow. He doesn't say it but I know he must be pretty cheesed off as he'd much rather play full-back.

Saturday 30th

Leicester 45 – Wasps 10

Leicester: S Vesty; G Murphy (rep: S Bemand, 69), O Smith (rep: D Hipkiss, 68), D Gibson (rep: Hipkiss, 63-67), A Healey (rep: A Tuilagi,

61); A Goode, H Ellis; D Morris (rep: M Holford, 61, sin-bin, 66-76),
G Chuter (rep: J Buckland, 61), J White, M Johnson (rep: Chuter, 71-78),
B Kay (rep: B Deacon, 78), H Tuilagi (rep: W Johnson, 30), N Back,
L Deacon.

Wasps: M van Gisbergen; P Sackey, A Erinle, J Lewsey, T Voyce; A King
(rep: J Brooks, 55), M Dawson (rep: W Fury, 68); T Payne, P Greening (rep:
T Leota, 58), W Green (rep: A McKenzie, 68), S Shaw, R Birkett (rep:
M Purdy, 55), J Worsley (rep: J Hart, 58), T Rees, L Dallaglio.

Leicester: Tries: Ellis, Gibson, Murphy, Back, Hipkiss. Cons: Goode (4).
Pens: Goode (3). Dropped goal: Goode.
Wasps: Try: Voyce. Con: Van Gisbergen. Pen: Van Gisbergen

Injured players at Leicester often watch the game from the main stand near
the press box, but this time I have been invited into the Orange hospitality box,
along with Benny Kay who is also injured.

I hate having to watch from the sidelines, but it's a cracking game. We score
five tries to finish the regular season on a massive high, and on top of the table.
The guys are showing so much confidence it's clear, right from the off, that
nothing Wasps do is going to come off.

Unfortunately I have the best seat in the house, just behind the posts, to
witness my great friend Henry Tuilagi suffer an horrific broken leg right in
front of us, after being hauled down just short of the try line by Tom Voyce.
Initially I couldn't see the injury and presumed he was just taking a breather.
But it was bad: apparently it was as if someone had sliced through his leg, so
clean and destructive was the break.

In normal circumstances Henry's injury would have put a real dampener on
the game, but this is a special day, the last home game for Martin Johnson,
Backy and John Wells. I will always regret not being fit for their final game at
Welford Road, as I would have loved to have run out with those guys one
last time.

Backy even managed to score his 125th try for the club and Goodey weighed
in with 20 points. Afterwards we all celebrate as if we've won the league. Well,
we might not have a trophy, but we have bloody well finished top of the table!

The lads present Backy and Johno with their changing room pegs and they make an unforgettable lap of honour cheered on by every Tigers fan. I might have detected a tear in Johno's eye but perhaps I'm imagining it. He's certainly choking up when he speaks to the crowd, but all I can think of is how fitting that the three of them should end their Welford Road careers with a thumping victory.

The next few months will be very difficult for all of them, as they give up the day-to-day routine and the mixing with the boys. Backy is going to be a coach at Leicester and perhaps one day Johno will return in a similar role.

Obviously I'm feeling a bit out of it, up here in the Gods, but after their lap of honour they come up – still in their kit – to have a drink with all the injured players. It's a nice touch, but that celebratory beer doesn't last long as so many fans follow them in we have to abandon it and make a dash for the European Lounge, where we all proceed to get right royally smashed.

Johno tells me that one of the first things he's going to do is pack up all the 'stash' he's accumulated over the years and send it off to eastern Europe. It's part of a programme run by a charity, so the shirts, shorts, tracksuits and boots can all be put to good use by people less fortunate than ourselves (and he can see his garage floor again). All I hope is that they can find a few people out there who are his size. That won't be easy.

I know that if I'm to stand any chance of playing in the Zurich Final I'll need some more physio in the morning, so I wobble off about midnight.

May

Sunday 1st

Harlequins were relegated yesterday after losing to Sale. It's a real shame. They've never been relegated, they've got a huge fan base and they've put so much money into the game. I almost joined them a few years ago and I really feel for them. The debate about whether we should have promotion and relegation to England's top flight has been raging since the game turned professional in 1995. I support the principle but, while it may sound harsh, for me London Irish would have been the best team to go down. They don't have their own ground, they don't play an exciting brand of rugby and they bring in players from all over the world, while Quins have a tradition of not only playing good rugby but providing a steady stream of players to the England team.

Worcester made a massive impact on the Premiership in their first year but I think a lot more could be done for National One clubs. We need to make sure their grounds and squads are developed so they are ready to come up and are not in the situation of having to borrow grounds and panic-buy a load of players when they are promoted. I'm sure Quins will bounce straight back. I hope so.

Monday 2nd

It's really strange not having a match this week, but I think it could be good for us to have a week or so off before we play the Premiership 'decider' at Twickenham. I say 'decider' because, well, we did win the League on Saturday and that should really be the end of it, but we'll do what we have to do... and I think it could be good for us to have a week or so off because we certainly celebrated like we'd won the League! We need to recover our focus, and quick.

Former Leicester boy, Adam Balding, has been named Gloucester's Player of the Year. He was stuck in a rut at Leicester a few seasons ago so I'm delighted he has made such a success of it at Kingsholm – even getting into the England squad this year. He was a great player but didn't really get the chance for us. Pat Howard tried to get Balders to run into spaces at Leicester, whereas Gloucester's coach Dean Ryan is happy to let him run over people, which he loves. Next thing you know he is captain.

Tuesday 3rd

I visit Henry in hospital. He's not the sort of bloke who would appreciate flowers and I'm not the sort of bloke who would buy them for another guy, so I take the usual selection of chocolates and sweets, as well as my great stock of jokes. Should be enough to cheer him up, I figure. Henry's obviously got someone on the outside working for him as he'd told me over the phone that the hospital food is awful, but when I get there he's tucking into his favourite meal, a Samoan speciality consisting of tuna, banana and coconut milk. He gives me a forkful to try and I have to admit, while it sounds horrible, it's actually pretty tasty.

He is in remarkably good humour for a guy who has just been ruled out of the game for four months. Clean breaks can be better than other injuries, no matter how horrific they look on the field. Seru Rabeni has just damaged his anterior cruciate ligament (knee) and could be out for nine months.

I'm delighted to discover that Leicester are employing a leading sports lawyer, Simon Cohen, to look after recruitment and rugby administration. Simon's arrival will give Pat Howard more time to concentrate on playing matters, which can only be a good thing. It can't be good to have the same guy negotiating your contract with you one minute and then coaching you the next.

England's Churchill Cup squad is announced this afternoon and with eight Tigers already selected for the Lions it is good to see another three – Goodey, Chuts (George Chuter) and Louis Deacon – picked to go to Canada. I'm surprised Balders (Adam Balding) didn't make it but well chuffed for Goodey. He was so close to coming on the Lions tour, at least now he'll get a chance to show what he can do.

Wednesday 4th

Backy, Whitey and Leon go to the Triumph motorbike factory today to pick up a bike each. Whitey goes for the biggest one, leaping on one with 1050cc engine, while Leon opts for something slightly more sedate. It took him five years to pass his test. I'm not too concerned as he wobbles off though – he rides his bike like a shopping trolley. Me? I've got the car, thank you. I almost bought a motorbike when I was 19, just before I went on tour with England in 1998. But after the tour I went on holiday to Ibiza and fell off a moped, at which point I thought, "Right, these things are lethal and not for me".

In the evening it's into the bow-tie and DJ and off to Twickenham for the Zurich Premiership's annual awards. It's a fantastic night for the Tigers: we collect the three main prizes and Johno is presented with a special trophy for his significant contribution to rugby. And the winners are... Zurich Player of the Season: Martin Corry; O2 Director of Rugby: John Wells and Land Rover Discovery Young Player of the Season: Ollie Smith. It is magnificent to see four of our players getting the sort of awards they deserve. I think Cozza and Ollie were the stand-out performers of the season and I was very surprised that Ollie took so long to come into the England reckoning – it is magnificent to see him in this summer's Lions squad.

Friday 6th

Johno puts his hand in his pocket today to give the boys one last big day out . He asked me to arrange for us to have a go-karting day at Stretton 2000 in Leicester, but we didn't think he was going to pay for it all. It's a magnificent gesture.

To give everyone a fighting chance we are split into three different races, based on weight and size: the Fat Boys, the Middleweights and the Lightweights, as apparently being a fat boy means you go better round the corners (although I thought it meant you were built for comfort not speed!).

Wipe-out! I think it's safe to say that none of us will be challenging Jenson Button in the near, or even distant future. Will Skinner sets a new standard for stupidity by managing to smash headlong into the tyres at the end of the pit lane when he was supposed to be slowing down, while Harry Ellis is a complete liability, accelerating hard out of the pits just as all the other guys are going past.

I'm concentrating too hard on taking people out by nudging them off the track to actually win. Not that it would matter if any of us actually had a strategy: whatever we do Austin always seems to win. If we go again we're going to have to sabotage his kart just to stand even the slimmest of chances. Of course, being the modest sort of chap he is, he keeps extremely quiet about it. He's not the sort of bloke that would go on and on about it for hours. Really.

Johno obviously thinks he hasn't spread quite enough love yet, because he takes us all out to Pause, a great Thai restaurant and bar in Leicester, afterwards where Austin insists on still not going on about his victory. Not at all.

Saturday 7th

I resist the temptation to spend the afternoon fretting over the TV to see who we'll be playing for the championship in a week's time and, putting all thoughts of Wasps v Sale to the back of my mind, pack Annie and the walking boots into the car for a weekend in the Peak District.

Now it really winds me up when people call me stupid, but I have to admit to feeling a bit daft today when I realise just how close the Peak District is to my house. I'd always thought it was miles away, but it takes us just 40 minutes to get to our hotel, the East Lodge in Rowsley, and if I'd realised it was just up the road I'd have come here ages ago. The hotel's gorgeous and right by Chatsworth House, so once we've checked in we head off for a wander around the beautiful grounds, checking out the tree that squirts water at you (ooh, they do have a sense of humour!) and the house itself, which is really impressive. It's really good to just spend some time together, but especially so as I will soon be off to New Zealand for seven weeks which will be really hard on us both. After an awesome dinner at a nearby restaurant called the Pickle, it's an early night for us.

Well, it is in a minute. I can't resist flicking on Teletext to find out who we'll be playing next Saturday. Just as I thought: Wasps. They won 43-22 at home and seem to have worked out exactly how to peak for these play-offs, winning the whole competition for the last two years. So we're in for a tough game next weekend then.

Sunday 8th

It's a beautiful day and, wandering round one of the local villages, we find a shop selling some really sweet name plaques for kids' bedroom doors which we decide would make great presents for our godchildren, Alex and Zak. We then realise you have to make them yourself so we end up spending an hour and a half painting them, which I have to say is quite enjoyable and therapeutic.

But we can't wait to get out in all that lovely fresh air again so we head to Matlock and head up a mountain called Heights of Abraham. Normally I'd love to walk up, but as I'm still a bit worried about my injury (although it feels fine after a week of intensive physio) we give in and take the cable car the 169metres to the top. The views from the top are stunning – we can see the River Derwent below and miles and miles of Derbyshire countryside – and I feel a million miles away from the stresses and strains of the season.

We collapse back at home just in time to catch Lucie's performance at the VE Day celebrations. I'd have loved to have gone down with Geordan to see her play live, but it was important to be with Annie this weekend – as she won't be able to come to New Zealand with me as her business is really taking off and I feel really chilled as we cuddle up on the sofa watching Lucie on the telly.

Monday 9th

I'm delighted to hear that Dean Richards has taken over at Harlequins after a year in France with Grenoble. He has moved to The Stoop on a three-year deal and deserves to do well. He led Leicester Tigers to four successive league titles and two Heineken Cups, so I'm sure it won't be long before he'll be leading the Quins back to the Premiership. Word also comes through that we are already starting planning for the new season by signing a new prop, Alejandro Moreno, who I bumped into when on holiday last summer with Tim Stimpson, Jamie Hamilton and Perry Freshwater. I don't know too much about about him as a player but he seems to have got the seal of approval from Whitey, which is the most important thing. At Leicester we have quality in the front row in guys like Wig and Whitey but after them we are into the youngsters so a bit more experience certainly won't go amiss.

After all my physio for my medial ligament injury, I'm finally able to start running in training and come through unscathed, so I know I'll be fit for Saturday, which is a great relief.

Tuesday 10th

I'm not one to disagree with Martin Johnson too often, because if I do he has this tendency to clock me one, but I can't just let him get away with a comment I read in the press today.

"I'M NO LEGEND," says the headline. Well, I'm sorry Johno, but I have to over-rule you on that one. You are a legend and we want to give you a great send-off at Twickenham on Saturday. Rugby, even at the highest level, is still about playing with your mates and I'm so glad I will be fit to play with one of my best mates one last time on Saturday. Apart from my first two seasons, Johno has been captain of every side I have played in, for Leicester and England, and I shall really miss him.

For now, though, I have to put all thoughts of Saturday aside and sort my life out. I want to make sure all the paperwork is in order before I head off to New Zealand, so I sit down at my office table and start compiling piles of bills and other stuff to wade through. I don't want to leave Annie to face it all.

Ten minutes later (can't remember who called who, honest) Danny Hipkiss, Will Skinner and I are heading into town. Yes, yes, I'll do it tomorrow.

Wednesday 11th

Wellsy names the team and I'm shocked to discover that I'm on the bench for Saturday. We have a rule that if you can't train fully on a Wednesday, when we do most of the key match preparation, you won't be in the starting line-up. There's obviously been some kind of a communication breakdown between the physios and coaches as, after I've taken part in the full morning session, Pat and Wellsy come up to me, really taken aback.

"Have you had some sort of miracle recovery? We were told there was no way you'd train today and you'd only be fit for the bench."

It seems if they had known I was fit enough to do the session I would have been in the starting 15.

What a nighhtmare. What's done is done – once you've announced the team it can't be changed – but I'm really annoyed. Now that I am going on the Lions tour I can't play in Johno's testimonial game in June, so playing on Saturday means a lot to me – especially as it will be my last chance to play with Backy and for Wellsy, too. I presume I'll get on pretty early on Saturday and will just have to hope that I do.

After training I do a photoshoot for one of my sponsors, Vulkan, who supply sports supports. In case anyone has seen the pictures, in my defence it's really difficult to pose in those sort of things and not look camp!

Friday 13th

After a successful team run, we all pile onto the coach down to London. The movie is Anchorman, with Will Ferrell. I've seen it before but it is very funny and it raises a few chuckles on the bus. It even gets Whitey going. He's one of those who laughs at the most random thing and, a bit like Frank Bruno, once he goes you can't stop him... within a few seconds we're laughing more at him than we are the film.

The trip to London means I can also sort out a replacement car. As I have a sponsorship deal with Renault, they kindly agreed to loan us a car. When I first went to pick it up a few months ago, the last thing Annie said to me was:

"I don't care what car it is, just make sure it is not in any ridiculous colour. It can be a Skoda as long as it is in black or silver or something normal."

When I got there, I discovered it was bright gold.

I didn't like to say anything, as it's a free car, but they obviously saw my bemused look and very kindly agreed to swap it over for a nice normal-coloured Megane. So Jamie Hamilton is kindly driving the golden wonder down to London and I'll drive the new black Megane home on Sunday. Hope she likes this one.

On checking in at our hotel in Sunbury we meet the England women's team who are playing South Africa tomorrow. They seem a good laugh and we end up playing cricket in the hallway with a few of them. I'm not sure you could really say there is a winner, as we're more worried about knocking things over than stumping people out, but it's good fun.

Saturday 14th

Leicester 14 – Wasps 39

Leicester: S Vesty (rep: A Tuilagi, 74); G Murphy, O Smith, D Gibson, L Lloyd (rep: A Healey, 51); A Goode, H Ellis (rep: S Bemand, 20); D Morris (rep: G Rowntree, h-time), G Chuter (rep: J Buckland, 80), J White, M Johnson, B Kay (rep: W Johnson, 80), L Deacon (rep: L Moody, h-time), N Back, M Corry.

Wasps: M van Gisbergen; P Sackey, (rep: R Hoadley, 83), A Erinle, J Lewsey, T Voyce; A King (rep: J Brooks, 83), M Dawson (rep: W Fury, 83); T

Payne (rep: C Dowd, 77), P Greening (rep: T Leota, 77), W Green, R Birkett, S Shaw, J Hart (rep: M Lock, 83), J Worsley (rep: M Purdy, 83), L Dallaglio.

Leicester: Try: Bemand. Pens: Goode (3).
Wasps: Tries: Voyce, Van Gisbergen, Hoadley. Cons: Van Gisbergen (3).
Pens: Van Gisbergen (5). Dropped goal: King.

It's a very strange, very emotional day for everyone connected with the club. I don't really want to talk about the game itself, suffice to say that it wasn't the way we wanted Backy, Johno and Wellsy to bow out.

One thing the game will be remembered for is Backy punching Joe Worsley, which may lead to a big ban for him if he is cited. I didn't see it that well but I know it is something Backy is capable of if he gets frustrated. I remember a very funny incident when Fritz van Heerden was still at the club and he and Backy got into a scrap in training.

Fritz was a hard man and 6ft 6ins with it, but the softest spoken bloke you could imagine, very polite and pretty religious. They clashed, I think while we were playing touch, and the next thing we knew Backy was swinging at Fritz who was trying to hold him off. Normally Wellsy lets players get it out of their system, but he came racing over to break it up. He pulled Backy away so Backy started swinging at Wellsy who promptly banished him to the clubhouse like a naughty schoolboy. Very amusing.

Anyway, writing that made me smile, but I'm still not happy. Today has to be one of the most disappointing matches of my career. When the championship play-off system first came in we were the only side to oppose it, as we were number one. The other teams thought it was a great idea. We did end up winning both the league and the play-off that year but ever since then the team finishing top of the table has lost in the play-offs. You have a league for a reason. In football the champions are the ones who perform consistently over the year and not the team that can win a one-off game. Can you imagine if Chelsea had been asked to play off against Arsenal or Manchester United to decide who the champions were? If you have to have a play-off, for financial reasons, I think we should return to the structure we had a few years ago when the team that finished top of the table won a trophy and there was a separate one for the side that won the play-off.

Johno made a very emotional speech after the game. I don't think he meant to make it that emotional but he could hardly stop himself. Everyone got a beer in the dressing room and went over to him to say: "Cheers, mate". But we didn't really know what to do. We didn't have a trophy to celebrate with.

The great thing about Johno is that he always picked his last game. He picked his last match for Leicester, for England (the World Cup final) and for the Lions (in 2001). No-one dropped him and no-one told him it was his last game and as a sportsman you can't ask for any more than that. It was only two years ago that people were writing him off as a captain and a player and now he leaves the game on a high, having achieved everything he wanted and with more honours than anyone before.

The key for him was in his preparation and the way he approached his training regime, never missing a session. In fact the only time I have ever seen him complain or not do a training session properly was a few weeks from the end of this season. You could see he was knackered and it was time for him to retire. He was grumpy. He still trained, even that day, but he did a lesser session than you might expect. You could see he was calling it time. You always know you can play matches, but it is at training when you really know it is time to go, when you can't get yourself up for one more session.

It was Sonia's birthday on Tuesday, so we're all due to have a few drinks tonight to celebrate. None of us really feel like it because we're still furious at ourselves for losing, but we go back to the Welford Road clubhouse and get smashed anyway. We end up playing ridiculous drinking games. I am a very reluctant participant in 'spin the bottle', with good reason as it turns out as it seems to point my way nearly every time. And, surprise, surprise, my forfeit is always having to snog one of the lads. I end up snogging nearly the entire team, and I have to say Jamie Hamilton and Vesty seemed particularly keen. Vesty even pushed me off my chair and onto the floor in a desperate attempt to have his wicked way with me!

Sunday 15th

Marco Pierre Healey gets his chance to impress today as we all pile round to Austin's house for an end of season barbecue. We don't have the Premiership trophy to drink out of, but most of the boys are there, along with their families, and despite the doom and gloom of yesterday, there's a nice atmosphere. Well, we can't do anything about it now so we might as well just enjoy the day.

Austin used to have a swimming pool in his garden but he has filled it in and replaced it with a trampoline (as only Austin would!) so we spent most of the afternoon bouncing around on that. Well the physios say it is good to build up the muscles around your knee! Of course, being us, it quickly becomes quite competitive as we try to be the first to do a somersault, two somersaults, a backwards somersault, and everything else we can think of. I manage two double somersaults, followed by a triple toe-loop, before remembering there's a barbecue and snaffling a couple of steaks before they're all gone. Austin's not a bad cook, but obviously his barbecues aren't a patch on mine.

Being the glamorous, hedonistic international sports stars that we are, Geordy and I finish the day watching telly round at ours with Annie and Lucie.

Monday 16th

I'm still a Leicester player! I finally sign on the dotted line today, and feel instantly relieved. Right, I can start thinking about the Lions now.

Before meeting up with them, I go for a final medical check-up at Bupa which I pass with flying colours, notwithstanding one or two minor trampolining injuries. Over the last few months I have developed a form of colitis, a kind of stomach bug, which is giving me some trouble and I've had to change my diet to cut out caffeine, some fruit (especially ones with pips) and dairy products, especially my beloved cheese. So I also stock up on some antibiotics, which should sort it out. I think the colitis developed as an adverse reaction to all the painkillers, supplements and other antibiotics I have taken over such a long period of time. But the doctors aren't worried and believe it will clear up soon.

Just one more job to do before I head off to join the Lions: a sneaky visit to a local jeweller. I've realised just how much I'm going to miss Annie and just how much she means to me, so I'm going to propose when I get back from New Zealand. I haven't told anyone yet, but I want to make sure the ring is really special, so I'm having it made up to my own design. And, no, I'm not telling you what that is yet. I think she should find out first don't you?

Tuesday 17th

As there are seven other Leicester players in the Lions squad we decided to meet at the local Hilton Hotel - where we gather before Tigers away games - and go down together. Annie drives me to the Hilton to say a tearful goodbye. I'm really going to miss her.

Day one with a new squad is pretty much like those army films you see on the TV, except we're not lined up and forced to have a short back and sides, thank God! We have a kit meeting with adidas, when we are allocated all the gear we'll need for the trip, and then we see the guys from Eden Park, who are supplying all the necessary formal wear. The Lions used to be told to turn up with just a toothbrush, as we'd be told what to wear day in, night out, but Clive's more relaxed about things like this so this time we're allowed to bring some of our own clothes. We're given a goody bag containing some nice gifts, like an i-Pod, and finally we see the medical teams, just to make sure there is nothing else we need for the trip.

I'm a bit shocked when I try on my formal trousers. Have I been eating chocolate cake in my sleep? I can't get the trousers anywhere near done up. Turns out they've given me a 32-inch waist by mistake, when I'm a 36-38. I can stop holding my stomach in now as they're getting some more sent to me before we fly off to New Zealand next week.

I'm not sure whether we will be sharing rooms in New Zealand, but we are here in Cardiff and my room-mate is Scotland hooker, Gordon Bulloch. It's nice to have the opportunity to get to know someone I'd never met before, although obviously we've played against each other. Gordon has just signed for Leeds so he wastes no time in quizzing me about the Premiership and we discover we share a love of wakeboarding.

Whitey and I make a beeline for Dave Campbell, one of the most important members of the Lions squad – our chef. He was England's chef during the World Cup and it's the first time we've seen him since then so we reminisce and tell him how wonderful he is in a pathetically badly disguised attempt to make sure some of our favourite dishes are on his menu for New Zealand. Dave hates it when players complain about the food and we give him a hard time about what he served us in Australia. All we seemed to eat for most of that World Cup campaign was chicken. Fair enough, Dave prepared it in every way you can imagine (and then some) but we got really bored with chicken tonight, and tomorrow night and...

Our favourite dish of Dave's was his mixed grill – chicken, sausage, bacon etc – so we're campaigning to have that on the tour itself. But Dave says he won't be able to do them this time because of the cost and the fact that all his menus have been pre-ordered. Shame. We'll just have to sneak out for a local fry-up then. We give him loads of stick, but Dave is a legend and we know it's going to be a tough eight weeks for him, working non-stop to feed us hungry Lions.

Wednesday 18th

After Monday I will be one of the few people who can say "I made my Lions debut in Cardiff".

Clive announces the squad for our game against Argentina at the Millennium Stadium by pulling back a page of his flipchart and I'm well chuffed to see my name there, next to the number seven. For my debut to be one of the rare times the Lions actually play in Britain or Ireland makes it even sweeter. I know it will be a pretty special night. Better yet, it's a Test game rather than a warm-up against a provincial side and my mates Geordan and Ollie will also be playing alongside me.

Training is a bit of a nightmare. Everyone is so nervous and concerned with getting it right that, inevitably, everything goes wrong. The session is cut short so we can go to a motivational talk, but I'm already worried that we're not spending enough time out on the pitch. All day we have meeting after meeting, media session after media session, team bonding exercises... I think we just need to get to know each other out on the pitch.

Thursday 19th

A few of us, including myself, express our concern to coaches Gareth Jenkins, Ian McGeechan and Mike Ford that we're not getting enough time to work on our line-out calls and scrums and that, while the off-the-pitch stuff is important, we need to prioritise. We have a power/endurance session where you're one-on-one against another player - in my case Michael Owen - wrestling, grappling weights and doing shuttle runs. This is followed by a one-on-one defence session, mine ending quicker than most as I land awkwardly on my knee.

Friday 20th

An 8am physio on my knee ensures I am okay to train today. Unfortunately not everyone in the squad is so lucky. The team to play Argentina are being opposed by the rest of the squad in a full-on training session and not long into it Scotland's Simon Taylor injures his hamstring and Mal O'Kelly pulls out with an abdominal problem. They are both good lads so I hope they recover in time to play a full part in the New Zealand trip. Simon only made it through one match in 2001 in Australia, after getting injured in the first game, so I hope he has more luck this time around.

I've had problems sleeping all week and tonight's no different. I lie staring at the clock, trying not to disturb my room-mate Gordon, until well into the wee small hours every night. The nerves are definitely starting to set in.

Saturday 21st

I'm no football fan, but when you get the chance to see Man United take on Arsenal in the FA Cup Final, well, you become one quite quickly, especially when the seats are right on the halfway line.

Football was never a big thing in our house when I was a kid and I guess because I got into rugby so young I just never really bothered about footie that much. I did play a bit though. Because of my size I was always the goalie (actually I think it was just because I loved diving around in the mud!) and my hero was big Neville Southall, so I was sort of an Everton fan... until he left, then I just lost interest.

I always watch the international games, of course, and some of the European club games, and my old friend and former housemate Ali Smith is a big Spurs fan, so I take an interest in them if only to abuse him when Spurs lose, which seemed to be all the time at one point.

The Man United team have shared the Vale of Glamorgan hotel with us this week, and I've bumped into a few of the players in the lobby. There's nothing exciting to report; we just nodded as we passed – it wasn't even a case of "Alright Wayne", "Alright Lewis."

The one thing I can't get over is how small they all are. When you see Roy Keane and Rio Ferdinand on the telly they look massive, but none of them are over 6ft 2in, which makes them midgets compared to most of the freaks I am used to playing with.

Anyway, the whole squad has been invited to the Cup Final. Brian O'Driscoll is a big Man United fan so he's really up for it and Gordon D'Arcy seems to be jumping up and celebrating whenever Arsenal go close, which isn't that often until after extra time when they win on penalties. It's a very enjoyable afternoon and really nice to be asked.

Back at the hotel Whitey breaks one of his golden rules. Whenever we go away with England or Leicester a Playstation or X-Box somehow seems to find its way into our team room. Whitey always takes great pleasure in abusing anyone who plays it for being a geek. But for this trip we managed to get a boxing game for the Playstation, which entices Whitey, especially as he could be the 'invincible' Rocky Marciano. He's very quickly hooked and forces me to stay up until the early hours playing it until he finally wins. I let him at around 1am as I'm knackered.

Sunday 22nd

After the excesses of last night's boxing marathon I'm glad of a lie-in today, and get up around 11am with the sound of the bell still ringing in my ears. As the kick-off for the Argentina game tomorrow is 7.10pm – as it will be for the matches in New Zealand – we have decided to do everything later, culminating in a training session at that time.

I think it is a good idea to try and adjust your body clock in this way. So we have line-outs at 3pm and a team run at 7pm. It's a surprisingly good session, given how little time we've actually had on the pitch together. Everyone's enthusiastic and it runs very well, which bodes very well for tomorrow. Or does it?

We have a massive cinema crew tonight, including the bus driver, who we not only convince to take us but also to come in with us. The unanimous decision is the new *Star Wars* film and I go along with Wally, Gordon, Geordan, Ollie Smith, Wig, Backy and chef Dave Campbell.

It's bloody long, but I am a big *Star Wars* fan so I'm not complaining, although even I have to admit some parts were a bit cheesy.

Monday 23rd

Lions 25 – Agentina 25

Lions: G Murphy; D Hickie, O Smith (rep: S Horgan, 62), G D'Arcy, S Williams; J Wilkinson, G Cooper (rep: C Cusiter, 58); G Rowntree, S Byrne (rep: S Thompson, 70), J Hayes (rep: J White, 49), D O'Callaghan, D Grewcock (rep: B Kay, 72), M Corry, L Moody, M Owen (captain).

Argentina: B Stortoni; J Nunez Piossek, L Arbizu, F Contepomi (captain), F Leonelli; F Todeschini (rep: L Fleming, 74), N Fernandez Miranda; F Mendez, M Ledesma, M Reggiardo, P Bouza, M Sambucetti (rep: M Carizza, 73), M Schusterman (rep: S Sanz, 71), F Genoud,

J-M Leguizamon.

Lions: Try: Smith. Con: Wilkinson. Pens: Wilkinson (6)
Argentina: Try: Piossek. Con: Todeschini. Pens: Todeschini (6).

It's a massive honour playing for the Lions on one of the few occasions they have played on British soil and all of us are fired up and keen to put down an early marker on the trip. Unfortunately, only a handful of people take that chance and it leaves some of us fearing we won't play again for a few weeks.

We were definitely under-cooked as far as training is concerned but the coaches know that – they talked about letting us just go out and play and have some fun. But we didn't get the chance to do that as we ran into a highly motivated and impressive Argentina side and in the end we had to rely on the left boot of Jonny Wilkinson to get us a draw.

There were glimpses of genius. I thought Ollie made a huge impression, scoring his try and running some superb lines. Jonny Wilkinson obviously made a big impression with the boot, scoring 21 points, and his distribution was excellent, especially his role in Ollie's try, but overall it was a disappointing performance from us and me personally.

After the match we have a farewell dinner on the pitch at Cardiff Arms Park but I don't really fancy it. The only saving grace is that Annie comes to the dinner and, with some room reorganisation, she is able to stay the night.

Tuesday 24th

Today is supposed to be a family day but, after a recovery session, I seem to spend most of it packing and re-packing my bags. Like most of the players I can't fit all the kit I've been given into the bags I've been given, so I have to send a load of gear home, as well as my guitar (Wally and I have decided it would be safer to buy new ones in New Zealand).

Having struggled with that, we then spend hours posing for all the official team photos (in kit and formal wear, but thankfully not swimwear!) and signing countless shirts for sponsors and the like. I finally get to see Annie at around 6pm and we join the rest of the squad for a farewell barbecue.

Wednesday 25th

There was something in my eye; I definitely wasn't crying (until after Annie had left, obviously). Annie was crying when she said goodbye this morning at 6am. Leaving is always the worst part of touring, although it does make it a little easier to say your goodbyes at the hotel, rather than the airport. Wellsy sends me a good luck text, saying:

"We've had a great time together, now go out there and make me proud."

The players are all in business class on the flight with the coaches in first class (oh, how the other half lives!) and we are seated in alphabetical order, which means that I am sat next to Josh Lewsey, which is good. It would be a nightmare to be on a plane that long next to someone you really don't get on that well with.

Just getting on the plane is a nightmare for Ben Kay. No, he's not a Denis Bergkamp, he's a massive Liverpool fan and has been going mental watching their epic Champions League final against AC Milan in the lounge. They've just, unbelievably, come back from 3-0 at half-time to 3-3, so the match goes into extra-time just as we're called to board!

"I'm not getting on that bloody plane!" he's shouting. "How can I get on that plane now?"

We force him aboard and, five minutes after take-off, he finally stops jigging about when the captain announces, to huge cheers, that Liverpool have won on penalties.

We've another reason to be in high spirits, as it's Jonny Wilkinson's 26th birthday. But it seems Jonny has made it known he doesn't want any fuss (pretty much like myself; my birthday's on June 12th) so his birthday goes by without much comment, and in fact due to the time difference he loses most of the day in the air anyway. Unless you are a bit of an extrovert, on a tour like this you want your birthday to go un-noticed; it's easier to let it pass, with just your mates knowing, otherwise you tend to have the mickey ripped out of you.

Thursday 26th

We had been given strict instructions by Otis (Dave Reddin, our fitness man) on how to avoid jet lag, which include not sleeping on the first leg of the journey to Singapore, but I think only our press man Alastair Campbell and Jonny Wilkinson manage to follow the advice. It's difficult staying up through the night just to get onto New Zealand time. I decide to have something to eat, watch a film and then have a 20-minute power nap, which turns into a full-on seven hour sleep. I'm a pretty good flyer. What could be better than to sit in a big seat and have people bring you food and drink while you watch movies?

We get off in Singapore, but as it's only a 40-minute turnaround there's just time to have a shower and change my T-shirt, so I look good for the press and the fans when we arrive. The last thing they want to see is a load of smelly rugby players with food all down themselves!

Oh, and I find time to call Annie and let her know we're en route. She's a bit surprised that I've called just to let her know we're on a plane. I think she'd kind of guessed that. Mmm, but it's good to hear her voice...

Friday 27th

For one moment we thought we'd lost him. Bill Beaumont certainly thought that Gavin Scott, one of our video analysts, had popped his clogs on the last part of the flight. Apparently Gavin decided to take his sleeping tablets 15 minutes before dinner (not the brightest idea), so he fell asleep with a bread roll in his mouth. Those sleeping tablets are obviously very powerful. What a complete mute. When he saw him with his eyes closed, crusty roll in his mouth, Bill actually thought that he might have had a heart attack, so he spent about 15 minutes trying to wake him.

With Gavin fully back in the land of the living we are given a massive welcome in Auckland, hundreds of fans (both Lions and All-blacks) and media waiting for us at the airport. It's not quite as big as the 8,000 who were waiting for us at Heathrow when we arrived back from Australia with the World Cup, but if anyone was under any illusions about how big this tour was going to be the fuss on arrival will have dispelled them.

I'm a bit shocked when I open the door to my hotel room and a king-size bed swings into view. Nobody has told us whether we're sharing rooms or not, so could this be one of Clive's more outlandish methods to get the team bonding? After all, we shared rooms in Cardiff and it cost more to get us over here, so maybe we're having to economise and share beds too! Fifteen minutes later it dawns on me that I'm in the clear and I can finally start unpacking.

To stave off the effects of jet lag, me and John Hayes, Donners (Donncha O'Callaghan) and a few of the Leicester boys grab a coffee (or three!) and head off sightseeing. We're staying at the Hilton right by Auckland's spectacular harbour, a superb venue and only a few hundred yards from the main shopping drag – it couldn't be a more perfect location.

Donners is one of those guys who once met is not quickly forgotten. He's quickly into Charlie Chaplin mode, pretending to knock over his cup or trip on an imaginary step and already I can see he is going to be one of the jesters of the trip.

I think the key to beating this jet lag is to stay up late on the first night, so after a conditioning session with Mikey Owen and dinner we head out for a few beers. As we move from bar to bar we start to notice that, instead of losing the odd straggler, we seem to be gaining a few. That's when we realise we're being followed by photographers, which is something of a novelty for us. They're getting on Whitey's nerves a bit, but we're not getting up to any mischief for them to photograph, so the night passes without incident and I flop into bed around midnight.

Saturday 28th

We've got the rugby blues, or at least the other guests at the hotel will have shortly as we've just invaded a music shop to get guitars. I think the shop owner thought all his Christmases had come at once as me, Denis Hickie, Jonny Wilkinson, Sos (Matt Stevens) and Wally piled in and each bought one.

The first jamming session of 'The Five Lions' (our new boy band!) goes moderately well, although it's quite clear there are musical differences, even at this early stage. Basically Denis, Jonny and Sos can play and Wally and I can't. We decide to leave the official Lions song *The Power of Four* for another day. Jonny's very patient with us and has clearly come on a lot since the World Cup. If only he lived a little nearer to me in England I could convince him to become my new guitar teacher, but at the moment the journey from Leicester to Newcastle might be a little prohibitive.

Matt is the king of the sing-songs. He is the first person on the microphone and you'll have to drag him off at the end. Jonny can play most things and both of them can tune the guitar by ear.

After our impromptu musical session I try to cure the dead leg I picked up against Argentina, via a new method of cups, something that one of our physios –Richard Wegrzyk – is an expert in. It is effective but is one of the most painful treatments I have ever endured. Basically a cup is placed on the affected area and air is gradually drawn out of it to create a vacuum, then it sucks your skin into the glass cup and they move it around in an attempt to separate the muscle fibres and get the bruise out so it doesn't calcify. It's horrendous, but no pain no gain I suppose. I'm not looking forward to my next session though and neither,

I guess, will Richard considering how much I swear at him.

Sunday 29th

As we have a squad of 45 and I played against Argentina, I knew I wouldn't be picked for the first game out in New Zealand and that is confirmed today when we get the team for the Bay of Plenty game. I think a couple of guys, like Cozza, who played in the Argentina game find their way on to the bench, but only due to injuries.

After the team announcement and training session we fly to Rotorua for the official Maori welcome, which includes the Hongi where they greet people by rubbing noses. Donners responds by giving all the assembled Maori a hug but that is him all over. He found a random Maori and just jumped on him. Especially considering he is teetotal, Donners is a raving lunatic and one of the most entertaining men I have ever met. I wish I'd remembered to bring my camera!

Once they had performed the haka it was up to us to return the compliment. Clive says he wants us to sing *Bread of Heaven*, so Sos steps up the plate to get us going with a rousing rendition. He loves singing and does a great job. I don't sing; I hide.

Back at the hotel I phone Annie. This will be the longest we've ever been apart and I make a point of phoning her every day. I'm missing her, missing being in my own bed. It's hard. I don't know how cricketers do it as they're away for months on end. It would have been easier if Annie had been able to come.

Monday 30th

My first wise move of the tour is to give the Zurich golf day a miss and head off with a few of the boys to go clay pigeon shooting. I do like playing golf but today's conditions are horrendous: gale force winds and torrential rain. About 20 of us go shooting including Donners, Whitey, Josh, Grewy, Gavin Henson, Michael Owen and Sos. The clay pigeon shooting is brilliant fun but the weather's so bad that we have to take refuge in a marquee while we're waiting to shoot and at one stage the marquee collapses on us under the weight of all the water and wind.

Josh is today's subject of all the abuse. As he has spent some time as an army officer everyone was expecting him to be a crack shot and whenever he misses his clay he comes in for some fearful stick, especially from Whitey. I don't know whether it's the pressure but Josh is absolutely rubbish. He blames the gun, the weather and us lot, but we think it's because he's just rubbish!

The guy running the shoot has a pump-action shotgun, nicknamed 'the Terminator.' As soon as he brings it out, you can see the lads' faces light up – especially Wig, who actually shouts "I'll be back!" at the clays as they're fired into the air.

We have a great afternoon before heading off to the golf course to take the mick out of the prize-giving. Geordan won the overall prize in a team with Clive Woodward, Stephen Jones (the journalist not the player) and Chris Cusiter. They actually won sombreros, which I think suits them down to a tee, seeing as how they're all bandits.

Tuesday 31st

Damn! My hopes that I had beaten the jet lag prove unfounded as I'm wide awake at 5.30am. I suppose it isn't too bad as I have a weights session at 8.30am so I would have had to be up soon anyway.

It's our first public training session today, in Auckland, all the others having been behind closed doors. As you can imagine, it's a very light-hearted event. We even have some local kids join in with the training at one point; well, we're hardly going to practise our line outs, giving away our calls in front of everyone. We go through a few running plays and it's a good PR exercise.

After lunch we get down to the real business with a proper training session at our base just out of town, in Takapuna. We are opposing the side that will play on Saturday and it's pretty heated, which is good. I much prefer training to have an edge as it often does at Leicester; to get people going you need to have a few bodies clattering into each other, giving each other cheap shots.

June

Wednesday 1st

Today is all about food, glorious food. It's the team meal tonight but before that we have to sit through Otis's first nutritional talk – perhaps they want to remind us not to overdo it tonight.

It has much the same effect on me as the safety speeches on airplanes: I've heard them before, and I know the drill, so I tend to switch off a bit. I consider myself to be a pretty healthy eater. Within limits. The food out here is pretty good, but they've not really got the snacks sorted – the other day we were offered an orange and carrot salad. Eurgh! I think Louisa Cheetham, our media manager, was the only person able to stomach it.

We head off into town for the weekly team meal out but this restaurant isn't quite prepared for 45 hungry mutes descending on them, ready to eat them out of house and home. The service is pretty slow and Whitey's having a sense of humour failure, but just as he resolves to storm out it all starts arriving. One and a half pizzas, two steaks and a bowl of potato wedges later, he's a happy boy again.

But not as happy as me! Well-fed and watered, I persuade a few of the boys, including Cuets (Mark Cueto) and Grewy, to go to the casino and I'm off to a flying start with a couple of small wins on the poker. Normally I lose on the poker and roulette and do my best to win back the £50 or so at blackjack, but tonight I am the man with the golden touch and everything I bet on seems to turn to chips. Very odd, but very pleasing and I return to the Hilton at 10.30pm in time for a rub on my leg from physio Stuart Barton and a nice little gloat to myself.

Thursday 2nd

The food's so bad we've decided to go out and catch our own! The guy who took us clay pigeon shooting on Monday invites us on a turkey shoot. The trip is great fun, but it nearly costs us Josh Lewsey. As we arrive at the farm, which is surrounded by an electric fence, the farmer asks Josh to jump out and open the gate.

"You have turned the electricity off haven't you?" Josh asks the farmer.

"Yes of course, we turned it off in the house," he says.

You can guess what happened next. Two seconds later Josh gets absolutely fried! Apparently they've left one panel of the fence switched on (accidentally, or maybe they're just really big All-Blacks fans) and when Josh touches the gate his hair stands on end and he starts shaking. He's left paralysed down one side but luckily it's only temporary. When we eventually stop laughing, ten minutes later, we decide it's the most hilarious point of the trip so far. Not sure he agrees.

I manage to shoot three turkeys, and in total we bag 16, and as it seems a waste to just shoot them and leave them there we decide to take our turkeys back to the hotel for our evening meal. We all enjoy a massive feed back at The Hilton. Donners complains that he's found pellets in his turkey but knowing him he'll have planted them himself.

Friday 3rd

I'm pretty happy this morning as training is a full-on bosh, with me on the side opposing the team that will play tomorrow in Rotorua. It's great fun. There is no pressure on us so we can run around like idiots, putting in tackle after tackle – just what I need to get the blood pumping.

Later, I enrol in the Wilkinson School of Excellence – picking, rather than kicking. Jonny is an excellent guitar teacher, as methodical in his approach to this as he is to rugby, and even better he doesn't appears to be charging me.

Saturday 4th

Bay of Plenty 20 – Lions 34

Bay of Plenty: A Cashmore; F Bolavacu (rep: A Stewart, 51), A Bunting, G McQuoid, A Tahana; Murray Williams, K Senio; S Davison (rep: T Filise, 64), A Lutui, B Castle, M Sorenson (rep: P Tupai, 64), B Upton, W Ormond (captain), N Latu, C Bourke (rep: W Smith, 46).

Lions: J Lewsey; M Cueto, B O'Driscoll (captain), G Henson (rep: G D'Arcy, 70), T Shanklin (rep: M Dawson, 78); R O'Gara, D Peel; G Jenkins, G Bulloch (rep: S Thompson, 66), M Stevens (rep: A Sheridan, 66), P O'Connell, B Kay, R Hill, Martyn Williams, L Dallaglio (rep: M Corry, 25).

Bay of Plenty: Tries: Bourke, Williams. Cons: Williams (2). Pens: Williams (2).
Lions: Tries: Lewsey (2), Cueto, Shanklin, Peel, D'Arcy. Cons: O'Gara (2).

On match days those who are not playing, but are fit, head off into the local community and today I'm visiting Matata, a town that suffered a terrible flood just before we arrived. Myself, Wig, Geordan, Chris Cusiter and Mal O'Kelly head off after lunch with our tour manager, Bill Beaumont. It's an absolutely stunning place and we are given a fabulous welcome.

The local kids treat us to a haka and a presentation and I feel really bad because the kids are the ones giving us presents – caps and T-shirts. It was very humbling. Bill has obviously brought a signed shirt and a few other things to hand over officially, but as we go around we don't have anything else to give them.

We meet up with the rest of the squad to watch the game and it starts well. We play some irresistable rugby in the first quarter, but then comes the sickening sight of Lol being carried off on a golf cart after it looks like he has dislocated his ankle.

As I am not playing I am sitting in the stand next to Will Greenwood, who is big mate of Lawrence's, and he takes the injury quite badly. It is always difficult when you see your mates get hurt like that. I remember getting ready to play France and watching the Ireland game on the telly when I saw Geordan snap his shin in half. It was a complete nightmare to see him so badly injured as I was preparing to play. It is much worse when other people get injured, rather than yourself. I immediately called Lucie to re-assure her that Geordy would be ok, I knew how worried and upset she'd be. The memories of that terrible day come flooding back now. Sometimes you take a step back and ask yourself, "isn't it ridiculous that we play this game, where you can easily get so badly injured?".

It is such a shame for Lol as he was clearly in magnificent form, perhaps the best of his career, so for his Lions tour to end that way is awful.

When I get back to the hotel, after the game, I watch Johno's testimonial against Jonah Lomu's side. It kicked off at 6.30am here in New Zealand but as this is the only country in the world with a Rugby Channel (not just a Sports Channel) on TV I knew it would be repeated a number of times throughout the day. A few of the lads had texted me to say that Leon got the winning try so there was no way I could miss that. I would definitely have played in the match, just for one last run out with Johno, if I wasn't on the Lions tour. Leon, Austin and Goodey seem to be having such a good time with him, and I think when they go up to receive the trophy there's a little tear in Goodey's eye. That doesn't surprise me as he's a bit of a crybaby on the quiet.

Sunday 5th

You know the episode of *The Simpsons* where Homer attends the 'all you can eat buffet' and is finally banned after almost making the restaurant bankrupt? Well it's being replayed in Auckland tonight, starring me, Josh, Whitey, Will Greenwood, Cus, Geordy, Sos and a restaurateur who must be regretting the decision to offer all you can eat when there are Lions in town on the prowl for food. The gimmick is that there's a red stick and a green stick on your table and if you're displaying the green stick the waiters just keep bringing you food. Presumably, normal people swap sticks at some point or just wave the white flag. Not us. The waiters are on the point of collapse by the time we're satisfied. Well, I've got an excuse as I'm celebrating. The team for Wednesday's game against Taranaki includes me!

Monday 6th

We are up at the top of the Sky Tower in Auckland. Wow it is high! As I have a game on Wednesday I have a legitimate reason for not taking part in the fantastically appealing idea of bungee jumping off the top, but Geordan and Benny Kay are bloody nutters and dive off (and come back up, I'm relieved to report). Wig's been talking it up, but when it comes to the crunch he wimps out too. I'll deal with heights if I have to, but I'd rather avoid situations like that. I'm not too happy being on solid ground either: there are some glass walkways up here which I pluck up courage to walk across. It's a really weird sensation, as though you're in mid-air and it's definitely playing tricks with my mind.

Tuesday 7th

The team run is at the unearthly hour of 8.30am, as we have to fly the 220 miles or so from Auckland to New Plymouth today. It isn't the best session but then with the Lions operating a Saturday and a midweek side it is only natural there will be teething problems early on, especially with players moving between both teams. But I am instantly impressed with the midweek coaching team of Ian McGeechan, Gareth Jenkins and Mike Ford. Geech is Mr Lions (although very laid-back) while the passion that Gareth shows for the Lions has to be seen to be believed. Fordy – who is a former Great Britain rugby league international – is top class after having worked with the Ireland team as their defensive coach.

The organisation has been magnificent on this tour and today is no different. Our bags have been packed for us and sent on ahead, so we don't have to check in, in fact we don't even have to visit the airport as the bus pulls straight onto the runway, almost up to the door of our own private charter plane. How cool is that?

It was frustrating sitting on the sidelines for our opening game last Saturday, so I'm looking forward to getting out there and putting my mark on the tour. I know I played for the Lions in Cardiff, but this feels like the real start of the tour. I will line up in the back row with Cozza and Michael Owen, who did a cracking job as captain against Argentina, and I'm looking forward to playing with him again.

Wednesday 8th

Taranaki 14 – Lions 36

Taranaki: S Ireland (rep: B Watt, 20); S Tagicakibau (rep: M Harvey, 41),

M Stewart, L Mafi, C Woods; S Young, C Fevre (rep: J King, 70); T Penn
(rep: H Mitchell, 73), A Hore (sin-bin, 57-67), G Slater, P Tito (captain),
S Breman (rep: J Eaton, 67), J Willis, C Masoe, T Soqeta (rep: P Mitchell,
59-67; rep: R Bryant, 67).

Lions: G Murphy; S Horgan, W Greenwood, O Smith, D Hickie;
C Hodgson, C Cusiter (rep: G Cooper, 80); G Rowntree, A Titterrell (rep:
S Byrne, 70), J Hayes (rep: G Jenkins, 51), D O'Callaghan, D Grewcock,
M Corry (c), L Moody, M Owen.

Taranaki: Tries: Masoe, Watt. Cons Young (2).
Lions: Tries: Murphy (2), Corry, Horgan. Cons: Hodgson (2). Pens:
Hodgson (4).

Cozza may have led us to an excellent victory tonight, but it won't stop him
picking up an as yet to be decided team fine. I would recommend $100. The
problem: he left the Lion mascot in the dressing room. Every Lions captain has
to run out with that lion before placing it on the side of the pitch, but he
stormed out of the changing room and forgot it this time. It was left to team
manager Louise Ramsay to grab it out of the dressing room. Cozza protested
that he was so pumped up he forgot it but that's no excuse, especially when we
can sting him with a fine. No excuse will do, he has to cop this one! Even
scoring a try to settle a few nerves at the start of the second half won't let him
off the hook.

We were told that every game on this trip would be difficult and anyone
with any doubt had that removed tonight as Taranaki put on a great show,
before going down 36-14. It took Cozza's try to break them down but we are
delighted with the way the defence went tonight. On one occasion I turned
the ball over on our own line, but no-one had spotted it and one of their
players rushed through and scored their first try. Gutted.

It was another magnificent occasion. Rugby is in people's blood out here and
it is inspiring to play in these sorts of stadiums, in front of these types of
crowds.

Geech presented the jerseys to us for this game, and even the guys who
weren't playing were there for the presentation. I don't need a presentation to
motivate me, no player would, but there is no doubt it focuses me more, even

if I cannot for the life of me remember what he said.

For this tour every jersey is embroidered in the bottom corner with your name, the date of the match and the opponents, making them real collector's items. As with England we change our kit at half time so we are given two shirts, although the one we start the match with is the only one that is embroidered.

There are one or two other subtle differences between the England and Lions set-ups that I noticed tonight. There is no music in the dressing room before the games, unlike what I'm used to with England, and although that is clearly a very small thing it is something else for me to adjust to. Before an England game you would probably get dance or rock music blaring out in the changing room. I find the music calms my nerves, takes my mind off the game and tonight I felt more nervous playing than I had done for a while. I suppose it is because the Lions is so different. I feel like I am starting again, trying to put in performances to win a Test place, so with that comes a little more pressure than normal.

After the game we enjoy a speech from each captain and a few drinks with the opposition. We end up getting on the Taranaki bus and hitching a lift to their local pub, which is something of a throw-back to the amateur days. It is good fun and I share a few beers with my opposite number, Chris Masoe, who scored their try at the end, which made for some banter between us. Everyone gets on very well together, even Grewy and his opposite number, Paul Tito, despite the fact that they exchanged a number of punches during the game. That sort of thing is usually all forgotten by the time you've had a shower.

At the end of the night we couldn't find our way back so Geordan ended up stopping a police car for directions and them coming up trumps with the offer of a lift home for the two of us and Ollie – a quality way to return to the hotel.

Friday 10th

Me cheering an All-Blacks victory? Damn right. They beat Fiji 91–0 and I'm delighted as it means they haven't had the workout they're looking for as a warm-up for us.

Saturday 11th

Maori 19 – Lions 13

New Zealand Maori: L MacDonald; R Gear, R Tipoki, L McAlister, C Ralph; D Hill (rep: C Spencer, 43), P Weepu; D Manu (rep: G Feek, 54), C Flynn, C Hayman, R Filipo (rep: D Braid, 75), S Hohneck, J Gibbes, M Holah, A MacDonald.

Lions: J Lewsey; T Shanklin, B O'Driscoll, G D'Arcy (rep: S Horgan, 23-31), S Williams; S Jones (rep: R O'Gara, 33-40), M Dawson; A Sheridan (sin-bin 40+4 50; rep: G Jenkins, 50), S Thompson (rep: S Byrne, 75), J White, S Shaw, P O'Connell, R Hill, M Williams, M Owen (rep: Jenkins, 42-50).

New Zealand Maori: 19: Try: L MacDonald. Con: McAlister. Pens: Hill (2), McAlister (2).
Lions: 13: Try: O'Driscoll. Con: Jones. Pens: Jones (2).

Clive pulls a masterstroke by asking Lol to present the shirts to the players before the game. Lol is a very passionate man and very good at judging the right tone and things to say to players before a game. Unfortunately we can't give him the win needed to send him back to England a happy man but it's clear the side have given everything they had. We certainly had the chances but the ball just didn't go our way. It was their night! Everyone is trying to put a brave face on it but looking around the dressing room you can see what a blow it is to lose this game, a big dent in our chances of beating New Zealand in the upcoming Test Series.

I had played against the Maori before – for England in 1998 – so I knew what a massive occasion it would be, heightened by the fact that they were saying goodbye to both Carlos Spencer and their long-term coach Matt Te Pou. That created one of the most incredible atmospheres I have ever seen outside of a Test match. It's pretty clear if the Maori entered the World Cup they'd do very well.

Sunday 12th

Oh God, I'm 26. I'm ancient! I got my present from Annie before I left – a

PSP, which she and my parents clubbed together for. An outstanding gift. So there are only a few cards to open this morning and then Annie rings me up to wish me happy birthday.

A birthday is just another day to me. I've never really made too much of a fuss about it and with it being in June, when most of the tours happen, I am getting more and more used to spending it out of the country – and you certainly don't want the lads making a big deal of it. I'd die if they wheeled in a big cake or something like that. Annie would have a party but for we normally go out for a meal, so that's the plan for later with Geordy, Ollie Smith, Wig and Rog (Ronan O'Gara).

Clive has planned the tour around three main bases: Auckland, Christchurch and Wellington so today we moved to Christchurch, which means a couple of hours on the plane.

Sadly we have to leave Lol and Simon Taylor in Auckland as their injuries mean they are on their way home. Lol is staying in Auckland for a while until the swelling on his ankle goes down enough for him to fly while Simon is heading to Sydney to spend some time with his brother. You feel for both those boys but especially Simon as he had to quit the 2001 Lions tour with an injury after playing less than half a match. This time Simon failed to play at all. Poor guy. I make a point of speaking to them both before leaving. Lol's obviously gutted but he seems to have come to terms with it and is already looking forward to next season.

As they leave, Ryan Jones arrives. He won't be able to play for a week as you need to be in the country for six days – due to the jet lag before it is safe to play.

Backy has finished his ban for punching Joe Worsley, so I knew I probably wouldn't be named to face Wellington, although I'm glad to be named on the bench and believe I may have a better chance of starting next Saturday against Otago. We see the Wellington game as the first run out of the Test team, and the first indication of Clive's preferred players, but I'm not too worried about being on the bench because it is Backy's first chance of playing. I expected him to be in.

Wally and Shanks (Tom Shanklin) are the first two players to almost lose it in training. Confrontations occur almost every week at Leicester and we have been going hard on this trip so far, so I think it was only a matter of time before two players were squaring up to one another. It doesn't come to blows; they grab each other round the throat and swear at each other. Nothing much really, but I am glad it has happened; you need that element of anger and I think this may give the edge that we've been lacking. We'd have a problem if people weren't at each other's throats. It always dissipates immediately you come off the pitch.

On the coach Denis Hickie decides there has to be a new fines system for players involved in any training ground dust-ups. Each player has the option of kissing the player they fell out with or paying a $100 fine. Shanks and Wally opt to kiss and make up, although, I have to say they seem a tad too keen for my liking!

Monday 13th

Does Shawsy (Simon Shaw) actually have it in for me, or is it just my luck that one of their heaviest members of the Lions squad lands on my knee, not once but twice in the same training session?

Due to the length of the season we've just had and the length and intensity of the tour, our training sessions are not usually that hard-core, but today is a press open day and we're going full-on to show we mean business, so we've been tearing into the rucks. Geordy Bulloch hits his head on John Hayes' shoulder and not long into the session Shawsy lands on my knee. Shanks manages to kick me in the eye at the same time so I feel properly done over. It's clearly an accident, but I'm forced to hobble off for treatment. The doc says "I don't want you to go back out!", but me being me I assure him that I'm fine and it's just a dead leg.

The doc knows he can't persuade me, so he puts a stitch in the eye and when I get back out the lads are just playing touch rugby. There's no way I can get injured here. I've been on the pitch barely two minutes before I touch Simon Shaw – well actually it's a bit more than touch, I grab hold of him and pull him down on top of me, he lands awkwardly on my leg again and ominously I hear a strange popping noise emanating from my knee.

I'm in agony, but I have to act like nothing's happened because I'd been told not to go back out, so I walk off the pitch as if I'm fine. I've been an idiot and gone against the doc's advice so I just tell him I must have done it the first time round, otherwise I know I'd get a ridiculous amount of abuse from the coaches.

The thing is, I was just frustrated; the full-on sessions don't come round that often and you want to impress the coaches and everyone's got something to prove to each other because it's the Lions tour. I always feel like a complete gaylord if I'm stood on the sideline and it's happened quite a lot lately. You're standing there watching and everyone comes off really battered and knackered and you're just stood there, shrugging and saying, "Er, yeah, I'm alright actually". I hate it. I didn't want to miss out any more and I had to prove something to myself.

The knee seizes up completely as I limp back and by the time I reach the physio's room I really am having trouble walking. Not having trouble talking to myself though.

"Why did you do that? You're such a moron!"

Back at the hotel I have a session with the physios and keep my fingers crossed. Those not selected for Wellington were treated to a jet-boating trip today. Brian O'Driscoll turned it down as he wanted some time on his own but Josh was there and regales me with stories about how good it was. I'll be even more annoyed if I don't make the game now as I missed out on that.

Tuesday 14th

Wow, that hurts. I can barely put any weight on my knee, let alone walk comfortably and I feel very battered indeed. One of the Lions (and England) physios, Phil Pask, is called in and immediately tells me that I won't make tomorrow's game, although I am pretty hopeful about being in the side for the trip to Otago on Saturday. The medical team aren't too sure what is wrong with my knee but treat it with ice, massage and rest.

It's strapped up with very strong tape. My knee ligaments are already so relaxed and overstretched through injury that if you push my knee one way there's more give, so with this new injury on the other side it looks like it would sway in the wind! But as long as you haven't done your cruciate or your posterior cruciate, which are the main ligaments that stabilise the knee, then you should be ok. Ligaments never completely regain their strength and tightness so you have to work on all the muscles around them, strengthening them with weights sessions so they can handle the extra workload.

If an injury like this had occurred during the season I would have had up to a couple of weeks off, but there isn't as much time on a Lions tour. The First Test is just over a week away, with the last game before selection coming on Saturday against Otago. This could be my last chance. If the team plays well then there's no reason to change a winning side. The physios advise keeping my weight off my feet and this time I decide to take their advice.

I'm climbing the walls, but at least it allows me to catch up on a few texts and phone calls I should have returned and overdose on Dr Phil and Oprah, which seem to form the bulk of daytime TV in New Zealand. So if nothing else, I glean some good advice on how to deal with any horrendous problems might that occur in my life. Unfortunately they don't discuss how to survive 24 hours in bed with only daytime TV to amuse yourself.

Wednesday 15th

Wellington 6 – Lions 23

Wellington: Paku (rep: Ellison, 77); Fa'atau, Nonu, Tu'ipulotu, Kinikinilau (rep: Jane, 68); Gopperth, Weepu (rep: Flutey, 74); McDonnell (capt), M Schwalger (rep: Mahoney, 59), Fairbrother, Andrews, Filipo (rep: Purdie, 71), Ormsby, Herring (rep: Thompson, h-t), T Waldron.

Lions: Lewsey (rep: Horgan, 67); Thomas, O'Driscoll (capt), Henson (rep: S Jones, 62), Robinson; Wilkinson, Peel (rep: Cusiter, 72); Jenkins, Byrne, White (rep: Stevens, 73), Grewcock, Kay, Easterby, Back, Corry.

Wellington: Pens: Gopperth (2).
Lions: Tries: Jenkins, Thomas. Cons: Wilkinson (2). Pens: Wilkinson (3).

The knee is much better today but while everyone else goes off to the game me, Shanks and Sheri (Andrew Sheridan) stay behind for physio with Pasky. I had been feeling fairly down about being injured again, but I thank my lucky stars when I hear about Shanks' knee injury. He has been suffering with it all tour and I gather in one session they removed several syringes of fluid from it. That's horrendous and I can see by his face that he has almost had enough of an injury – and the treatment – which looks like it will put paid to his chances of being a Test Lion. You can see he is at the end of his tether as he is sore after every training session, let alone matches. Shanks has played really well on this tour and I think he was one of those players who could have made a real challenge for the Test team, either in the centre or on the wing.

Pasky tells me he believes I will make Saturday's match, which makes the thought of yesterday's enforced telethon more bearable. After our physio session, the four of us watch the Wellington match in a small bar in the hotel. It's a much better performance from us and there are a good couple of tries, including a kick and chase from Alfie (Gareth Thomas) who is playing his first game on tour, having joined up later than most as he had to wait until the end of the French season.

Clive moved Jonny to inside centre for the last 20 minutes – is this the tactic he's going to employ in the Tests, I wonder? Gavin Henson was a little surprised to be replaced in the second half, apparently saying to Clive: "I've never been taken off before!."

That's one thing you can say about Gav, he says what he thinks. You can see he is trying to bite his lip on this trip. Pasky takes me, Shanks and Sheri out on the town for a curry to cheer us all up, which is good of him.

Thursday 16th

For a few moments this morning I thought my Lions tour was over and my knee was really knackered. It was the most innocuous of incidents. I was just walking down the street in Christchurch with a few of the lads, on our way to lunch, when one of them gently pushed me from behind (playfully) and my knee just buckled. I had to hold on to one of the other lads to stop me falling on the floor.

My first thought was "I am going home". I went back to see Pasky, he calmed me down, treated it and it improved immeasurably. I haven't trained all week because of the knee, but I am named in the side to play Otago at the weekend, in the knowledge (although this is kept quiet outside the squad) that I will need a fitness test tomorrow. I am named on the blindside with Martyn Williams starting at seven, alongside the new boy Ryan Jones.

Friday 17th

My chances of playing in the First Test are over. I have no chance of stating my claim for a spot. I know I will be fit enough for that game, but Otago would have been the chance to prove it. Running on the grass in my fitness test my knee was fine, but once I ran on a hard surface it was very sore. Pasky was quite surprised how much I could do and in the end it was a really close call. The final decision was taken out of my hands, which is lucky as I might have given it a go.

Pasky's view is that if I did play this game it might knacker my knee for some time. I'm not happy, but Pasky reminds me that there are still six games left on this tour so there's no point in taking a risk. Clive tells me I will definitely play on Tuesday so any thoughts that I'll be going home are banished from my mind.

As I'm not playing tomorrow I decide to give the normal cinema trip a miss. Whitey provides the evening's alternative entertainment, giving me a bit more abuse than normal as he can see I'm really grumpy.

Saturday 18th

Otago 19 – Lions 30

Otago: G Horton; H Pedersen, N Brew (rep: J Shoemark, 49), S Mapusua, M Saunders; N Evans, D Lee (rep: C Smylie, 82); C Hoeft, J Macdonald (rep: J Vercoe, 65), C Dunlea (rep: J Aldworth, 55), F Levi, T Donnelly, C Newby (capt), J Blackie, (rep: A Soakai, 86), G Webb.

Lions: G Murphy; D Hickie, G D'Arcy (rep: O Smith, 55), W Greenwood, S Williams; C Hodgson (rep: R O'Gara, 74), C Cusiter (rep: M Dawson, 65); G Rowntree (rep: A Sheridan, 65), G Bulloch (capt, rep: S Thompson, 65), M Stevens, S Shaw (rep: D Grewcock, 65), D O'Callaghan, S Easterby, M Williams, R Jones (rep: M Owen, 84).

Otago: Try: Lee. Con: Evans. Pens: Evans (4)
Lions: Tries: Greenwood, Jones, S Williams. Cons: Hodgson (3). Pens: Hodgson (3).

Every morning we have the day's diary put through our door, explaining exactly what is happening, where we need to be and why. A bit like a Butlin's holiday camp, but without the redcoats. But today's missive was laid out a little differently and it has clearly confused a few of the players.

We're supposed to be in a meeting at 8.45am, but it soon becomes clear that only around half the squad has realised, as the room is almost empty. The top of the diary page is normally reserved for management only meetings, but on today's sheet it included a listing for everyone... clearly we are easily confused.

On this trip we have been running a buddy system. Each week you get a new buddy. It's excellent for the new boys as they can ask their buddy the stupid questions you wouldn't want to ask in a team meeting. I don't think it would have gone down too well to ask Clive and the management team where you put your dirty underpants.

This week my buddy is Shane Horgan, so I bang on his door but there's no reply. Gordon D'Arcy has taken charge of phoning everyone, ticking them off a big list as he speaks to them. Shane's response on hearing D'Arc tell him to get his arse downstairs now "as we have a meeting" is, "Who's got a meeting?" The call clearly woke him up.

We finally start 15 minutes late; Clive is seriously annoyed as one of his big things is timekeeping. You know never to be late for a meeting with Clive. Everyone pleads innocence and I suppose there is safety in numbers on this occasion.

I am one of the ten or so injured players who stay behind as the team travel to Dunedin to take on Otago. With the team away there is no food provided, so we get in a takeaway to cheer ourselves up. Very naughty. We have a mixture of Chinese and pizza, then we all watch the game together.

Ryan Jones took my place at six and plays really well, which is frustrating and again I'm worried about my chances. It often happens that players arrive on a Lions tour late and make a huge impact. It happened to Cozza in 2001 and he ended up playing in every Test match. Clive had already hinted to me that I had a great chance of playing in the Test matches at six – with Backy at seven – so to see someone else come in, take their chance and play so well in that position is very difficult and I'm feeling a bit depressed as I head off for bed.

Sunday 19th

I am probably the only one in the room to be pleased to be named in the side to travel to Invercargill to play Southland on Tuesday. Being selected in that team means you won't play in the First Test, although that is a long way from my mind after a week on the sidelines with this knee injury. I'm just glad to be out there playing again and it means I can start to state my case for the Second Test, in Wellington.

There are a few very disappointed faces, Gavin Henson in particular, but knowing that Gareth Jenkins and Ian McGeechan will be coaching the midweek side softens the blow a bit. It is a pleasure to be coached by them as their passion and motivational skills shine through. They're both very laid-back. Gareth motivates you with his commitment. He's someone you are happy to follow. Geech wants to see good rugby played and for everyone to take the field with a smile on their face. There is a definite upside to be being picked for the midweek game as they have created a very relaxed, enjoyable environment to work in.

As part of the preparations for the First Test, the coaching team have decided to bring in a new set of line-out calls and, although I'm not in the team, I need to learn them as well.

The feeling is that the All Blacks may have cracked our line-out codes as we have been using the same ones for each of the five games we have played so far. Security has been as tight as it could be for our training sessions and the grounds we use are sealed off, but you'd be amazed at the lengths some teams go to to find out your calls. They employ lip-readers to watch videos of games, they try and send spies round to watch you train, they have people earwigging when you run through your line-outs at the start of a game. It does help massively if they can work your codes out.

For me the change is a real headache as I find it difficult enough to learn the line out calls at the best of times, let alone when they are given to us at the last minute. It always takes myself and Julian White twice as long as anyone else to learn them. I don't know whether we're just that bit keener to make doubly sure we know them, but we always end up in the hotel's conference room or somewhere at night, with Danny Grewcock and Ben Kay practicing the calls. It's like musical chairs. We get a row of chairs to represent the other players and get into position. Ben or Danny will make a call and then we'll move the chairs into position. It sounds daft (and must have amused many a passing waiter over the years!) but it really helps, otherwise if you just try and memorise them in your head you don't really get a good idea of where you're supposed to move to. I'm sure I do it subsconsciously in the supermarket checkout queue – we probably look like that scene in The Full Monty where they all start tapping their feet and practising their moves.

It's quite complicated. There are around 30 calls just for line-outs, with all sorts of variations. If it's a four-man line-out there will be ten calls for that, ten for a five man lineout, six man line-out... it's endless. You've just got to rehearse the moves and there is not always enough time in training, because you've got loads of other things going on like practising backs moves or going through team plays.

So now, less than 48 hours before our next game, they've changed all the calls! So a call we used in the last game is now something else completely, at this point in time I'm not entirely sure what. I think it is often better going with what you know. Even if the opposition knows your calls, you'll still get the ball if they are executed perfectly.

The plan is to operate the old system for the Southland game, while learning the new one that will take over next Saturday in the First Test. My first reaction is, "What a nightmare". It is like being the understudy in a play and having to learn everyone else's lines. Anyone could drop out of the Test team this week so I not only have to learn the old calls for six and seven, but the new ones as well.

In the olden days they never used to lift at line-outs, they just used to throw the ball in and hope for the best. Now we practise maybe 40 different calls and have to remember which ones we are planning to use in a particular game. My head hurts. I want a time machine!

Monday 20th

We land in Invercargill to be greeted with a very strange sight. Two men in bright yellow boilersuits and a guy with a plate of oysters! Apparently in 1993 England hooker Brian Moore had said Invercargill was like Chernobyl with oysters. Most of us scurry past oyster man, especially as there is a photographer with him. Shanks stops to eat one before catching a glaring Clive out of the corner of his eye and then he runs past as well. Maybe Clive is worried that too many oysters will put Shanks in the mood for loving, not rucking!

The spirit in this team – the 'Midweek Massive' as our doctor Gary O'Driscoll calls us – is excellent. You might think a few heads would have dropped as we all know we won't be playing Test match rugby this weekend, but conversely we can play without any pressure on our shoulders so everyone is looking forward to it. Yes, people are annoyed, yes, people are unhappy because they didn't make the Test side, but that doesn't make us any less determined to do well. As a team we're having a good laugh – they are a good bunch of boys.

I've heard that on previous Lions trips people have "gone off tour", gone on the lash and forgotten about rugby once they failed to make the Test team, but it's not happening here. I don't know whether it is because we are four more years into the professional era and we are actually being paid to be here, or whether it is because of the atmosphere Geech and Gareth have created, but it hasn't even crossed our minds. For me, whether it is midweek or not, it is an opportunity to play and impress. We'll have enough chance to go off tour once the Third Test has been played.

After the way it has gone for me over the last week, the only attitude I can take into this match is to treat it like it's my last. I can't leave anything on the pitch tomorrow. If I play well it could be a way into selection for the Second Test, but it could also be my last game as a Lion so I may as well enjoy it.

I'm back at six tomorrow, which means I play a bigger part in the line-out and have more calls to make. When you are a seven it's easier at line-outs as only one or two calls will bring you into it. When you play at six you'll have lifting and jumping calls to memorise.

I manage to recruit Gordon Bulloch for my pre-match trip to the flicks. There is a white board in the team room where people write up activities, so I put up the cinema details to see if anyone would be interested in joining me. The only showing is at 9.10pm, which seems to be a little late for some of the boys, or perhaps the fact that we're going to see *Batman Returns* put a few people off?

Tuesday 21st

Southland 16 Lions 26

Southland: J Wilson; M Harrison, B Milne (rep: P Te Whare, 63), F Muliaina, W Lotawa; R Apanui, J Cowan (rep: A Clarke, 80+7); C Dermody (captain), J Rutledge (rep: D Hall, 60), A Dempsey (rep: J Murch, 53), H Macdonald, D Quate, H Tamariki (rep: R Logan, 82), H T-Pole, P Miller (rep: J Wright, 40+1).

Lions: G Murphy (rep: G D'Arcy, 82); M Cueto, O Smith (rep: T Shanklin, 50), G Henson, D Hickie; R O'Gara, G Cooper (rep: C Cusiter, 51); M Stevens (rep: A Sheridan, 41), A Titterrell (rep: G Bulloch, 51), J Hayes, S Shaw, D O'Callaghan, L Moody, M Williams, M Owen (captain; rep: S Easterby, 69).

Southland: Try: T-Pole. Con: Apanui. Pens: Apanui (3)
Lions: Tries: Henson (2). Cons: O'Gara (2). Pens: O'Gara (4).

My normal pre-game routine nearly leads to me missing today's game. Sitting in the cinema for two and a half hours means my knee has seized up, so this morning I'm panicking a bit as I get out of bed and very gingerly put my weight on it. It takes three or four rubs from Barty (Stuart Barton) to free it, but after the last one it feels fine again. The massaging is pretty painful and I'm swearing a bit at Barty – imagine having a massage over a bruise for about 40 minutes.

But it's great to be out on the park at last. I really enjoy the game and the knee holds up very well. I'm actually pretty relieved to be selected at six, with Martyn Williams at seven (despite the extra line out calls) as that means that Clive is still considering me for the Tests. I really enjoyed playing with Martyn. I think he was very unlucky not to make the Test team.

It was a super human effort from the guys who played on Saturday, to front up yesterday for training and play today. We got a great start and I think the team thought it would be easy to go on and build a lead, so we just tried to go too wide, too early before the game was won.

I am one of four players asked to do the post-match press conference. I'm happy to do so, as I know not many people will be hassling me for quotes when I'm sitting alongside the man of the moment, Gavin Henson. Gav had been so disappointed to be left out of the First Test side and responded in great style with two tries. Almost every question in the press conference is directed at him. He's a very honest guy and when he's asked near the end whether he thought his non-selection for the Tests could have been due to anything that happened off the pitch he replies: "That's a stupid question!"

Ronan O'Gara and I while away time keeping an eye on Alastair Campbell as we had been winding him up before the press conference, telling him all the terrible things Gav was going to say (we might have exaggerated the odd detail). Alastair is priceless – we can see him squirming every time Gav is asked a question. But in the end Gav does really well and fails to cause any international incidents.

John Hayes, the Munster prop, had spent some time playing in Southland a few years ago and I think it was here that they moved him from the back row to the front row. So when the post-match dinner speeches start there are many references to him, which you can see he hates. It get worse for him as there are so many that he is asked to go up on stage to give his own speech, the idea of which you can tell he's hating even more. He sits there cringing and moaning for ages, but eventually a loud chorus of "Can't take it, can't take it'" forces him up to mumble a few words and sit down in record time.

There have been many big characters in the midweek side, none more so than Denis Hickie who has been the life and soul of our bus trips. It was Denis who started one of the Midweek Massive traditions: "Ask Richard!" Richard Smith, our QC, looks nothing like Jeeves, but he has turned into something of a general knowledge nerd so on every trip someone has to "Ask Richard!" a suitably absurd question like: "Which city has the biggest land mass in the world?" This morning we went past a Lamborghini garage and he was asked how many they had to sell a year before they brought in a profit? He had to come back by the end of the day with the answer and comes through with flying colours as usual.

(It's Mexico City and just the one, by the way!)

Wednesday 22nd

Much to my surprise my knee feels fine this morning. Perhaps actually playing will be my miracle cure.

Clive announces the Test team to a very nervous 45-man squad. It's the complete opposite of all those televised award shows, where you really want the camera to show the stars' disappointment: we all spend the next ten minutes or so making like we're on the Tube by completely avoiding making eye contact with each other, only steaming in to congratulate those who make the squad once the final name is read out.

From the line-up he has clearly gone with experience. I had thought that Chris Cusiter might have a chance of making the bench as the back-up scrum-half, but Matt Dawson is hardly going to let anyone down. I think most coaches will go with what they know so the number of English players in the team, despite Wales' recent Grand Slam, doesn't surprise me.

Those of us not picked for the Test are given a 'night pass' to let our hair down. When you are so far from home the social side is very important and the management sensibly recognise we need a bit of down-time. So, for the first time since we got to New Zealand, we go out as a squad of 45 – while the management go up Christchurch's gondola for an informal get-together with the media. At least we know whatever we get up to tonight won't get reported!

Obviously the Test 22 can't stay out as late as the rest of us, so once the meal is over they head back to the hotel leaving the rest of us with the beer. It's a great night just chilling out. I think a lot of time, effort and sometimes money can go into 'bonding' a group of rugby players when all we really need to do is go out for a few beers, as we prove tonight.

Tuesday 23rd

Grewy's missus, Natasha, arrives this morning and she fills me in on what I've been missing back home. Not much, apparently, although she rubs in the fact that the weather has been scorching since we've been away. Ah, the lot of an international rugby player: we chase the winters around the world! I suppose if I'd wanted to stay in the sun all the year round I should have persevered with my fast bowling action. As more and more fans are arriving this week I also take the chance to catch up with a friend from school – JD O'Brien - who has come over from Australia, where he now lives, for the Tests.

I drag him off to the casino which, unfortunately for me, is only about 100 yards from our hotel. The casino management give us all gold cards, which means we can go upstairs into the high-rollers area. We waste 15 minutes up there trying to learn baccarat, which has to be the most complicated game in the history of the world. A croupier tries to teach me and Shanks how to play but we don't even get close to understanding it.

We beat a hasty retreat downstairs to lose all our money at roulette, poker and black jack. Sam Vesty's not around to control my spending, so I quickly empty my pockets but at least I can understand the games I'm losing at.

Friday 24th

We are given two free tickets for each match and have the opportunity to buy a further two so, as my folks are in town, there isn't really any discussion about who gets the freebies. The ones I had to pay for go to another university friend, Nick Townsend, who has also come over for the tour.

As I'm not involved in the First Test today is a day off, so I kick that off in time-honoured style by lazing in bed until 11am. I meet my parents for lunch – it's fantastic to see them out here and we have a great time catching up. Then Geordy and I take Virginia (Ben Kay's missus) and Natasha jet-boating, leaving their far worse other halves to get themselves in the mood to take on New Zealand. It's hair-raising stuff, but that's not why we're white-knuckled – the water feels like it's about -18 degrees and the wind chill is really stinging our faces. What temperature did they say it was back in England?

It's not too cold to make the 100-yard dash to the casino, however. To try and change my luck I take Rog (Ronan O'Gara) with me this time. I tell him we're not leaving until we've won all my money back. He informs me that he'd actually like to play in one of the Tests before leaving New Zealand...

Saturday 25th

New Zealand 21 – Lions 3

New Zealand: L MacDonald (rep: M Muliaina, 69); D Howlett, T Umaga (capt, rep: R Gear, 75), A Mauger, S Sivivatu; D Carter, J Marshall (rep: B Kelleher, 67); T Woodcock (rep: G Somerville, 67), Keven Mealamu (rep: D Whitcombe, 75), C Hayman, C Jack, A Williams, J Collins (rep: S Lauaki, 77), R McCaw, R So'oialo.

Lions: J Robinson (rep: S Horgan 57); J Lewsey, B O'Driscoll (capt, rep: W Greenwood, 2), J Wilkinson, G Thomas; S Jones, D Peel (rep: M Dawson, 74); G Jenkins, S Byrne (S Thompson, 57), J White, P O'Connell, B Kay (rep: D Grewcock, 57), R Hill (rep: R Jones 18), Neil Back, Martin Corry.

New Zealand: Tries: Williams, Sivivatu. Con: Carter. Pens: Carter (3). Lions: Pen: Wilkinson

Although I am hoping to be playing in the Test side next Saturday I am still training with the midweek side, as if I will play against Manawatu on Tuesday, another game no-one wants to be selected for. But as the team isn't announced until tomorrow we all throw ourselves into training before heading off to Lancaster Park for the First Test.

The whole squad is called to the team room at 5.15pm for the shirt presentations and our last chance for a quick "good luck" to the boys. Clive has asked Geech to give out the shirts, which I think is an inspirational choice. His speeches are pretty good, if maybe five minutes too long, and he delivers some stirring words before calling players up individually to receive their shirts. I want one of those!

I manage to find Backy, Whitey, Hilly and Cozza to wish them good luck but unfortunately I can't find Ryan Jones anywhere.

It is lashing down and I don't think in our wildest nightmares we could have imagined a worse start than we get: in the first 15 minutes we lose our captain, Brian O'Driscoll, who has to leave the field on a golf cart, and one of our key players, Richard Hill. Nightmare!

To add to those injuries I don't think I've ever seen a line-out misfire as badly as ours does today. The drills are a tiny bit slower and we miss a couple of throws because people didn't get up in time. No surprises there: the guys were still walking through the line-outs late last night and it's clear that people still don't know the calls as well as they need to. I suppose the line-out is one of the areas that show how hard it is to bring players from four nations together in such a short space of time. Shane Byrne of Ireland was the hooker and Ben Kay of England a key line-out jumper. At club and international level they both operate completely different systems and for their countries both call their own line-outs.

Back at the hotel Clive calls a brief team meeting and tells us, despite the fact that we're all disappointed with the performance, that we all have to go out and mix with the fans who have travelled across the world to support us. He thinks it's very important that we don't hide in our hotel, that we go out and give something back to the fans.

I do meet some fans, sort of. Two of mum's friends from Jakarta, Alan and Eileen, are also in town so I meet them and mum and dad, at around 11.30pm. It's Alan's 60th and Eileen treated him to this trip as his present. If only we could have put on a better display for him. It's around 1am before I get to bed.

Sunday 26th

Grewy's post-match attempt to drown his sorrows was rudely interrupted by the news that he is being cited. Not Tana Umaga or Keven Mealawu who dropped Brian O'Driscoll on his head to put him out of the Series and could have broken his neck, but Danny Grewcock. He has been accused of biting Mealawu!

When the news filters through this morning all the players are stunned. The hearing will start at 10am, so Danny has had to sit up for most of the night with the team QC, Richard Smith, going through the tapes of the game and preparing his case.

To have the hearing within 24 hours of the match is better for everyone because we are travelling today and everyone prefers a quick decision. It's not quick enough for Danny to come with us today, though. We all depart Christchurch for Wellington, leaving poor Danny behind to face the hearing on his own.

When we arrive in Wellington we find out he has been banned for two months. The sentence itself shows that the case wasn't proved as the normal sentence for biting is six months. Danny was in a ruck and the next thing he knows one of their players was trying to drag him out of the ruck via his mouth, so the natural instinct is to bite him to get his hand out of your mouth. I would have done exactly the same. What would you do? How you can get away with dragging someone out of a ruck that way amazes me. That seems to have been totally ignored. There wasn't any video evidence, so all they went on was the word of other New Zealand players. I just can't believe that Danny was cited for an incident that was not visible on any TV angle while Tana Umaga and Keven Mealawu walk away without any hearing at all.

The incident with Brian was simply a disgrace. They both picked him up, off the ball and dumped him on his shoulder, dislocating it and putting him out of the tour. His role as captain of the Lions lasted no more than 40 seconds! Sometimes things happen in a ruck, or when you are trying to play the ball, but it shouldn't happen off the ball – and for them to deny it afterwards – it is awful. If Brian had been carrying the ball at the time and they'd done that it would definitely have been a penalty, so I can't understand why nothing is being done. The way the citing system works any citing must be made by the commissioner within 12 hours, so we know nothing is going to happen to either of them. It is a contact sport but to see nothing done is ridiculous. I'm furious, as are the rest of the squad.

As well as losing Danny and obviously Brian, there is more bad news this afternoon: Hilda and Shanks are also ruled out of the tour with their injuries. Players dropping out of the tour are part and parcel of a trip like this, but to lose so many after a defeat isn't exactly the morale boost we were looking for.

At training the Test team, although they had been well beaten in Christchurch, pitched up to train with the side that is going to take on Manawatu on Tuesday.

The Midweek Massive had done the same thing for them last week and the return of the favour proves the spirit that is flowing through this Lions squad.

Monday 27th

Danny arrives in Wellington and is clearly unhappy with the decision of the hearing, but off the field he is such a laid-back guy he is more philosophical than I imagined he would be or indeed could be, given the circumstances. He is so unlucky, remember he was ruled out of the World Cup with a freak injury (Ben Cohen stood on his toe during a warm-up).

Biting is obviously something you don't want on your record, but within the squad – and I believe within the game – people know what really happened. It is like when someone puts their finger in your eye. What do you do? I would break someone's finger if they stuck it in my eye and I would have done exactly the same as Danny did on Saturday. In my view he would have started the Second Test next Saturday so it is a big blow to see him leave the squad.

It's the start of a big few days. In a three-Test Series it is clearly make or break this Saturday. It was horrible having to sit in the stand and watch the guys going down in the First Test, now we have to find something deep within ourselves. We have to ask ourselves, "Are we going to go out there and compete in the Second Test or just disappear?" The answer is that we are more determined than ever to compete.

Denis Hickie has been one of the tour comedians, but it comes back to haunt him a little today. Like me, as he wasn't named in the team to play tomorrow he thought he was in with a shout of making the Test team until Clive says to him:

"Denis we are going to need you this week. We are going to need your sense of humour."

So he's now the joker rather than the player.

Clive's policy has changed in that being selected for Tuesday's game doesn't rule you out of the Test match, but I see it as a big positive that I am not picked for the trip to Manawatu, although I can't take it as any more than that. I can't second guess him at all. In my experience Clive rarely takes players to one side to explain a selection or non-selection. He just announces the team. He's certainly never told me in advance of naming a team if I am in and if not why I have been left out. I am one of the three back row forwards (along with Simon Easterby and Ryan Jones) not to be picked so either it means we are playing on Saturday in the Second Test or, just as likely we won't play in either game. One of us will probably have to step aside for Cozza as he is such a great player and leader.

We finish a hell of a day with a de-brief on the First Test. No player would ever be singled out in a meeting like this. Those who didn't play well will know it and they don't need a room full of people to tell them that. There is a lot of focus on the problems in the line-out and the forwards are in apologetic mood, taking most of the blame, saying the backs couldn't play if they weren't given any ball. I am asked to be involved, but it is difficult for me to comment when I didn't play in the game.

Tuesday 28th

Manawatu 6 – Lions 109

Manawatu: F Bryant; B Gray, J Campbell, M Oldridge (rep: N Buckley, 54), J Leota; G Smith (rep: B Trew, 48), J Hargreaves (rep: D Palu, 75); S Moore, N Kemp (captain; sin-bin 32-42), K Barrett (rep: P Cook, 66), T Faleafaga (rep: P Maisiri, 49), P Rodgers, H Triggs (rep: C Moke, 49), J Bradnock (rep: S Easton, 80, sin-bin 86), B Matenga (rep: Easton, 38-42).

Lions: G Murphy; J Robinson (rep: M Cueto, 53), O Smith, G D'Arcy, S Williams; C Hodgson (rep: R O'Gara, 51), C Cusiter (rep: G Cooper, 41); A Sheridan, G Bulloch (captain; rep: A Titterrell, 42-80), J Hayes (rep: M Stevens, 62, sin-bin 79), S Shaw, D O'Callaghan (rep: B Cockbain, 41), M Corry (rep: Bulloch, 84), M Williams (rep: N Back, 41), M Owen.

Manawatu: Pens: Hargreaves (2)
Lions: Tries: S Williams (5), Cueto (2), O'Gara (2), Corry, Murphy, Robinson, Hodgson, Smith, Back, D'Arcy, Cooper. Cons: Hodgson (7), O'Gara (5).

My knee problem is still in the back of my mind so Pasky and I decide I shouldn't go and watch the game against Manawatu in case it adds to the swelling. Wally also stays back so we head to a sports bar near our hotel, called Chicago's, to watch it. It's not that full and of the rugby fans who are actually in there the vast majority are Kiwis so no-one really bothers us. We might have expected some stick, but as the Lions score 17 tries and more than 100 points there isn't much they can say.

The victory gives the whole squad a lift, especially the guys who played in the game. Everyone knows we have come here to win a Test Series, but to see the Midweek Massive win again, and so emphatically, is tremendous.

To address last Saturday's problems in the line-out, we decide to go back to the first system and use the calls we had used on the rest of the tour, which is easier for everyone. And we also decided that Paul O'Connell would call the line-outs, another change from Saturday. With Tommo playing at hooker that is what he is used to anyway so that was no problem for him.

Wednesday 29th

After Shane Williams' performance in scoring five tries last night, I think he has to play on Saturday and when the team is announced no-one is surprised to see him in it.

The team is read out in numerical order, from 1-22, and for one horrible second I think I've blown it. I thought that Clive would pick me at six, so when Simon Easterby's name is read out as the blindside for the game my heart sinks. But it rises again almost immediately as I am confirmed as the openside. My theory about the back row doesn't work out either as all three of us left out of the Manawatu game are included in the starting line-up, with Cozza on the bench.

I don't have a chance to phone Annie and tell her the good news, because we're straight out onto the training pitch for a fairly light session focusing on attack and clearing out the rucks.

After training it's time to do the rounds with the TV, radio and print journos – it seems like there are hundreds of them. I have a number of TV interviews to do and I am getting more and more annoyed with the questions as they all seem to ask:

"Do you really think you can win this Test match?"

It's ridiculously negative and I'm getting quite hot under the collar while trying to remain as professional as possible and sensible with my answers.

The British press are always so negative towards their teams, but the Kiwis are the opposite, whether their teams are playing poorly or not they will still talk them up. So I'm getting abuse from both sides! It doesn't bother me though: I tend not to read any of the papers. I don't even use them as motivation like some guys do. I know when I have played well or badly, so I don't need someone else to tell me, especially, with respect, the press.

Back at the hotel there is a mountain of text messages and missed calls to return after news of my selection has winged its way around the world. I finally speak to Annie and my parents, who are delighted. The first thing Annie says is:

"I want to come out and see the match! I want to be there for you!"

But I talk her out of it. There is no need and it would be a waste of money. I don't want her business to lose out either. Our days are pretty packed out here so I wouldn't see her that much if she was here and we are going on holiday for two weeks once I get back so I'll have the time to catch up with her then. It's great to have my parents out here, but I have to concentrate on the rugby. It's winter in New Zealand so it is not like Annie would be able to enjoy the weather when she got here. It's better she stays at home and we have a proper holiday when I get back.

I am missing her, though. Being apart from each other for so long is tough, especially on the phone bill. O2 gave us about £500 of credit as part of their sponsorship deal and my bill's normally around £150 a month, but it looks like it's going to be around £600 this month. Ouch! We speak every day, although they're not always the best conversations, as due to the time difference one of us is always getting up while the other one's going to bed. I love touring, being with the lads, having a craic, but in a way it is the worst part of the job.

Thursday 30th

Backy makes a point of finding me to offer me his congratulations and his best wishes for Saturday, despite the fact that I'm taking his place. Sometimes I genuinely think he wants it to be me, and no-one else, who takes over his role whether it's with Leicester, England or the Lions.

I remember, when he got his 50th cap, we beat Australia and he was captain. He came up to me and said:

"Don't worry, one day you'll be in this position and you'll have 50 caps."

He said a similar thing in the World Cup when he insisted that if anyone had to take his place he'd like it to be me. It is very difficult for both of us. It is hard to make sure you sound sincere with someone who has taken your place. I usually just shake their hands as I am genuinely happy for them - it is difficult to convey what you feel. Backy was undoubtedly unhappy with the selection for Saturday's match but he wasn't about to take it out on me.

I'm also feeling awkward because Geordan wasn't picked for Saturday. Before we left the UK I believed he was far more likely to play in the Test Series than me, so I'm finding it really hard to know what to say to him. I'm gutted, too, because I enjoy playing with him and it would have been great to have him out there with me on Saturday. Geordy knows what I'm thinking though.

Our training session today is based around defence, and at the end Alfie, the new captain for the weekend, calls us all in for a few words. It's very funny. He says:

"I've just got two words to say boys: 'Make sure we don't ****ing panic!'"

Everyone just bursts out laughing. We know what he means. Alfie is a great man – a full-on lunatic, but a lovely man. He is so passionate about playing for the team and I know he'll be a great captain on Saturday.

By the time we get back, having done an extra line-out session, only the dregs of the team meal are left, so I order a chicken and brie sandwich and Wally and I watch an old favourite in the team room, a DVD of *Dodgeball*. I've seen it before but we were very bored.

July

Friday 1st

I've been very anxious in the last couple of days and perhaps more nervous for this match than I have been for a while. I have been struggling to get to sleep since the team was announced and when I do get off I keep waking up during the night, thinking about the game, what I'm going to do, worrying. Lucky that we are not sharing rooms as I think I'd have become the room-mate from hell.

Tomorrow is an opportunity for us to set the record straight, which I think is what has put me on edge. It is clearly one of the biggest games I will ever start. Once I'm at training it is all fine, but away from training – and particularly when I'm on my own – the nerves start to take over.

We know we didn't turn up last Saturday and we can't afford to let that happen again. Win or lose we are going to play some rugby. The main objective is to go out there and hammer them in the forwards.

Annie may not be with me, but I use some of my day off to head into Wellington and buy her a couple of presents. Lingerie, since you ask, but you're not getting any more details than that. I didn't realise quite how expensive it was until I got to the till, but she's worth it.

Geordy, Wally, the Doc (James Robson), Munch (Shane Byrne) and his missus join me for the weekly trip to the cinema. *War of the Worlds* is pretty gripping, but unfortunately peters out towards the end. Tony Ward, our Kiwi liaison man, sorted it for us and even got us into the gold members area of the cinema, where you get big armchairs and free food and drink. It's almost midnight before we get back to the hotel so it's straight to bed, if not straight to sleep.

Saturday 2nd

New Zealand 48 – Lions 18

New Zealand: M Muliaina; R Gear, T Umaga (captain), A Mauger (rep: L MacDonald, 41), S Sivivatu (rep: M Nonu, 81); D Carter, B Kelleher (rep: J Marshall, 72); T Woodcock (rep: C Johnstone, 87), K Mealamu (rep: D Witcombe, 78), G Somerville, C Jack (rep: J Gibbes, 83), A Williams, J Collins (rep: S Lauaki, 73), R McCaw, R So'oialo.

Lions: J Lewsey; J Robinson, G Thomas (captain), G Henson (rep: S Horgan, 78), S Williams; J Wilkinson (rep: S Jones, 66), D Peel; G Jenkins (rep: G Rowntree, 66), S Thompson (rep: S Byrne, 87), J White (rep: Rowntree, 61–66), P O'Connell, D O'Callaghan (rep: M Corry, 81), S Easterby, L Moody, R Jones.

New Zealand: Tries: Carter (2), Umaga, Sivivatu, McCaw. Cons: Carter (4). Pens: Carter (5)
Lions: Tries: Thomas, Easterby. Con: Wilkinson. Pens: Wilkinson (2).

My Lions Test debut and I am very nervous. Nervous of not performing and nervous of letting everyone down, from my family to my team-mates and the supporters who have come all this way to follow us. After being given this opportunity I want to play as well as I possibly can on what is a massive stage.

I get up late, we have a quick line-out session and then I get a rub on my knee from physio Barty. Once that is all over I decide to return to my bed – as it is a 7pm kick off – with a heat pack on my knee, just to make sure it is 100 per cent for the game.

I spend the afternoon watching TV, packing and then repacking my kit. I haven't got that much to put in my bag – boots, gumshield, shoulder pads – as most of it is at the ground, but I am still scared I will forget something. The team meeting is at 5.25pm today, as the ground is only a short drive from our hotel in the centre of town.

Tour manager and former Lion Bill Beaumont presents us with our jerseys and delivers a speech which is brief, but I can't say whether it's to the point, as all we can hear are the hundreds and hundreds of Lions supporters who have congregated inside and outside our hotel. While he is talking to us they break out into a rendition of *Bread of Heaven!* It's brilliant to know so many people have made the effort to come and see us off and to know that they will be there in the stadium giving us all the support we need. The fans have been so amazing on the whole trip.

People started arriving outside the hotel at about 11am and they created an amazing, uplifting atmosphere. As we leave the team room Geordan comes up to me, gives me a big hug, and wishes me luck. It means the world to me.

We have to walk down a flight of stairs from the team room to the lobby and onto the bus. The whole area is packed and the security guards have had to clear a path for us to get through. I know my folks are in the crowd somewhere, but I can't see them; there are just too many people. It's a phenomenal send off, similar to what we experienced in Manly before the World Cup Final.

Normally I sit on my own on the bus but I am pleased to see Paul O'Connell sit down next to me. There isn't much chat at this stage though; I just stick the i-Pod on and try to relax as much as possible. Apple gave us all an i-Pod for the tour and each player was asked to nominate their favourite song (mine's Hurricane by Bob Dylan), so each i-Pod is loaded with each of the players' favourite songs. That's one hell of a concept album. Gethin Jenkins picked The Way to Amarillo and, unfortunately for Gethin, not only is there a listing for each song but the player who nominated it has his name next to it, so there's nowhere to hide.

We often get questionnaires from our clubs or England and we rarely take them that seriously, but this time your answer has a repercussion because you got stuck with the song you chose. Julian White didn't bother to fill in the Lions questionnaire for quite a while and the Lions media manager, Louisa Cheetham, was chasing him for weeks. We had to nominate our favourite book, film, pet hates, etc, all of which went into the media guide. It finally got to the stage where Whitey got a call from Clive who went through his questions on the phone with him. I can't imagine how embarrassing that must have been.

When we get to the ground, my shirt for the second half is hanging on the peg and I immediately check my bag for the hundredth time to ensure my starting shirt is actually in there. I would normally drink half a can of Red Bull before running out for the game but I've just discovered the colitis is aggravated by caffeine so water it is. The antibiotics seem to be doing their job, at least I'm not having to dash to the loo every five minutes.

Finally, the moment is here. The fans are making an incredible noise and a shiver of anticipation and nerves hits me as we run out. As soon as I'm on the field, I'm lost in my own little world. Focus, focus, focus.

The first kick-off doesn't go well: Rodney So'oalo lines up on his side off the field, directly opposite me, and when Jonny Wilkinson kicks off he runs straight towards me, nowhere near the ball, just to take me out. There's little I can do except try and draw the referee's attention to it but he seems to be ignoring it.

"He stood his ground, he stood his ground," he says, but I know that isn't the case.

Clive was complaining about the role of touch judges earlier in the tour. They seem to be getting more and more involved in what is going on around the ball when surely they should be focusing on what happens behind it? I don't blame the referee as he is watching the ball.

We make an incredible start though: Alfie scoring in the first few minutes, but they really pile on the pressure after that and score off the first turnover. I put in 22 tackles today and it feels like 122! It's far more than usual: I would normally expect 14 or 15 in a game. I think the most I've ever put in is 25 when we played Wasps, so 22 is a lot and I'm pretty pleased on a personal level, but gutted for us. I really don't think the scoreline reflected the match as we were far closer to them than 30 points.

There is still a lot of ill-feeling over Tana Umaga's role last weekend in injuring Brian O'Driscoll and throughout the game I can hear some of our players calling him a "cheap shotter".

I'm not sure whether this leads to him boycotting the after-match function, but he doesn't turn up for the speeches and his vice-captain, Richie McCaw, stands in for him, something I have never seen before. Win or lose the two skippers always turn up to the after-match function to thank the other team for the game. We're told that Tana had to meet someone but it was very unusual – a bit bizarre. I would have thought this was his chance to bury the whole incident, in front of both teams, so I was surprised he didn't take it. Why couldn't he just say he was wrong and he shouldn't have done it? Tana made a huge deal about how he was treated in the press, but Brian could be out for months. If I had to choose between getting a hard time in the press or missing all the Lions Tests I know which one I would pick. It disappointed me that Tana wouldn't take responsibility for what he had done.

I managed to hold on to my first Lions Test shirt, despite being asked to swap by Richie McCaw. Earlier in the tour I had been swapping my embroidered shirts, but I had no intention of doing that today. We lost so it could be my first and last! When I explained to Richie that it was my first Lions cap he was happy to take the non-embroidered shirt. When we last played the All Blacks, for England at Twickenham, Marty Holah was their seven but they refused to swap their shirts.

It's not like that at Leicester: we don't swap shirts in the league, possibly because we only get one new shirt every five games and have to give it back after the game. They give us a shirt to keep at the end of the season but, unless it really means something to you personally, you tend to let friends and family have them. I've got my first cap, my World Cup shirts and my Heineken Cup winners shirt framed in my office, but I've always wanted an All-Blacks shirt – and now I've got one.

After the match almost the entire squad heads to a bar called Jet in Courtney Place, the main nightclubbing area in Wellington, to let our hair down. Some of the All Blacks are in the same bar but as it's on a number of floors we don't bump into each other. It is one of the last nights out for Shanks and Hilda, before they go home, so I was determined to make it. We don't get over there until midnight so we stay out until around 5am. It's a great release.

Oddly, the time you're most relaxed is immediately after a game. Win or lose, it doesn't matter (well, obviously it matters hugely!). You've had to keep your emotions in check all week and cope with all the nerves and the immediate aftermath of a game is wonderful, a total release as all the adrenaline rushes out of your body. As the accommodation situation is pretty dire in Wellington, my uni mate Nick ends up sleeping in my room, so for one night only I do end up sharing.

I'm not sure he appreciates the offer, though. The worst thing after a game is trying to get to sleep. Your blood's still hot, you're scratched all over and itching because of it, you've got stud marks down your legs, scabs on your knees and the worst thing is that you have friction burns on your ears and they get very sticky and scabby and you end up sticking to the bed sheets. I usually spend most of the night after a match tossing and turning, groaning and moaning, stinging and whingeing and trying not to disturb anyone.

Sunday 3rd

We travel back to Auckland today, so after three hours 'sleep' I wake Nick up, run round like a loon for five minutes stuffing everything I have into every bag I can find, and then blearily dash downstairs to the team meeting. I hope Nick doesn't go back to sleep, the lazy sod.

I was a little worried about how the supporters would now react to us after two bad defeats, but when I come out of the team meeting I find hundreds of them in the street outside our hotel, all of them cheering us on the short walk from the lobby to our bus. It's humbling to think of how much time, money and sacrifice these people have made to follow us across the world and then to see their unstinting loyalty.

The journey to the airport is pretty quiet, but again the supporters are on great form when we arrive back in Auckland and as we pull into the road that houses the Hilton Hotel about 30 of them rise from their tables at a restaurant to toast our appearance. Thanks guys.

Monday 4th

So far so good today, as I'm not named in the side to play Auckland which points (and I stress points) to me keeping my place for the Third Test.

I'm really knackered so, for the first time on the trip, I take one of the energy drinks that are always on offer on the side of the training pitch. I normally have a Red Bull before a match to fire me up, but this is a different one which is supposed to do the same thing. It kick-starts my brain so training is fantastic, I'm running around like a nine-year-old, but when I get back to the hotel, man I feel rough. I can't get to sleep the whole night. It's like coming down off some massive high – great for the session but "oh, the after-effects". I'm certainly not taking one of them again. Red Bull only from now on.

Tuesday 5th

Auckland 13 – Lions 17

Auckland: B Ward; I Nacewa (rep: G Williams, 73), B Atiga (rep: I Toe'ava,

80), S Tuitupou, J Rokocoko; T Lavea, S Devine; S Taumoepeau (rep:
C Heard, 66), S Telefoni (rep: J Fonokalafi, 80), J Afoa, B Mika (rep:
J Kaino, 46), B Williams, J Collins (captain), D Braid, A MacDonald (rep:
K Haiu, 70).

Lions: G Murphy; M Cueto, W Greenwood (rep: S Horgan, 51), G D'Arcy,
D Hickie; C Hodgson (rep: R O'Gara, 23), M Dawson; G Rowntree,
G Bulloch (captain), J Hayes (rep: M Stevens, 62), S Shaw, B Kay (rep:
B Cockbain, 40+1), J White (rep: M Corry, 56), M Williams, M Owen.

Auckland: Try: Nacewa. Con: Ward. Pens: Ward (2).
Lions: Try: Williams. Pens: Hodgson (4).

The physio room is like a scene from *MASH*. Not quite blood and guts but
certainly a load of bodies. The man who leads the team that helps rebuild them
is Dr James Robson and he keeps a board in the room with the lists of the
walking wounded. He breaks it down into "off-tour", "non-contact" and
"having treatment" and out of the 45-man squad he has about 15 down as
"off-tour" and almost the same as "non-contact". It means that we are unlikely
to be able to train tomorrow.

It's fantastic to be able to go along to Eden Park to cheer the Midweek
Massive tonight, as they finish the tour unbeaten. We all hit the dressing room
at the end for a quick celebration and whoever plays in the Test match on
Saturday will have been boosted by their victory. They could have scored a few
more tries and Denis Hickie came in for a fair bit of stick for the one he
missed in the second-half, juggling a crossfield kick not once, not twice but
three times before dropping it. It was like one of those agonising cricket
catches. He had it and then it went away from him! But they've done
fantastically well and I've been proud to play for them.

Wednesday 6th

The 'Free the Wig One' T-shirts are just about to go on sale in the hotel
shop this morning when we finally hear that Wig has been cleared of any
wrong-doing in last night's match against Auckland.

It's incredible to think that Tana Umaga and Keven Mealawu drop Brian
O'Driscoll on his head and get nothing while Wig does absolutely nothing

and is then cited and accused of hitting someone in a ruck. His excellent record obviously counts in his favour, but he wasn't that confident going into the hearing after what happened to Danny. He had a minor clash at a ruck, something you would see dozens of times in any Zurich Premiership game, but once you are cited you can never be that certain.

As expected training is cancelled with so many of the squad ill or injured, including captain Gareth Thomas who has come down with the flu, so I take the opportunity to enjoy a morning in bed.

In the afternoon I get a severe case of writers' cramp, not from putting the finishing touches to this diary but from our signing session. Each player is allowed to enter five items into the signing session, but realistically everyone sneaks in a few other items (the management are usually the worst offenders!) so the session can last a couple of hours. As there are around 80 people involved in the tour it can add up to a lot of ink and it is hard for me to understand my own signature by the end of the session. Donncha O'Callaghan wins the award for the most bizarre thing to be signed by putting in two massive maps of New Zealand.

Two and a bit hours later I head back to bed as I am feeling a little rough. I think I have got a small dose of Alfie's flu. I call Annie and she cheers me up as she's got a big contract for a showflat for a prestigious new waterside property development. I'm so proud of her.

Thursday 7th

It's time to meet the press today and Stephen Jones is paying for his lack of organisation yesterday. Stephen hadn't been out to buy any items for yesterday's signing session so he put in his white polo shirt, one of the items we were given at the start of the tour. And what are we told to wear for today's press session? Our white polo shirts. So Steve has two choices: wear one with the whole squad's signatures on it or beg, borrow or steal one from someone else. He sensibly chooses the latter option.

Clive announces the team for the Third Test but takes the unusual step of speaking to most people at breakfast to tell them whether they are in or out. I can't remember him doing this before, but maybe he's doing it because he thinks there were some tight calls. He doesn't speak to me but I suppose as I'm staying in the team he doesn't feel he needs to.

But he does finally speak to Geordy! He's elated but would have been happier if the call had come a week earlier. Mark Cueto is beaming all over his face after speaking to Clive so it's not difficult to work out which piece of news he got either.

From what I can gather Clive offers Gordon D'Arcy a place in the Test team, but Gordon says he's "too fatigued" to accept, that his body isn't up to it and that he's knackered, which is a remarkably brave and honest thing to say.

D'Arc has had something of a nightmare season, missing most of the Six Nations and culminating in him getting stamped on the head in the Auckland game. I know how much playing in a Test for the Lions would mean to him so it takes a very big man to turn it down on health grounds. He knows he isn't fit enough to do the shirt justice and I have the ultimate respect for him for saying that.

Leicester have brought over a big group of about 100 supporters so tonight I'm going to spend time with them, along with some of the other Tigers players in the Lions squad, at one of the hotels in town. They're a great bunch and it's a good laugh, but one of the organisers, Jimmy Overend, has been out buying wigs and when I see them come out I make my excuses and beat a hasty retreat. I know what's coming next.

The day is going pretty well until everything comes to a stop around 10pm when news starts to filter through about the bombings in London and it clearly puts something of a perspective on what we are doing here. I have a few friends who work in the city – some I used to play with – so like many of the lads I spend an anxious hour or two trying to get in touch with friends, to make sure they are ok. Luckily they seem to be the sort of people who get into work at 6am so they were at their desks when it happened.

We'll have a meeting in the morning to discuss what has occurred and to make a mark of respect towards those that have died, and their families.

Friday 8th

The Tigers announce they won't be moving to Leicester City's Walkers Stadium next season as planned, staying instead at Welford Road.

Welford Road is a great ground but I'm disappointed, not only for the players but for the supporters who would have got the stadium and the facilities they deserve at the Walkers. But it seems both clubs have agreed that a joint venture is not possible.

I believe moving to the Walkers, especially with its bigger capacity, would have helped take the club forward. Leicester have been the best-supported club in Britain for a while now but it is clear that other clubs are catching us up. I only hope we can now move ahead with the development of Welford Road to keep us at number one and keep us setting the benchmark.

In the evening I'm expecting a motivational video and pre-game talks from the coaches, explaining how they expect us to play, but Alfie (not quite recovered from the flu, but determined to play tomorrow) takes over, throws all that out and decides that he will be the only one to address the players.

Alfie says he wants everyone to relax and that we should remove all the hype and stress that is normally associated with the build-up to a major Test match, so we go over some moves just amongst the players. I quite enjoy the psyche-up talks, the videos and the coaches, but I can see the validity of Alfie's approach. He's a top man. One of the great things about a Lions tour is the friendships you make and I have certainly enjoyed my time with Alfie.

Geech and Gareth Jenkins have had T-shirts made for everyone who played for the Midweek Massive, which actually turns out to be every player in the squad except Paul O'Connell. They also clocked up the number of minutes people had played and brought people up in order of the 200-club, 300-club etc, with Geordy and Denis Hickie being the most senior members of the Massive. There were also a few presentations to staff to thank them for all their hard work on the tour, but afterwards Whitey comes up to me.

"They've left our kit men, Dondo (Don Pearson) and Reg (Dave Tennison) out. That's disgraceful! Will you give Dondo your shirt from tomorrow's Test as a gesture, and I'll give Reg mine?"

Of course I agree as both those guys have put in so much work on this trip. They were the two guys who were permanently on the move. They were both so dedicated on the trip and if anyone needed anything they were there.

After the presentations it's pretty late, but there's just enough time to squeeze in the traditional pre-game cinema trip. Tommo isn't feeling that well so it is just Geordy and I who head off to see *Fanastic Four*. We nearly don't make it as the taxi driver drops us at some art house cinema. Our request for "Two tickets to *Fantastic Four* please!" doesn't go down too well and there are a few quizzical glances. Another frantic taxi journey later we just make it. The film is average, easy watching and nothing too taxing on the brain, Perfect, in fact.

Saturday 9th

New Zealand 38 – Lions 19

New Zealand: M Muliaina; R Gear, C Smith, T Umaga (captain; sin-bin, 9-19), S Sivivatu; L McAlister, B Kelleher (rep: J Marshall, 47); T Woodcock (rep: C Johnstone, 45), K Mealamu, G Somerville, C Jack (rep: J Ryan, 77), A Williams, J Collins (sin-bin, 55-65), R So'oialo, S Lauaki (rep: M Holah, 41).

Lions: G Murphy (rep: R O'Gara, 66); M Cueto, G Thomas (captain; rep: S Horgan, 51), W Greenwood, J Lewsey; S Jones, D Peel (rep: M Dawson, 49); G Jenkins (rep: G Rowntree, 49), S Byrne (rep: G Bulloch, 70), J White, P O'Connell, D O'Callaghan, S Easterby, L Moody (rep: M Williams, 76), R Jones (rep: M Corry, 68).

New Zealand: Tries: Umaga (2), Smith, Williams, Gear. Cons: McAlister (5). Pen: McAlister.
Lions: Try: Moody. Con: S Jones. Pens: S Jones (4)

All through the tour we have done everything we could to keep our line-out calls and moves from the All Blacks, but it seems all of that has gone out of the window today. We walk to a nearby park where hundreds of kids are playing mini-rugby to do our final line-out walk-through. They all stop to watch us – although none of them seem to have mobiles, so I guess we should be safe!

Unfortunately we are without Tommo who's pulled out this morning with the illness that prevented him coming on last night's cinema trip, Shane Byrne coming into the side and Gordon Bulloch onto the bench. I thought Tommo would have pulled through. He must have been bad to miss a Test match. Losing him is a big blow, with respect to Shane and Gordon, as he was so much at the forefront of our comeback last Saturday and I know he would have carried on in the same manner today. Any change this close to a game does affect you, but we know Shane isn't going to let anyone down.

I spend most of the rest of the day packing my bags. I'm going to Australia tomorrow for some R&R before heading home, but I want the majority of my bags to go back with the team to save me carting them around Oz. So that means all bags have to be ready by 9am tomorrow which, considering how much I like my sleep and because we will surely have a big night tonight, means I have to get them ready today. I'm not sure if it's the packing taking my mind off the match, but I feel a lot more relaxed this week than I did seven days ago. It's not always a good sign but the nerves of the First Test seem to have disappeared.

We meet at 5.20pm to hand out the shirts. Geech does the honours but this time his speech is short and sharp. He really nails it.

Sadly, though, it doesn't work. The performance we put in is spirited, but the bare fact is that we lost again, and that hurts every member of the playing and management teams.

I managed to score our try and although it wasn't that glamorous – being driven over by the forwards – I'll take and enjoy it, on behalf of the whole pack. It was magnificent to score for the Lions and at that point, in the second half, we only needed two converted tries so the belief never left us, especially as we exerted quite a lot of pressure on them.

We never gave up, and I think that has been one thing you can say about this squad, we played for each other. Bringing together a group of players from four nations and expecting them to become the best team in the world in seven weeks is a big ask.

A 3-0 Series defeat really hurts, but it has been a fantastic seven weeks. I have enjoyed every minute and everything about my Lions experience makes me want to be there again in 2009, when the Lions go to South Africa.

Naturally there had been some security worries around the match so we were told to make our time on the pitch at the end of the game brief, but we knew we couldn't leave without going over to our fans. The officials didn't really want us walking round the pitch but as the fans have followed us around the world and spent thousands of pounds we went to give them a small "thankyou" from the squad. We had to. They've been magnificent.

I attended the press interviews after the match which meant I was about an hour late for the dinner. As it was the end of the series the tables were mixed and we were also allowed two guests so mum and dad were delighted to join me on a table.

Alfie and Dwayne Peel had to go and get x-rays so it meant that Alfie missed out on making his after-dinner speech, Paul O'Connell stepping in on his behalf. Paul spoke very well and very quickly:

"Now we are going to get slaughtered!," he says.

Sunday 10th

We finally opted for a quiet night, which turned into a quiet morning as we sat in the Hilton Hotel bar for most of it, drinking beer and telling tall stories. Myself, Michael Owen and Geordan walked back to the hotel from last night's dinner, which at the time seemed a good idea, but it took us about four times longer than everyone else to get back as we were being mobbed by everyone.

We eventually met up with Cozza, Whitey and Shane Byrne in the hotel bar. Cozza disappeared for about an hour to see his missus and his little one and when he came back he was clearly intent on making up for lost time, buying ridiculous black drinks that tasted like rocket fuel and which came in a tupperware bowl. We finally got to bed around 4am.

As the majority of the squad disappeared back to England I headed up to Christchurch to meet Annie's family for some snowboarding, before catching a plane to Australia – with Geordan and a couple of mates – for a quick holiday.

It's been a season of complete highs and lows for me, so I'm ecstatic to be able to finish it off on a high. We're on holiday in our apartment in Puerto Banus in Spain and I have taken Annie out for a meal as a way of saying thankyou for getting the flat kitted out. I gave a friend, Adam, my spare keys and told him to do his worst. As the starters arrive, I complain that I'm feeling a bit dodgy. I torture myself by pushing my delicious-looking starter around my plate and melodramatically grabbing my stomach. The main courses arrive and I start laying it on really thick.

"I'm not sure if it's too much sun or I've eaten something dodgy," I groan.

Except now I really can feel my stomach starting to churn.

Annie is all concerned so we pay the bill and head off home. I let her open the door and she gasps as she walks into the room. The entire apartment is covered with rose petals, flowers and candles (cheers, Adam, it looks amazing).

"I just wanted to say thank you for all your hard work in getting the apartment ready," I lie, before uncorking the champagne, grabbing two glasses (and Annie!) and heading out onto the balcony...

She said yes.

Acknowledgments

Lewis Moody

I feel like this could turn out to be one of those terrible Oscar speeches where they go on thanking everyone they have ever met, culminating in a "Praise be to God", but there are a few people I absolutely must thank.

I would like to personally thank all the players and coaches from all the teams that I have had the privilege of playing with this year. It has been a pleasure playing with you.

Rugby is one of the few opportunities in life where you can battle side by side with your mates and lay your body on the line for them in the knowledge that they will do the same for you, for the collective good of the team. So to my Leicester colleagues I would like to say it has been, and will continue to be, one of my life's singular honours to take the field alongside each and every one of you.(Even though you are all a bunch of mutes really).

I'd like to thank Paul Morgan and Karen Buchanan.for putting up with my lack of memory and being the first people to actually force me to remember parts of my life that would have otherwise disappeared into the empty cavern known as my brain.You made this a truly memorable experience.

To my friends and colleagues who are mentioned in this book, for making life so enjoyable, to all the physios for getting me back on the pitch and keeping me on it and all those at the Leicester Tigers from the groundsmen to the boss.

Also to all my sponsors – Nike, Gilbert, Renault, Timberland, Vulkan, Red Bull, International Rugby News, and Spirit of Sport.co.uk.

Paul Morgan

Thanks to Karen Buchanan, a world-class editor, and as always to Jo, who has the patience of a saint.

Also from Vision Sports Publishing...

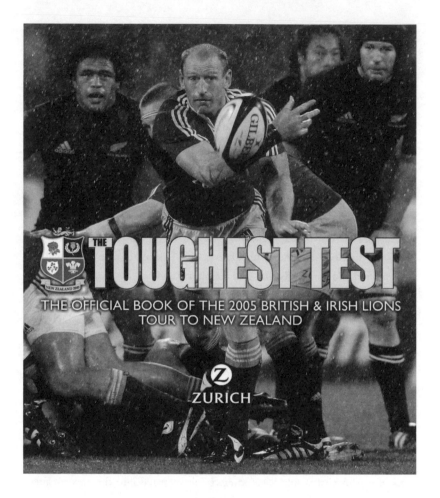

1-9053260-4-1

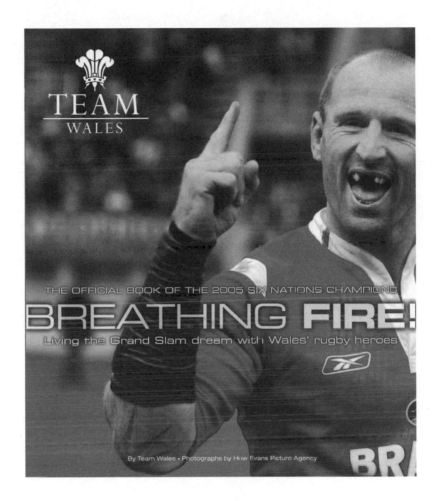

0-9546428-8-0

www.visionsp.co.uk

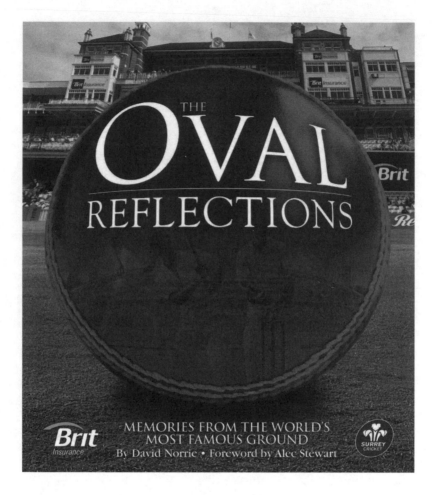

THE
OVAL
REFLECTIONS

MEMORIES FROM THE WORLD'S
MOST FAMOUS GROUND
By David Norrie • Foreword by Alec Stewart

1-9053260-5-X

www.visionsp.co.uk

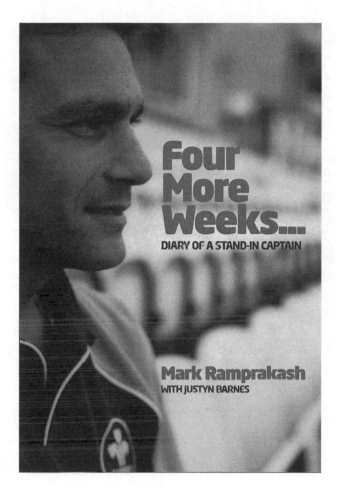

1-905326-01-7

www.visionsp.co.uk

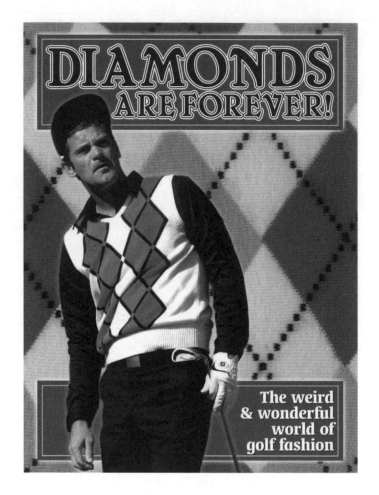

0-9546428-7-2

www.visionsp.co.uk